THE A303

'There's a reason people like Fort and me prefer the 303 and it's the romance of the thing ... The A303 is an ancient route, steeped in history, and Fort meanders from it in search of bygone ages ... It's a nostalgic experience, informative, humorous, charming' *Daily Mail*

'Anyone who has holidayed in the West Country will enjoy *The A303, Highway to the Sun*. Tom Fort's diligent digging under the tarmac has uncovered a great stash of tales, with swindlers and druids rubbing shoulders with King Arthur and Margaret Thatcher' *Sunday Times*

'A lovely book ... It's most famous for running by Stonehenge (lots of jams there) but Mr Fort has found scores of other reminders of the past ... At last someone has celebrated the romance of the British road' *Guardian*

'A delightful book, nostalgic, slyly witty, perceptive ... it achieves an admirable universality in its insights into travel, holidays, agrarian longing, conservation and the general sense that things were better sometime in the past. This is a wonderfully charming book. It is also stealthily profound' Justin Cartwright, *Spectator*

'Elegantly written, with a dry humour and an eyebrow raised ... His object is to reveal the special beauty of the landscape, particularly Salisbury Plain and Stonehenge. Mr Fort is a charming and knowledgeable guide, who can people the hills with shepherds, and the manors and rectories with eccentric antiquarians; who can tell you about an ancient system for flooding water meadows or the common names of chalk-loving flowers and butterflies. It is enough to make Wiltshire your next holiday destination' *Economist*

'Fort has an eye for the quirky, the absurd, the pompous — and a style that, like the road, is always on the move' *Sunday Telegraph*

'Highly enjoyable. Fort has explored this A-road and its environs by car, bicycle and foot ... Keep his book in the glove compartment, to read at points where two lanes squeeze into one' *Independent*

'What Tom Fort has done in this excellent primer is to combine English history and myth with a host of nerdish facts about the road, some cultural analysis and not a little literary reflection to boot. Fort's book is also a meditation on the motor car itself ... Charming, like the road itself' *Independent on Sunday*

'Here Fort unearths a tenth-century story of internecine lust, treachery, betrayal and murder worthy of the Icelandic Sagas' *Times Literary Supplement*

'Entertaining and impeccably researched. A melange of history, sociology, geography and op-ed ... It's also very charming, containing a gargantuan amount of genuinely fascinating trivia and opinion' *Metro*

THE A303

HIGHWAY TO THE SUN

TOM FORT

**SIMON &
SCHUSTER**

London · New York · Sydney · Toronto · New Delhi

First published in Great Britain by Simon & Schuster UK Ltd, 2012
This paperback edition published by Simon & Schuster UK Ltd, 2019

3 5 7 9 10 8 6 4 2

Simon & Schuster UK Ltd
1st Floor
222 Gray's Inn Road
London WC1X 8HB

www.simonandschuster.co.uk
www.simonandschuster.com.au
www.simonandschuster.co.in

Simon & Schuster Australia, Sydney
Simon & Schuster India, New Delhi

A CIP catalogue record for this book
is available from the British Library.

Paperback ISBN: 978-1-4711-8609-7
eBook ISBN: 978-0-85720-327-4

Printed and bound by CPI Group (UK) Ltd, Croydon, CR0 4YY

To the memory of my father and mother

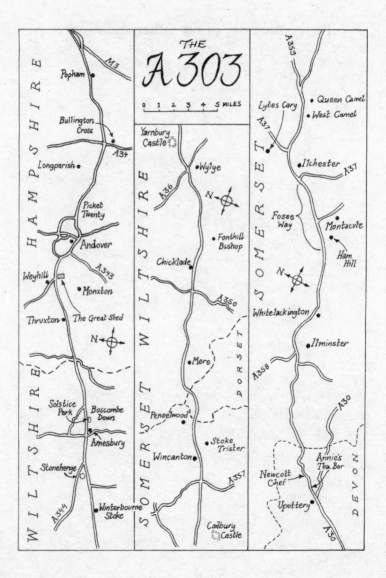

THE
A303

0 1 2 3 4 5 MILES

HAMPSHIRE

M3

Popham

Bullington Cross

A34

Longparish

Picket Twenty

Andover

A343

Weyhill

Monxton

Thruxton

The Great Shed

N

WILTSHIRE

Solstice Park

Boscombe Down

Amesbury

Stonehenge

A344

Winterbourne Stoke

Yarnbury Castle

A36

Wylye

N

Fonthill Bishop

Chicklade

A350

WILTSHIRE

SOMERSET

DORSET

Mere

Penselwood

Stoke Trister

Wincanton

A357

Cadbury Castle

A359

Lytes Cary

A37

Queen Camel

West Camel

Ilchester

A37

Fosse Way

Montacute

Ham Hill

N

Whitelackington

Ilminster

A358

A30

Newcott Chef

Annie's Tea Bar

Upottery

A30

SOMERSET

DEVON

CONTENTS

FOREWORD

Of the nine books that I have written and that have been published, this has been by far the most successful commercially. I am delighted that this should be so, but also mildly perplexed. Each time I write a book, I think that it is better and more important than the one before. But none of the others pressed the button that this one did, and still does.

Of course, it has helped that it was accompanied by a BBC Four film that – by the standards of the channel – turned out to be a considerable hit, having been shown well over twenty times. My father and mother-in-law, bless them, watch it every time it's on. One Sunday afternoon, in the course of a village cricket match, the opposition's wicket-keeper recognised me and revealed that he, too, had seen it multiple times. When I suggested that he must be bored with it by now, he replied very emphatically: 'No, I could never get bored with the 303.'

Perhaps that is the secret. I'm inclined to think that, by

accident, I hit upon a subject that could touch a distinct sector of the book-buying public in a surprisingly potent way (I must emphasise that the original idea was not mine, but came from someone then working for the publishers whose creative thinking had been stimulated by the repeated experience of sitting in unmoving lines of traffic on the approach to Stonehenge). After the book came out I gave a talk at the Mere Literary festival, at the end of which the owner of the Willoughby Hedge café – which welcomes travellers in a layby near Mere – told me he had sold four hundred copies. At a transport café!

It turned out that the A303 was not like other roads. It connected people to memorable events or times in their lives – childhood holidays, honeymoons, taking the kids or the grandchildren to the seaside, fleeing work for their precious caravan or second home. It also had – has – history, landscape, landmarks, pubs, diners and that indefinably quality summed up as character. And Stonehenge, never forget Stonehenge.

Even when motorists and truck drivers were cursing it, they retained a sneaking affection. 'Bloody 303,' they'd say, as if it were a wilful pet or a tedious old uncle. No one talks about a motorway like that.

Its character hasn't changed at all, nor have most of its features. But some of the details have, as have some of the contexts in which I wrote about it the best part of a decade ago. Fat Charlie, the logo of the Little Chef diners, with whom I had a lot of fun, has disappeared as has the Little

Chef brand itself. An era in roadside feasting has ended, and the annexation of the old sites by Starbucks – no Olympic Breakfast on offer there – is a cause of continuing regret.

There has been a steady casualty rate among the pubs where I sought rest and nourishment. The Great Shed at Andover that stimulated me to look into the subject of distribution centres has been surpassed by a much Greater Shed outside Amesbury. King Arthur Pendragon's well-used caravan on the byway beyond Stonehenge has gone (or perhaps fallen to pieces). *Top Gear* has migrated from the BBC and changed its name.

Most striking are the changes that have taken place and are threatened at Stonehenge. The tatty old visitor centre has been replaced by English Heritage's glass, steel and timber 'experience', and the A344 link with the A303 has been grassed over. Much more significantly and ominously, it looks as though the government is resolved on reviving and realising the old vision of hiding the A303 away inside a tunnel. If this vainglorious folly actually happens – and I cling to the hope that it won't – it will result in years of upheaval and chaos, and will impoverish that section of the road for ever.

But much more remains unaltered since I walked and cycled and drove the 90 odd miles of the A303 to research this book. Outside the Holiday Inn at Solstice Park, The Ancestor still raises his great arms – in horror, or is it amazement? King Alfred's Tower pokes above the woods of Stourhead as you crest the last western ridge of Salisbury Plain. Annie's Tea Bar continues to offer the finest English breakfast just before the road's end, even if it is now Emma's Café. The traffic jams still crawl along the familiar pinch-points and the view of Stonehenge is still – for now – free.

Rather than rewrite or ditch whole sections of the book affected by changing times, I have taken the easy way and, in general, alluded to them in footnotes. I have deleted a few passages entirely that were completely out of date and struck me on re-reading as not very interesting, and I have corrected the occasional error that crept through the original editing.

Apart from that, *The A303: Highway to the Sun* stays as it was. I'm thrilled that a new edition is now called for. Since writing the book and doing the TV programme, I have retained, maintained and even deepened my relationship with the road. I will never walk it or cycle it again – that was not fun at all – but I still drive sections of it every fortnight or so during the fishing season (May to the end of December) and I still find its company both stimulating and comforting. We are old friends, and may we never be parted.

INTRODUCTION

Many of us have a road that reaches back into our past. It was not the road itself that mattered, but where it led. It took us to another world which, because it offered a vivid and thrilling alternative to our lives at home, had special status. It was the world of our family holidays, where we spent some of the most precious times of our growing up, times experienced with peculiar intensity. The memories of them, of the special places at the end of the road, retained their definition through the decades that followed.

As children we probably didn't have the dimmest idea of where to find the road on the map. But it was as familiar to us as the way upstairs to bed. We knew the landmarks that measured its progress: maybe a pub sign, a red post-box, a old, sagging stone wall weighed down by ivy; a church steeple, a big, ancient tree. In our hearts we embraced each as it passed. Each delivered the same message. *Nearly there now.*

The special place stirred something very deep inside us. It offered adventure, excitement, a particular kind of intense happiness. Part of it was because it was different from home, but part of it was that it also had something of the same familiarity. We knew where the key was left, where to find the path that led to the sea, where the wood was stored. We knew to watch out for the low beam in front of the fireplace, the tight turn on the stone staircase.

Even though we were there for only a fortnight, we felt able to claim a kind of ownership. For that time it was ours, shared with no one else; certainly not the tenants who came before and after. Not knowing them, we were somewhat inclined to despise them because they could not possibly possess all the secret knowledge that we possessed, and therefore could not prize the place as we did. We would leave, aching with regret, but consoled by the thought that it would be ours again next year or the year after that, or one day.

Later in life, if things work out that way, we may pick up the road once more. Then we come back with our own children, hoping to give them the magic that we found. Because the magic was real, and because they have something of us in them, it can work for us through them. Holidays make us children again. They legitimise sandcastles and picnics and cricket on the beach and scooping at rock pools with nets. What has changed is that now we have to know the number of the road and how to find it.

For me and my elder brothers the road led to a low,

grey, thick-walled cottage at the southern end of Coniston Water in the Lake District. It was owned by my grand-mother's elder sister, and for a fortnight most summers it was annexed by us and assorted cousins, friends and hangers-on under my grandmother's benign supervision. There was a shack crowded with beds where the children slept, and a path past dripping laurels (it rained more often then) down to a long, green boat-house with a corrugated iron roof that nestled in the reeds at the lake's edge.

Those were pre-motorway days. I, naturally, took no interest in the route north from our home in Berkshire. Looking at the family copy of the 1959 *AA Road Book*, I would guess that we picked up the A423 Oxford road at Henley-on-Thames, and the A34 at Oxford. This would have taken us to Birmingham, Stafford and west of Stoke to Manchester, where we must have joined the A6 past Lancaster. A few miles short of Kendal we turned left on the A590 Barrow road for the south Lakes, at which point I would be roused from my daydreams by the appearance in the west of the dark Lakeland fells, their rough-edged heights pushing at the sky.

It was the best part of 300 miles and it took a whole day. We left early in my grandmother's sky-blue Morris Traveller. She was not a particularly slow driver, but it was rare for the speedometer to get above 60 m.p.h. Sitting in the back seat behind her, I could sense from the crescendo of engine noise and the slight shuddering of the chassis when we were approaching top speed. I would lean forward over her shoulder to watch the needle tremble as it reached the sixty mark. Silently I would urge it onwards; I longed for it to reach seventy, although I think that even at that tender age I was aware that the top speed of eighty displayed on the speedometer belonged in the realms of make-believe. Sixty was exciting enough, but on the single carriageway, traffic-clogged arterial routes of those days, it was never maintained for long.

For most of the way, I stared out of the window but saw very little. I was sustained by my imagination working on the special place, building dramatic scenes of slaying pike, slicing the canoe into the reed-beds and preparing an ambush, laying eel lines in the big pool down the river, playing cowboys and indians in the bracken. That first sight of the Lake District, with the westering sun flooding through the clouds, would recall me briefly to the real world, but it was followed by another slow, boring crawl as we skirted around Morecambe Bay towards Ulverston.

The real excitement began as we crossed the River Crake where it entered a branch of the bay, and turned north on the Coniston road. The river was intensely familiar to me because its mouth was just along the shore from our cottage, and it flowed through many of my favourite imaginings. From there onwards the road followed its valley. One either side were green meadows speckled with sheep and separated into irregular shapes by the wandering lines of the dry-stone walls. Higher up, the fields gave way to the rock and bracken of the fells.

From then on my senses were on full alert, trained on a succession of landmarks: grey pebble-dashed farmhouse, overhanging copper beech, small slate-roofed church; a pair of high, rusted metal gates, never open; Coniston Old Man ahead, its lop-sided summit lit by the evening sun (if it was clear, which it sometimes was). The climax was the first sighting of the lake. There were always false alarms, because the road went up and down and twisted left and right many times, and I could never remember exactly which rise in the land would reveal that first sight of water. So when it came – a liquid gleam against pale green reed-beds – there was the shock of recognition followed by a jolt of delight.

As a grown-up I have been back many times with my children. The road is the same, although the trees are taller and the cottage seems even lower. The moment at which the lake reveals itself feels exactly as it did half a century ago.

I did not know the A303 then. It was later, much later, that I found it. I was in the process of discovering two rivers that would become places of enchantment for me; the road opened my way to them and thus became important to me.

The first of the rivers, travelling west, is the Avon, which winds south from Amesbury towards Salisbury. It's a chalkstream of rich feeding where the trout grow big, and pewter-scaled grayling shoal in the hatch-pools and in the deep holes on bends where the current has scoured out the bank. Further on, beyond Stonehenge, through the village of Winterbourne Stoke and past the grassy earth-works of Yarnbury Castle, is the valley of the Wylye. It is half the size of the Avon, although it has surprising depths, and it runs through woods and meadows and past old beamed houses with mullioned windows, connecting a string of the prettiest, sleepiest villages in England. You can lose yourself on the Wylye, and fish for hours without seeing a soul or being aware of anything much beyond these willows and alders and the sound and movement of water, or the likelihood of finding a feeding fish where the gravelled shallow shelves down to the head of a pool.

I would drive the A303 sometimes on my own, but often with a particular friend. In summer we would gener-ally go down in the evening, towards the sun, reaching the Avon as the shadows of the trees stretched across the water, and finish late with the bats out and owls hooting across dark meadows. In winter the fishing days are short and the water can seem lifeless. But even the coldest of them can startle you with a magical hour around noon when insects suddenly hatch and the grayling wake up to eat them. And always the A303, holding out the promise of delight on the way there, the way back always more muted, the radio on to cover the silences, the landmarks passing unnoticed, their meaning forfeited.

The A303 extends from just west of Basingstoke to a few miles east of Honiton in Devon. The distance is little more than ninety miles, which makes it a baby among major arterial routes (the A1 is 400 miles, the A38 290). But the A303 straddles spheres. It can take the adventurer from cosy, commuter-belt Hampshire to the threshold of another land entirely, one of wooded dales enclosing tumbling streams, steep hillsides and old stone farm-houses, purple treeless moors, eventually rocky headlands and sandy beaches and the surging sea. It is a road of magical properties.

From the late 1950s, for ten or twelve years, Linda followed it each year with her father, mother and younger brother from their home in Buckinghamshire. Their first car was a Hillman Minx, their destination a caravan site near Weymouth. As their circumstances improved, they migrated west for the annual holiday, to Devon and later Cornwall, and it grew from one week to two.

Linda's father, a clerk with the Gas Board, would really have preferred to have spent his leave entitlement at home tending the garden that he loved with a deep, quiet passion. But Linda's mother insisted that they must go away, and as he loved to drive, he drove. He wrote down the route on an envelope: across to Basingstoke, A303 to Honiton, A30 further west – the destination always a caravan site. Linda's mother did not drive and could not read a map, so Linda sat next to her father, passing on the instructions when it got complicated. The end of the road varied, but there was one constant. Linda would ask if they were going past Stonehenge and when they did, they would stop and climb on the stones and wander among them and wonder at them. Each year, the monument which had delivered different messages to so many over thousands of years told them that they were on their way.

Linda's father liked the A303 because it was faster than the narrow, winding A30. The A303 gave the journey a firm, propulsive shove. He liked it even more when they widened stretches of it into dual carriageway. Stuck behind a crawling lorry or – worse still – a tractor dragging a stack of hay, he would become silent and tense. Then a section of dual carriageway would beckon and the mood in the car – later a Triumph Herald, later still a lime-green Ford Capri – would lighten as the accelerator pedal went down.

Simon and his family went every year to Devon or Cornwall, always staying on a farm, always taking the A303, always stopping at Stonehenge for their picnic. Simon's father was an Austin man: the family progressed from Austin 7 to Austin 55 to Austin 60. He had all the maps covering the south-west and had – or felt he had – no need of a map-reader. 'Dad was in charge of getting us lost,' Simon remembers. When Simon, as a young man, took his girlfriend to Yorkshire for a holiday, he felt they were going the wrong way. It was unnatural not to be on the A303. The road was in his blood.

There are plenty who still follow the same path. I went to find a random sample of them on a Friday in the 2011 summer holiday season. It was grey and drizzly, the forecast dodgy. The traffic was heavy but not exceptionally so, just the usual solid stream. The car parks at the service areas were full; the Little Chefs were packed, with queues outside. Humour was good despite the weather and the traffic.

A family from Hatfield in Hertfordshire – father, mother, two kids, two grandparents – were heading for Exmouth, their seven-seater packed to the roof. 'Always take the A303,' Dad said, 'less boring than the motorway, and you've always got Stonehenge.' Derek from Newmarket was taking a cup of tea from a Thermos in the shelter of his boot-lid as the drizzle drifted down, his team – wife, daughter, two grandsons – tightly packed into a blue saloon bound for Bridport. Derek had seen a BBC Four programme I'd made about the A303. 'Here, meet the wife,' he said proudly. She, he confided to me, would rather be heading east to see the sun – Yarmouth or somewhere like that – but he made the decisions and one of them was the A303.

An elderly couple in the queue for a cup of tea were doing as they had done most years since 1957, when as honeymooners they set off for Devon in their Austin 7. Now they had their ten-year-old grandson with them. They had had their foreign holidays since then and there was nothing wrong with them, but there was something about the south-west, something special, and this was the way to find it. An old rocker with a pony-tail told me that it had begun for him in the mid-1960s folded into the back of the family Mini, and he'd finally settled in Cornwall and not come back. 'It was part of my childhood, the

A303,' he said, speaking slowly and nodding in that old rocker's way. 'So part of me.'

There were more the same, taking the road not because they had deep feelings about it or had ever thought much about it, but because it was part of a familiar and comforting act of escape. Everyone knows the motorway is quicker: M25 around London, M4 to Bristol, M5 to Exeter. But the A303 belongs in the ritual and the motorway doesn't. We go this way because we always went this way, and we're still doing the same thing only we're older now and the car's rather smarter and the traffic is just as bad as it ever was. All those I spoke to explained their preference on the grounds that the motorway was boring. There was more to see on the A303 and more time to see it. Stonehenge, always Stonehenge. Two of the drivers were ex-truckers. They said most truckers would take the A303 if they could, for all the same reasons, plus better, cheaper, hotter, fresher-made breakfasts at the cafés along the way.

Everyone moaned about the traffic, but in a good-humoured way, almost affectionately. It was part of the A303; what else could you expect on a Friday afternoon in the holiday season? Don't fret, mate, we'll all get there in the end.

Coming back is something else. Same road, but not the same at all. For a child, there is an almost physical ache as the special place is left behind, and even as adults we feel the sadness. The road is complicit in the loss. The landmarks in their reverse order remind us of what we are leaving behind. We twist our heads for a last glimpse of the cottage or caravan or campsite, catch a last gleam from the lake or the sea. Ahead is home, work, school, routine, daily shaving, uncut lawn, unpicked veg, duties, appointments. It is the road that is returning us to this enslavement and we resent it. It's then that the jams seem against us, an extra injury. A man in my cricket club was telling me about coming back from his holiday in Devon, infant daughter fractious, wife testy, the traffic solid. 'Fucking A303, I hate it. Don't talk to me about fucking Stonehenge, sick of the sight of the fucking thing.'

★ ★ ★

'You can let yourself go on the 303,' pounded forth Kula Shaker. 'You can find your way home on the 303.' The song celebrated in enigmatic lyrics the way to 'the land of the summer sun' – presumably Glastonbury, where the band was born at the 1993 festival. Each June the Glastonbury faithful still follow the road in pursuit of some kind of escape or release, a few days of another kind of life.

For the generation before them, the lure was Stonehenge and its Free Festival – music, drugs, free love, hugs and acid smiles and signs of peace, a repudiation of the cheerless world of career and mortgage beyond, and the grim, dangerous world beyond that. Down the A303 the Love Convoy rolled, until Mrs Thatcher and her ministers and the *Daily Mail* decided that society had had quite enough of that sort of useless parasitism, thank you, and put a stop to it.

There was no psychedelic rock for me at the end of the road, and certainly no free love, just flowing water and the sweet, fulfilling joy of casting a fly for a fish. Like most travellers, I did not trouble myself about the road itself – not at first. It was nothing more than a means to my end. The idea of looking into its story took form slowly. But once I began to pursue it, the feeling was like that of pushing open a door into a walled garden full of interesting vegetables and trees laden with apples and plums and pears; or into an attic where there were old chests in which the records of old adventures had been left to gather dust.

As I wandered about poking my nose in here and there, I began to wonder not just about this road but about other roads and roads in general, and our relationship with them, and the place of the motor car in that relationship. It is a truism that we take our cars for granted, and another that we could not imagine life without them. But it could be that we are edging towards a watershed in that relationship.

Since 1945 the car – a vehicle built of steel, powered by petrol, owned by us – has become a dominant influence on the way we live. It has enabled almost all of us to embrace a frantic fluidity of movement that has progressively determined how, mechanically, society should function. Other forms of transport – horse, bike, train, bus – have been unable to stand against it. It made possible the immediate gratification of every fleeting desire to be somewhere else. It put within everyone's grasp a vision of mobility that abolished constraint and reduced the world into a mesh of manageable journeys. We were all seduced by its central principle: go where you like, when you like, as you like.

Its flaw is that it is fabulously wasteful. It consumes resources of energy, space and time as if they were inexhaustible. They are not. Little by little the vision's sources of nourishment are beginning to run out. The price of fuel has risen to a point where only the rich and the stupid no longer pause to consider if a journey is worth it. At the same time insurance premiums have been driven up to levels way beyond the means of many recently qualified drivers. The roads remain clogged; journey times rise inexorably.

A new model of mobility is needed. Already in the cities some people are giving up their cars in favour of a rental service available via phone app that enables them to pick up a vehicle when they need it and drop it off when they have finished with it, paying an hourly rate for the use. Far from finding their freedom of movement restricted, they discover that they have rid themselves of a bundle of irritations (breakdowns, punctures, where to park, getting fuel, remembering tax and MOT) not to mention the expense.

The age of the motor car has been with us for little more than half a century, and there is no reason to believe that it will last for ever, any more than did the age of the train or the stagecoach. True, for much of the world it has only just begun and still has its course to run, as the people of emerging economies joyfully embrace its life-enhancing possibilities. But in traffic-strangled western Europe its days are probably numbered. It is no longer feasible to dismiss as a sociologist's utopian fancy a system of small, plastic mobile pods powered by fuel cells (probably hydrogen), communally owned, with a digital control network determining availability, route, speed and price; a system in which people and businesses will be careful of their mobility allowances.

When the new age comes, its people – the children of our children's children perhaps – will look back at our system and consider it startlingly wasteful, destructive and crude. It's a fair bet that they will not be hopping into their micro-cars on a whim and nipping eighty-odd miles down the A303 for an evening's fishing and eighty miles back again. But there will still – unless we mess everything up – be fishing. And there will be an A303. It will still be assisting tomorrow's travellers to accommodate the chronic restlessness of the species. It will still enable them to pursue their dreams and to live and relive remembered joys in one way or another.

1

IGNITION ON

The weather might have been kinder for such an auspicious occasion. It was a gusty, rainy September day. The photographs show the worthies of Hampshire in raincoats, umbrellas raised against a leaden sky, hair disarranged by the breeze. They included the chairman of Hampshire County Council, Sir Richard Calthorpe; the chairman of Andover Rural District Council, Mr J. D. Threadgill; the Mayor of Andover, Mrs Anne Thorne, and a gaggle of aldermen and county and borough councillors. They had been summoned to welcome a distinguished guest and to mark a red-letter day in the history of the county and the ancient town of Andover.

In fact the guest was not as distinguished as he should have been. The programme originally submitted to the county council by the Ministry of Transport stated that the Andover bypass would be opened by the minister himself, Richard Marsh, one of the smoother and more televisual

1

talents in Harold Wilson's Labour government. But late in the day word came that Mr Marsh was being diverted to the Basingstoke Northern bypass. His place at Andover would be taken by his parliamentary secretary, Bob Brown, a Newcastle MP and former trade union official.

The guests may well have been disappointed by this substitution; may have sniffed somewhat at hearing Mr Brown's Geordie accent rather than Mr Marsh's melli-fluous Home Counties tones; may have nursed the regret in their hearts – this was Hampshire, after all – that this long-awaited moment should have arrived when a Socialist rather than a Conservative government was in power. Never mind. Mr Brown could cut a ribbon as neatly as anyone else. He could deliver a celebratory speech written by some nameless official without making a fool of himself. He would do. The great matter was the road.

The main photograph in the *Andover Advertiser*'s coverage of the day's events shows Mr Brown with scissors at the ready. The road surface beneath his feet is dark and smooth and slick with rain. The scene revealed in other pictures is one of ruin: a landscape ripped asunder, woods and copses torn up, fields assigned in Domesday devoured, hillsides thrust aside; vast ramparts of soil, stone and chalk heaped up, the countryside violated in the name of progress. In our time we have largely forgotten the brutality of road building. But then it was familiar enough. Then was 1969.

The *Times* of the next day, Friday 12 September,

reported the opening of the £2 million Andover bypass as well as that of the Basingstoke Northern bypass in a single paragraph. The newspaper was more interested that morning in the discussions about mutual tensions and interests between the Russian premier, Mr Kosygin, and the Chinese premier, Chou en Lai. It reported extensively on a wave of industrial unrest in western Europe involving French railwaymen, Italian metal workers and German miners, and on the expulsion of an unruly rabble of hippies from Ibiza. The paper's education correspondent examined the sagging morale of teachers. The Northern Ireland correspondent analysed an official report laying the blame for Belfast's incendiary condition on militant supporters of the Reverend Ian Paisley. The Israelis had shot down eleven Egyptian aircraft, and a new constitution for Rhodesia had been published. The Bank of England was concerned about the tightening squeeze on credit. Letter writers were exercised about Britain's place in the Common Market.

In the *Andover Advertiser* the bypass was the big story, but not the only one. Andover Ufologists had held a meeting to talk about sightings of 'moving lights and blurred illuminated objects' and agreed to hold a further skywatch. Grateley and District Women's Institute had thanked Mrs Mann for her talk on How To Make a Skirt. Basingstoke Chamber of Commerce was reported as having urged Andoverians to 'come and shop in the "Space-age Town of the South"'. Members of Andover

Borough Council had voted not to wear ceremonial robes for the Battle of Britain service on 21 September – Alderman Porter said there was nothing worse than six people turning up in regalia and the rest not bothering.

If you had cash to spare there were ways to spend it. Pontings of Andover were offering a one-year-old Hillman Minx Estate in white, with fitted wing mirrors, for £700. You could rent an 'all-channels 19-inch tube TV set' for forty-six shillings and two pence a month, with a forty-shilling deposit. And on it, the night of the bypass opening, you could have watched Patrick Cargill in *Father Dear Father* on Thames, followed on BBC 1 by an episode of *Dad's Army* entitled 'The Armoured Might of Corporal Jones'.

It so happened that I got my full driving licence in 1969. At the time our family car was, I think, a Ford Consul, but I have no memory of ever being allowed to drive it. My three elder brothers and I shared the use of the sky-blue Morris Traveller that had been our grandmother's until she upgraded to a Morris 1100. The Traveller served us well until its rear offside wheel fell off while I was driving it through the outskirts of Guildford, inflicting fatal structural damage to the undercarriage. As I had been responsible for putting the wheel on after a puncture repair – apparently with the nuts the wrong way round – I had only myself to blame.

That autumn I went to university, where one of my

brothers passed on to me a bulbous, mud–coloured Austin A40 which he had bought from our local garage for £45. It had a bench front seat covered in soft chestnut leather worn and cracked by the many backsides of previous owners and passengers. It had no functioning heater and in cold or damp weather it was necessary to haul the choke out to its full extension of eight or ten inches to have a hope of starting it. The window wipers were very short and moved so slowly that in anything like a downpour it was safer to steer by leaning out of the window, or preferably to stop altogether.

The A40 was followed by a 1959 Austin Cambridge that I bought from the same local garage for £55. In its distant youth this car had had a twin–tone white body with black roof and tail. Over time the black had faded to dingy dark grey, and the white to dirty dishcloth, both extensively blistered and pockmarked by rust. Because it was the first car I had bought for myself I was rather proud of it, but it had many faults. On anything more testing than a 1–in–20 uphill slope the engine would start coughing in a tubercular manner. Genuine hills could be conquered only in first gear, with queuing traffic behind obscured by a trailing cloud of bluish smoke. This condition required regular return visits to the garage for a process known as 'de-coking'. Each time she would run smoothly for a while. Then the coughing would resume. Gradually the intervals between the treatments became shorter.

The Austin Cambridge came with a starting handle. I

doubt if one in a hundred of today's pampered motorists would be able to recognise one, let alone know what to do with it. Actually my own notion of operating it was hazy. I knew where to insert it, but no one had told me about the dangers of kickback, or that I needed to keep my thumb on the same side as my fingers. By now the health of my car had deteriorated to such a degree that it would start only if pushed. One morning there was no one to help push it, so I resorted to the handle. My fractured wrist was in plaster for fifteen weeks.

Other vehicles came and went in our lives. Our grand-mother progressed from a Morris 1100 to a Morris 1300 to a very smart, almost luxurious Vanden Plas 1300 with grey leather seats, soft carpets, and a lacquered walnut dash-board. She was as generous in letting us drive her cars as in everything else. My brother Matthew overturned one of them on a local lane, and her one concern was that he was all right. I skidded in her Vanden Plas when taking a bend far too fast and shot backwards into a field, puncturing both back tyres, and she did not even rebuke me for my recklessness.

The brother who had passed the Austin A40 on to me acquired a Morris Minor which he was very taken with, until one day he lifted the carpet on the driver's side and saw the road underneath. My eldest brother had a Humber Super Snipe (I liked the name but the machine was not to be relied on) and subsequently a Vauxhall Cresta with gears on the steering column (vulgar but excitingly powerful). For the family car we had the Ford Consul, followed by various Cortinas, then a horribly ponderous Morris Oxford.

The feature common to all these cars was that they were British. They were made by British workers in British factories owned by British companies (Ford UK had been here so long it felt British). In 1968 British Leyland produced a million cars, and the ad campaigns of that year had a pleasingly home-grown flavour. 'Great cars don't happen overnight' was the slogan for the ever-popular Morris 1300. The Triumph TR6 offered the thrill of its 'long, power-breathing nose', its petrol injection, its 'body-hugging bucket seats'. The admen at MG were inspired to free verse: 'One day/ when time has clipped/your sports car wings/when all the proud cars of your years/line up to take the cheq-uered flag of memory/you will remember how you caught/the sunrise/rode the misty wings of morning/in your MGB GT'.

There were ominous signs, though. 1969 saw the launch in Britain of the Honda 1300, the Datsun Sunny, and the Toyota Corolla, heralding the Japanese invasion of our car market. At the mighty Longbridge car plant on the outskirts of Birmingham – the heart and lungs of British Leyland – a Communist shop steward called Derek Robinson was deploying his menacing, monotonous Midlands voice to take control of the works committee, thereby sowing the seeds of the industrial conflict that, a decade later, would make Red Robbo a leading hate figure for the right-wing media and Conservative establishment.

For the moment, however, a roll call of familiar names still gave the British car market its distinctively and comfortably British complexion. There were new or newish models to draw the gaze of the rapidly expanding army of car buyers – Wolseley (the 18/85), Riley (the Kestrel), Hillman (the Husky), Singer (the Gazelle), Sunbeam (the Rapier), Rover (the 3500), Humber (the Sceptre) – as well as the various Morrises, Austins, Triumphs and Vauxhalls, the exciting new Ford Capri, and the darling Mini. We thought British and we bought British. And – as the opening of the Andover bypass illustrated – the experience of driving British was expanding fast.

'Every new mile of highway brings a warm glow even to a Transport Minister's heart,' Mr Brown told his damp, windswept audience as they stood beside Andover's Picket Twenty interchange. The minister's heart must have been unusually suffused with heat that September day. Not only had Richard Marsh himself opened the Basingstoke Northern bypass and Bob Brown the Andover bypass, but twelve miles further west the chairman of Wiltshire County Council, Sir Henry Langton, was declaring the Amesbury bypass open, offering the hope that the people of Amesbury would at last be able to enjoy a decent night's sleep.

It's likely that Richard Marsh's inner warmth was

short-lived, as within a few weeks of that happy day he was sacked from the government for daring to oppose *In Place of Strife,* Harold Wilson and Barbara Castle's ill-fated plan for bringing the obstreperous unions to heel. But for the great majority of the citizens of Andover and Amesbury the comfort was huge and permanent. Andover in particular had acquired the reputation over the previous decade of being one of the most hellish traffic bottle-necks in the country. Queues several miles long were standard at holiday times, as up to 20,000 vehicles a day tried to fight their way through the twisting streets of the town centre. At night the houses along Bridge Street and London Road shuddered in a fog of diesel fumes as a procession of trucks ground past.

'You cannot expect diamonds the size of bricks,' Mr Brown said later in his speech. The meaning of this cryptic metaphor seems to have been that the £2 million spent on Andover might seem modest, even insignificant, in the context of an annual road-building budget of £300 million – but that schemes like this added up. What the country was finally getting, Mr Brown boasted, was the 'sophisti-cated road network' it needed and deserved – and all thanks to the wisdom and ambition of a Labour govern-ment. At last a vision was being realised.

We had always lagged behind our continental competi-tors in this great endeavour. In Germany the first *autobahns* had been constructed, as ordered by Hitler, at incredible speed, 'as flawless and powerful as National Socialism itself', in the words of one evangelist. Italy had its first *autostrada* even earlier, while in France the network of *autoroutes* had been spreading steadily during the 1950s. But in Britain the fine words had never – until comparatively recently – been matched by fine deeds.

As long ago as 1903 a Conservative MP, John Scott Montagu, had proposed a motorway between London and Birmingham. In 1905 Scott – by then Lord Montagu of Beaulieu – set forth this vision: 'Large towns will have special arterial routes. There will be but little noise, no smell, no dust. No bacteria will breed in fermenting horse-manure, and the water-cart will be unknown. Europe will become for the motorist one vast holiday area. The country with the best roads will become more and more prosperous. Roads will be justly regarded as the necessary hallmark of civilisation.'

Autocar's blueprint for the way ahead

Few disagreed. But somehow the vision did not inspire the resolve to realise it. Every government had a plan to modernise the road network. No government managed to produce the resources to make it happen. In August 1936 *Autocar* magazine asked what progress had been made on the programme announced 'with gusto' a year and a half earlier to spend £100 million on new roads and major improvements. The answer, in effect, was almost nothing. The war came, everything was postponed. Peace came, and with it austerity. In May 1946 the Labour Transport Minister, Alfred Barnes, set out proposals to Parliament to improve road safety, repair bombed and blasted roads and reduce traffic congestion – all subject, he said, to the availability of 'such resources as may be at my disposal'. The resources were not abundant.

Little by little the pressure increased. Much of it took the form of a growing clamour from the swelling ranks of middle-class car owners sick of traffic jams and crawling along narrow, winding roads dating back to the turnpike era. At the same time a new generation of road builders, led by Lancashire's forceful county surveyor, James Drake, at last managed to get the attention of ministers and their officials. The builders argued that without a network of fast dual-carriageway roads, Britain would be unable to retain its place at the top table of world economic powers. The equations were simple enough. The car industry was vital to the economy and would become more so. Greater prosperity would mean more people buying more cars.

Everyone wanted to go somewhere, but they must be able to get there.

'The purpose of motorways,' Drake wrote, 'is fairly obvious. They should provide safer travelling, they should reduce the time taken to make the journey, and they should carry more traffic.' At that time the possibility of an inherent contradiction between the second and third axioms did not occur to anyone.

In March 1958 the Conservative Transport Minister, Harold Watkinson – described by Joe Moran in his terrific book *On Roads* as 'the first politician to see the votes in motorways' – blew a horn to inaugurate the building of the M1. At the end of that year the prime minister himself, Harold Macmillan, opened the first stretch of British motorway, the Preston bypass (which would form part of the M6). Two years later, work began on the M4, and two years after that the first section of the M5 was opened. In 1962 Watkinson's successor, the irrepressible Ernest Marples, promised a thousand miles of motorway over the next ten years. By 1966 it was possible to drive on motorway from London to Birmingham, much of the way from London to Leeds, and across the Severn Bridge into Wales. A year later responsibility for planning, building and maintaining motorways and trunk roads was transferred from the county councils to the Ministry of Transport.

The eyes of the planners and the engineers roamed far and wide. Among the routes on which they rested from time to time was the A303. Although the M5 was well on its way to penetrating the south-west, it was really a western highway. Even when married with the M4 it would represent a very long way round for motorists on the southern and eastern sides of London who were anxious to taste the delights of Devon and Cornwall.

Something better was needed. An old dream, of a London–Penzance trunk road, began to shimmer alluringly on the horizon once more.

2

THE ROAD TO MANDERLEY?

The question for students and critics of Daphne du Maurier's *Rebecca* is: did the second Mrs de Winter and her creepy husband take the A303 to get to his 'secretive and silent' Cornish hideaway? The best I can offer is that they might have done.

There are not many clues. As newlyweds they leave London in the morning and arrive at the house in time for tea at five, but there is nothing about signposts or map references. Subsequently, driving from Cornwall with stuffy Colonel Julyan, they stop for lunch 'in one of those inevitable hotels on the main street of a county town' where the colonel puts away soup, fish and a roast. Since they reach the suburbs of London by three o'clock, we can assume that he laid down his napkin not later than two hours from the capital. This could place the old-fashioned hotel in Amesbury or Andover on the A303 (each had the George), or in Salisbury (a very early lunch) or Stockbridge

14

(the Grosvenor in the High Street would fit the bill) on the A30. Basingstoke, Bagshot, Egham and Staines – other likely lunching venues on the A30 – can, I think, be ruled out on the grounds that they do not really qualify as country towns.

When Mr and Mrs de Winter – without Colonel Julyan – return from extracting Rebecca's dark secrets from Dr Baker in Barnet, they leave a restaurant in Soho at quarter to eight in the evening. Maxim de Winter says they should reach Manderley by half past two in the morning. 'There won't be much traffic on the road,' he forecasts. But which road? She, annoyingly, sleeps instead of reading the map. They stop at a garage where a bitter wind blows. I like to think that this was a Salisbury Plain wind – it is autumn, when the Plain winds can be bitter indeed. That would put the garage on the A303 – Amesbury? Mere? Wincanton? – but I concede that the inference is tenuous.

Certainly de Winter would have been aware that he had a choice of route. Motoring west from central London he would have taken the Great West Road as far as Hounslow, then the A30 through Staines, Egham and Bagshot and on beyond Basingstoke to a junction near Micheldever railway station. Here the A303 forked right to Andover and the A30 slipped south towards Stockbridge and Salisbury. The two roads thus framed to the north and south a segment of land about eighty-five miles long and shaped like a toucan's beak, before coming together again near Honiton. There the A303 became defunct, as it still does, while the A30 continued to Exeter and eventually Penzance.

When Daphne du Maurier was first enchanted by Cornwall and its coast in the 1920s, the vast, tedious task of numbering Britain's more important roads had been completed, on paper at least. But it took some years for the numbers to reach road signs and maps. A *Geographia* cloth road map for south-west England and south Wales – dating from about 1926 – classifies both the A303 and the A30 as Class 1 (A) Ministry of Transport Roads, without numbers. The A303 officially came into existence on 1 April 1933, but the maps did not hurry to catch up. The 1937 *Roadmaster* map of England, Wales and Scotland – 'specially designed for motoring' and 'prepared according to the Berquvist Easy Reference system' – designated both roads as first class, with their numbers but without the 'A'. The map attached to the Trunks Road Act of 1936 showed the A30 as the route to the west, with the A303 nowhere.

If de Winter was following Ministry of Transport advice, he would definitely have taken the A30 via Salisbury. But he might have known better. Even then – the novel was written in 1937 – traffic jams were becoming a familiar problem, and the likeliest place to encounter them was where a main road had to squeeze and twist itself through the centre of a busy town on a course designed for carts and horse-drawn carriages. It may well be – I put it no more strongly – that having got through Staines, Egham and Bagshot, he quailed at the prospect of

Salisbury and Yeovil, not to mention Shaftesbury, Sherborne and Chard.

It's also possible that he had a copy of the *National Road Book* compiled by R.T. Lang and published in 1936. This indispensable volume contained, in a way characteristic of its age, an address to 'the Good Companions of the Road, helping each other along the ways in that good nature and cheerful spirit which is bred by love of the countryside'. Dealing with the task of getting from London to Land's End, Lang recommended leaving the A30 at Basingstoke, taking the old coach road via Overton to Andover, then forking left onto the A303 for a 'wild, open run across Salisbury Plain' and on to Honiton – 'a direct and mostly falling road through what Defoe called "the most beautiful landskip in the world"'. Who could resist such an invitation?

Nevertheless, on the trunk road map that accompanied Alfred Barnes' statement on future plans to Parliament in 1946, the A30 remained the senior route to the west. But within a few years officials looked at the situation again. They noticed that the A30 was afflicted with an undue number of town centre bottlenecks, and they decided that the less encumbered A303 might be a better bet. The *AA Roadbook* of 1957 advised motorists heading from London to Cornwall to turn from the A30 onto the A303 at Micheldever. On 1 April the *London Gazette* recorded that the A303 – as far as it went – was hitherto to be regarded as the trunk road to Penzance.

Since then, the A303 has always been the favoured of

the two sisters. Despite being much longer and much more steeped in history, the A30 was left to meander between the old coaching stops that had once nourished it, rarely chosen for major improvements, neglected and overlooked, condemned by its largely single-carriageway status to be loathed and despised by the motorists forced to use it. The A303, in contrast, was spoiled and pampered. Andover and Amesbury got their bypasses, and stretches east and west of Andover were converted to dual carriageway, with a link near Basingstoke to the M3. By the mid-1980s a gleaming highway stretched to Amesbury, while further on a string of towns and villages – including Wylye, Mere and Wincanton – had been graced with dual-carriageway bypasses.

The assumption underlying the piecemeal upgrading of the A303 was that one day all these stretches of smart new road would be unified into a great arterial route to Exeter; and eventually from Exeter onwards. That was the dream.

3

HESTON SERVICES

T. S. Eliot's celebrated musings on ends and beginnings in *Four Quartets* – 'In my beginning is my end . . .' and '. . . in my end is my beginning' – are highly suggestive of roads. For all I know they may even have been suggested to him by the A303. They occur in the second of the poems, 'East Coker', which Eliot named after the village near Yeovil where his ancestors came from. It is entirely possible that when he first visited it in 1937, he used the pre-war A303 to get there from London.*

For the Exeter man with business in London, the A303 begins a few miles east of Honiton and ends when it meets the M3 south-west of Basingstoke. For the Londoner whose soul yearns for the wooded dales of Somerset, the purple heights of Exmoor or Dartmoor, or

* Another clue that the A303 was in his mind could be the reference in the fourth line to houses being replaced by 'an open field, or a factory, or a bypass'.

the crashing surf of Cornwall, it is the other way round. Neither end, neither beginning, can claim precedence over the other. But it makes sense for a narrative about a road to move generally in one direction or the other, which is how I have organised this one. The alternative would be either a degree of topographical to-ing and fro-ing that would rapidly become irritating, or even a second, back-to-front version of the whole thing. My choice to go east to west was a matter of convenience for me, no more. I would not want anyone to interpret it as implying condescension towards those whose concep-tion of the road is the reverse. After all, most of us end up driving back the way we came.

I have tried to imagine this road as a river, flowing through time as well as space, shaping the landscape, accepting tributary roads as it goes, its story composed of itself and the stories of those who have lived and died on it, and travelled it. I am aware that the analogy is far from exact: that, for instance, a river starts as a trickle and keeps growing, is born in high ground and is extinguished by the sea, must go downhill and downhill only, and is possessed by a one-way force. But I still see a likeness, and in both cases exploration requires location of a source.

This can be tricky with a river. It's not always easy to tell which spring or which puddle caught in some boggy upland has primacy. Sometimes – as with the Danube – there are two competing branches, and the arguments over which is the senior rumble for centuries. With the eastern end of the A303 there is also a degree of – shall we say? – mystery.

On the map it emerges from a lopped branch of the M3, standing out to the right as the motorway curves from the south-western edge of Basingstoke towards Winchester. There are slip roads either side of this stump. The northern one provides access for eastbound traffic onto the A30 into Basingstoke (curiously, the A30 as a westbound proposition ceases to exist altogether at this point, but springs back to life several miles away as an offshoot of the southbound A34). It is on the southern slip road – leading from the M3 to the A303 – where the search for the source must be concentrated.

Getting close

You are driving west along the M3. You pass a junction that leads in one direction to the A30 into Basingstoke, and in the other to Dummer, home of the Duchess of York's late, louche and luxuriantly eyebrowed father, Major Ronald Ferguson (but let's not be distracted). Soon after this junction, a sign summons you to consider the A303. An invitation is also inscribed across the road surface. You deviate left. The slip road arcs past field and woodland and back under the M3. The blue colouring of the marker posts indicate that this is still classified as motorway. But which motorway? Is it still M3? Or could it be unidentified M303? Or should it be A303(M)? I said it was a mystery; I didn't say it was an interesting mystery.

The Highways Agency does not tell, and anyway in a moment or two limbo-way ends with a sign showing a thick red diagonal line across the motorway blue. This is the beginning of the A303 (or, for the last time, the end). You may now legally mount a horse, start pedalling a bike, set forth on a scooter, or walk. None of these methods of locomotion is to be recommended. Fortunately Basingstoke Crematorium, with its chapel, its neat rows of tablets to the departed, its lawns and groves of trees and memorial pond and splashing fountain, and its thoroughly modern facilities for disposing of the victims of accidents, is very close at hand.

In terms of scale and the speed of traffic, this newborn A303 is hardly distinguishable from the motorway that sends it forth into the world. There is one important difference, however, (apart from the rules allowing horses and so forth). There is no hard shoulder, no lane of refuge for the halt and the lame and the punctured. Instead there are lay-bys. The first of many soon appears.

Our lay-bys are not intended as places to linger. The British lay-by does not lead – as its equivalent in France may do – to a bosky clearing suitable for rest and picnicking. It is a stingy affair, shallow and rarely even offering protection in the form of a screen of shrubs or trees from the racket and pressure waves produced by the traffic blasting past. The traveller who wishes to eat, rest or make a phone call is advised to stay in the car. The traveller wishing to urinate or have a crap must take his or her chance in the undergrowth. Facilities are minimal, often restricted to a rubbish bin, less often including a noticeboard on which is displayed what is euphemistically referred to as Tourist Information about the locality.

Law of the lay-by

There is usually another sign, of the bossyboots variety, telling you to take your litter home with you. Perversely these are generally placed next to the rubbish bin. The message is thus confused. Are you supposed to use the bin only if you are not going home, or if you have no home? Or are you supposed to divide your litter, leaving some and taking some away? Judging by the amount invariably distributed all around these cheerless places, many people – perhaps understandably – have decided to chuck it on the ground rather than grapple with these difficult questions.

Ancient monument

Beyond the bin and the bossy sign in the A303's first lay-by is a small, pale, upright object with a rounded top, which turns out to be a minor and overlooked national treasure. It's a milestone installed in the 1760s to inform passing travellers that they were 53 miles from London, 14 miles from Stockbridge and 7 miles from Basingstoke. The fact that it appears in the British Listed Buildings Schedule is, I think, rather marvellous. What trouble we still take over tiny relics of our past. There it stands, this stubby fragment of transport history, and I doubt if anyone pauses to inspect it from one year to the next. But some dedicated architectural historian from English Heritage has taken the trouble to record its details and praise it as 'a good example of eighteenth-century milestone'. Eight furlongs further on – or 1760 yards if you prefer – there is another, with the distances appropriately adjusted. But there are no more on the A303 after that, because the old turnpike road then veers south in search of Stockbridge.

By then the traveller on the A303 has sped past, or yielded to, the temptations of the road's first contemporary version of the coaching inn of old. This announces itself with a sign displaying a plump, elfish fellow with a perky grin, a hanky tied in a knot around his neck, and an outsize chef's hat at a jaunty angle on his head. Elsewhere – but not here at Popham, because there is no room on the sign – he is shown holding up a warming dish with a cover on it shaped like a perfectly rounded breast and nipple. With or without the warming dish, his business is clear. His name is Fat Charlie and if you care to listen, he can tell you a good deal about the nation's eating habits.

Fat Charlie says hello

Fat Charlie is the logo and mascot of the Little Chef chain of roadside diners. Just the mention of Little Chef is enough to bring on an attack of queasy snobbishness among the newly food-conscious, and to rouse the plump and bilious food critic to spasms of disgust. The cream-and-red livery, the hats and uniforms, the formica tables and plastic-covered benches, the clusters of cruets and the laminated menus embody a small-town culinary philistinism that shames the *extra vergine* classes. And the food! Where else but Little Chef could you have found the Hunter's Chicken marinated in BBQ spices and served with a slice of cheddar cheese and crispy bacon? Or the tuna and chicken cheese melt? The Works flame-grilled burger and the chicken breast in batter 'on a bed of tangy relish, mixed leaves and tomato', served with chips or jacket potato? Who else but Little Chef could have proclaimed the Knickerbocker Glory as 'the taste of long summer afternoons in a glass'?

By rights Little Chef should long ago have gone the same way as Watney's Red Barrel beer and the turkey twizzler. But somehow it clings to its niche, because it offers a particular kind of person what they want in particular circumstances, and there are just enough of them to keep it going, although not as many as there used to be – in January 2012, 67 Little Chef outlets were closed. And Fat Charlie is more than just the creation of a design department. He has a life of his own and a place in the public's affection. A few years ago, after an upheaval in the ownership of the chain, a slimmer, semi-skimmed version of Fat Charlie was introduced, considered by some buzzy, finger-snapping PR sharpshooter to be more in keeping with growing consciousness about healthy eating. There was an outcry from Little Chef's constituency, and Full Fat Charlie was restored.

In summer 2009 he underwent a more subtle image change. He lost his neckerchief and took to sporting a bumfreezer chef's jacket with four buttons on the front. Not many realised it, but Charlie was aping a new and improbable mentor. By then Little Chef had acquired a jargon-spouting Christian evangelist named Ian Pegler as chief executive. As well as the good book, Pegler believed in the mystic power of PR, and his great coup was to recruit Heston Blumenthal, the genius of the Fat Duck restaurant in Bray and the Zeus among Olympian kitchen gods, to bring Little Chef's moribund laminated menu to life. Channel Four were on board for a TV programme about his involvement, and the 'eatery' at Little Popham was chosen as location for the rescue mission.

So Heston and his team journeyed from Berkshire to Hampshire to goggle in amazement at Little Chef staples such as the Mega Mixed Grill (rump steak, chicken breast, gammon, onion rings, chips) and squawk like outraged virgins at the horrible things done with microwaves. Over three nights on prime-time TV they were shown dragging Popham's willing but ignorant staff into the age of braised ox cheeks and rope-grown Scottish mussels.

The Heston wagon rolled on (oddly enough, Popham Fat Charlie never got the chef's jacket). The Pegler cart soon followed. But the Popham Little Chef lives on, and from my extensive acquaintance with it does solid business. Most of Blumenthal's daring innovations – the ox cheeks, the *coq-au-vin*, the mussels, the beer and vegetable casserole, the trifle with sponge soaked in green tea – proved too radical for Little Chef regulars to stomach, and have followed their creator out of the door. Fish and chips, steak and ale pie, and prawn cocktail survive from the Heston reformation. His influence is still felt on the 'Today's Specials' board, casually scrawled as if in response to a sudden inspiration in the kitchen. When I first visited in October 2009, two of these specials were Lamb Shank with Creamy Mash and Belly Pork on a Bed of Salad. Fifteen months later they were still there – today's, yesterday's and tomorrow's specials.

The only dish I have eaten there is the 'Olympic Breakfast', and very good it is. I do tend to reflect, as I wipe the brown sauce from my plate, that a slice or two of fried bread to complement the outdoor-bred sausages, the rashers of Wiltshire-cured bacon and the griddled free-range eggs would hardly contravene the Olympian spirit. But the coffee is good and the service genuinely cheery, even though I could do without the foodie quotes from George Bernard Shaw and A. A. Milne on the backs of the uniforms and the stand-up comic jollifications piped into the men's lavatories.

Outside I pause to pay my respects to Fat Charlie, a notable survivor. Famous chefs may come and go, and food fads blaze and die, but Charlie's grin stays as wide as ever. 'Little Chef Has Changed', the sign proclaims. It hasn't, not really. It can't. It can only go on as it is, or disappear.*

★　★　★

The Black Wood presses against the A303 just beyond Heston's Little Chef. It is well named. The tall, straight beeches stand close, the canopy blocking the sunlight from reaching the mantle of leaf-fall and dry, cracked beech nuts that covers the ground. An old Roman byway runs along the western flank of the wood, forming a junction to

---

* And disappear it has. Fat Charlie is no more. The Olympic Breakfast is no more. In 2017 the Popham site was taken over by Starbucks, which can tell you nothing about the nation's eating habits. The other A303 Little Chefs closed one by one, and the brand has now been erased from Britain's gastronomic map entirely.

the south with the great Roman highway between Winchester and Silchester. The assumption is that it provided access to Popham Beacons, a vantage point on the north side of the A303 from which an eye could be kept on a wide tract of country extending to Winchester in the south, Alton in the north, and across the Test Valley in the west to the military camp at Quarley Hill.

It's a while since the centurions tramped along in the shade of the beeches, but the surface of the road – compacted chalk and flint – is firm enough beneath the dead leaves and twigs. It still has its uses. Someone has driven down here to dump old lorry tyres, broken plastic chairs, and a heap of propane gas canisters.

Popham Beacons gets its name from the anxious time when Philip of Spain menaced Elizabeth of England, and signal-fires were heaped on hilltops across the land to warn of the expected Catholic invasion. The fire-builders left no trace; nor did the Roman guards. But there is a cluster of Bronze Age burial barrows close by, which does speak quietly of the very ancient history etched into the landscape of this very modern road.

'The Road is the humblest and the most subtle but . . . the greatest and most original of the spells which we inherit from the earliest pioneers of our race. It was the most imperative, and the first, of our necessities.' These words were written by Hilaire Belloc in a book called *The Old Road,* which appeared in 1904. It is a typical product of

Belloc's warm-hearted and energetic personality; typical, too, of its time and of a particular way – amateurish in the best sense, you might call it – of embracing and identifying with the past. Belloc was no archaeologist, nor a professional historian, but he was an enthusiast. He was a meat-eating, ale-quaffing Englishman, and a devout Roman Catholic, and he invested his Road with sacred significance. As our ancestors travelled it, he wrote, they brought with them 'letters, customs, community of language and idea' – and, inevitably, religion. The Road came first. Everything else followed.

In that innocent Edwardian age, interpreting prehistory was simple. Belloc's book included a map showing five great ridges of southern England: North Downs, South Downs, Dorset Downs, Cotswolds/Mendips, Chilterns/Berkshire Downs. His thesis was that to follow the ways of our ancestors you merely had to step along one or other of these ridges. He himself, for reasons of faith, chose the eastern way, between Winchester and Canterbury. But he could just as appropriately have tramped the Icknield Way and Great Ridgeway, or one of the others. On his map, and in his mind, they all converged on Stonehenge. To walk any of them was, Belloc enthused, 'to plunge right into the spirit of the oldest monument of the life men led in this island'.

This belief in the interconnectedness of southern England from the earliest times inspired others to investigate the ancient routes more closely than Hilaire Belloc had time to. Among them were a retired Manchester schoolmaster and his wife, Harold Timperley and Edith Brill, whose inquiries resulted in an influential and much-quoted book, *The Ancient Trackways of Wessex*. One of these trackways is of special interest to students of the A303, the Harrow Way. According to Mr and Mrs Timperley, the Harrow Way had its eastern 'terminus' near Dover and its western near the mouth of the Axe in Devon; it was, they maintained, the Great Ridgeway's 'only competitor' for the title of Oldest Road.

They sketched its path from Dover over the North Downs into Surrey and Hampshire, thereafter plotting its course in majestic detail around the north of Basingstoke, Whitchurch and Andover to meet the A303 at Weyhill, and then on past Amesbury to Stonehenge, and from Stonehenge on towards Devon. The sober presentation and wealth of topographical referencing lent considerable plausibility to their route for the Harrow Way, and subsequent writers tended to accept it as established fact. Paul Rowntree, in his invaluable pamphlet *From Trackway to Trunk Road: A History of the A303*, notes the coexistence and often coincidence between the ancient way and the modern road from Weyhill to between Wincanton and Sparkford. 'By the time of the Bronze Age,' he writes, 'the Harrow Way was a major arterial route.'

Well, maybe. It is certainly a beguiling picture, of an ancient land traversed by time-honoured tracks along which our enterprising and inquisitive forbears roved;

some seeking a pagan festival, others trading drinking vessels and weapons, others impelled by the eternal hope that life would be better across the next valley and over the next hill. Unfortunately evidence to support this account of primal travel is sparse. For instance, it used to be asserted confidently that the prehistoric tracks connected the upland settlements preferred by prehistoric people on the grounds that they were safer than the wooded, predator-infested valleys – until it was shown that settlements were established and maintained on all kinds of terrain except bog, and at all levels. It was also pointed out that, in some cases, supposedly primordial paths overlaid Celtic and even Roman field systems, which strongly suggested that the fields must have come first and the paths later. Nor did they appear on the earliest medieval maps, and no convincing evidence has ever been produced to indicate that a coherent system dependent on a network of trading routes ever existed.

The sceptical view was well put by the road historian Hugh Davies in his book *From Trackways to Motorways: 5000 Years of Highway History*: 'What seems to have happened is that the ridgeways are the outcome of an *idea* of what ancient Britain was like, promoted by Victorian and earlier antiquaries keen to reconstruct a communication system worthy of those who built such dramatic monuments as Stonehenge and Avebury.' The desire to seek patterns and infer meanings in the landscape is understandable, but can lead to trouble – witness the theory of ley lines advanced by Alfred Watkins in the 1920s and subsequently promoted by some of his followers with an ardour bordering on lunacy. At the same time, however, debunking need not go too far. The A303 may not have been Neolithic man's way to the west. Nevertheless marvellously ancient ways do lie buried beneath that smooth band of asphalt and chippings, and a vast amount of ancient history is stored along its way.

★ ★ ★

The hurtling motorist is most unlikely to notice a melancholy relic below the bridge that takes the A303 over the A34 between Basingstoke and Andover. I spotted it only because I was walking, which is no fun but does reveal a thing or two that you would otherwise miss.

It is a battered pub sign displaying a faded, flaking silver cross, and is all that remains of the Bullington Cross Inn. Researches in the Hampshire Records Office and elsewhere have failed to reveal anything much of the history of this hostelry, possibly because it was isolated from any village. It was certainly in business in the nineteenth century because it is described as 'a lonely inn that stood where four roads meet' in a book called *On Southern Roads* by a popular late-Victorian travel writer, James John Hissey (other titles include *Over Fen and Wold* and *On the Box Seat*). It stood right beside the Newbury–Winchester road. When the massive interchange with the A303 was built in the 1980s, the A34 was diverted away from the Bully, as the regulars knew it, allowing it a garden and some breathing space. Sadly for the Bully, the interchange also incorporated the resuscitated A30, as a result of which its design – involving two roundabouts and nine slip roads – was so complicated that the way into the pub became almost impossible for passing motorists to find. The Bully fell into decline, and now the site is occupied by a car-crushing and metal-recycling yard. Giant grabbers nod at transporters heaped high with shattered vehicles, and the murmur of beer drinkers and the music of the juke-box have been replaced by the sound of yesterday's Mondeos and Escorts being reduced to manageable size.

Farewell the Bully

The fate of the Bullington Cross has been replicated up and down the A303. The old coaching inns have either been bypassed (the George in Andover, the George in Amesbury, the George in Ilminster, for instance), fly-overed (the White Horse at Thruxton), turned into fancy hotels (the Park House at Cholderton), or have disappeared altogether (the Deptford Inn at Wylye). The only hostelries still standing on the road are the Bell* at Winterbourne Stoke, and the Eagle a few miles west of Ilminster, which is a sad state of affairs.

★   ★   ★

The enormous bridge over the A34 is followed a couple of miles later by another bridge, flat, functional and insignificant. Beneath it is a thing of beauty. There is a big alder one side and a little willow the other, and between them water as clear as glass hurries in a band of competing threads of current over a bed as pale as bleached bones, and over and around tresses of bright green weed. Another stream joins from the side, swirling through a pool scoured from the gravel. They come together briefly, then slip either side of an island as they head south through Bransbury Common for Chilbolton.

Upstream, the two flows are briefly united, but divide again at Middleton before becoming one below one of the mills at Longparish. There are three bridges between Longparish and the A303, each built of red brick, each full of charm, each paying courteous attention to the river, which is the Test. Now, I have made a promise not to write of

* The Bell subsequently closed for some time, although at the time of writing (March 2019) it is open again.

fishing in this book. My mother and one or two others whose opinions I value objected that there was too much fishing in previous books of mine. But there must be rivers, because my road crosses them. And surely, with rivers I must be allowed fish; and with fish perhaps an angler or two.

A mile or so above Longparish the Test is joined by another stream, even more graceful. This is the Bourne, whose source is a spring far to the north, towards the Berkshire Downs. In 1902 a very tall Irishman of striking presence and with a fine baritone voice brought his wife and infant son to live in Hurstbourne Priors, a village of brick-and-flint houses and thatched cottages straggling along the lower valley of the Bourne. His name was Harry Plunket Greene and in his day he was one of the best-loved singers in the world. He was also a keen angler and he grew to love the Bourne almost as if it had been another member of his family. When his seasons on it were done, he wrote about the joy and occasional sadness it had given him, and called the book *Where the Bright Waters Meet,* a quotation from the Irish poet Tom Moore. In time, Plunket Greene's fame in the musical world faded, but this book bestowed on him a sort of immortality.* Since its first publication in 1924 it has almost never been out of print. It regularly appears on shortlists of angling classics

---

* Plunket Greene was a formidable interpreter of Elgar – he sang the title role in the first performance of *Dream of Gerontius* – and Parry, whose daughter he married. He was a great advocate for German *lieder*, then very much a minority taste; you may catch him on YouTube singing 'The Hurdy-Gurdy Man' from Schubert's *Winterreise*.

for the simple reason that it bursts with an irrepressible and irresistible delight in people and nature and flowing water and the business of trying to persuade a trout to take a fly – in the end, a delight in life itself.

Cricket pavilion Hurstbourne Priors

There used to be a footpath by the meeting of the bright waters – where the Bourne flows into the Test – but it has been diverted so that the owners of the big cream house overlooking it can enjoy it in peace. But you can still stand on the bridge at Hurstbourne Priors and look across to the undulating cricket ground where Plunket Greene captained the village side against The Artists and Old Marlburians and other wandering clubs, and at the creeper-clad church where he worshipped and sang. The clarity of the water deceives the spectator on the bridge into thinking that it is no more than a few inches deep. A little way up there is a pool where you may, when the light is right, make out the shapes of grayling. Plunket Greene referred to them as 'the grey squirrels of a trout stream', observing the orthodoxy of the time which was to treat them as vermin. In fact they are wonderful fish, just as fine as trout, and as wild as can be, which cannot always be said of their spotted cousins.

These streams – Hampshire, Wiltshire, Berkshire and Dorset have them, and they crop up in parts of East Anglia and Yorkshire as well as across the Channel in Normandy – are different from streams elsewhere. They look different and they behave differently. The special quality is given to them by the rock over which they flow and which forms their valleys and watersheds. Its influence spreads far beyond the bright waters where the trout and grayling grow fat.

4

DEAD MEN AND ALGEBRAIC EQUATIONS

Chalk is the bedrock along more than half the overall length of the A303. It sets the tone of the landscape from Popham as far as the Wiltshire/Somerset border south of Penselwood – 'a rolling ocean of green', as the travel writer Robert Byron characterised it, 'over which the cloud-shadows play like a cinematograph – an ocean suddenly frozen, as it were, into green cliffs whose pastoral escarpments guard the valleys and vales like giant fortifications.'

The chalk gives the land its pallor. It determines its texture and what will grow. There are comparatively few oaks on the chalk downland; its trees are beech and yew. There are not many ponds or ditches, and little bracken. Left to itself it reverts to a scrub of hawthorn and dogwood. Cleared and opened to sheep and rabbits, the thin soil favours a cover of springy turf, a carpet of grasses and flowers like hawkweed, ribwort, buttercups, daisies and burnet. For many centuries the high ground was left for grazing, while the growing of crops was concentrated in the valleys. During the second half of the twentieth century the development of modern fertilisers and the advent of the tractor made it possible to convert much of the upland to arable use. But the chalk is still at the surface, and after ploughing the furrows gleam white in the sun, speckled with flints. The flint is hard and glassy to the touch and is extensively used in the chalk country to face houses and cottages and farm outbuildings and churches.

The chalk was laid down around seventy million years ago in the convulsions that signalled the end of the Cretaceous period (*creta* is the Latin for chalk). As the oceans receded, a layer composed of algae and the crushed shells of molluscs was deposited. The depth of the layer varied from a few metres to several hundred. There are extensive chalk deposits in Russia, America, Australia and Israel. But the greatest of them was left in a crescent across eastern, southern and south-eastern England, under the Channel and into northern France.

Chalk is composed almost entirely of calcium carbonate grains that are uncemented and hence unusually porous. It is the geological equivalent of sponge. Beneath the surface it is split by vertical, horizontal and sloping fissures. The rain seeps down and along these cracks. Sometimes, through erosion, they become rivulets which combine into subterranean rivers. Where a layer of marl or flint blocks the downward seep, the water will migrate sideways, for miles if need be. There may be two or more such strips at different angles in the same block of chalk, so that the water falling on the different sides of the same hill can end up flowing in opposing directions.

The water that feeds the chalkstreams is filtered through the chalk and enriched by the minerals within it. It is these minerals that nourish the weed that nourishes the molluscs, crustacea and invertebrates that nourish the trout and grayling in their turn. The volumes of water stored in these hidden sponges of rock are enormous, and guarantee that the streams flowing from them will not dry up. They hardly ever flood, either, because even the heaviest and most sustained downpours will mostly soak into the hillsides rather than run off the sides gathering silt. Sustained winter rains will, however, cause the water levels within the chalk to rise. Where that water finds a break in a slope, it will gush forth in a spring, causing a fine little stream – known in these parts as a winterbourne – to flow until the water table drops again.

* * *

By and large the list of ministers who have taken charge of transport over the past fifty years amounts to a rollcall of political mediocrities. Not one went on to become Prime Minister. One – Alistair Darling – became Chancellor. One – Malcolm Rifkind – became Foreign Secretary. Among Labour holders of the office, Barbara Castle (December 1965 to April 1968) is the single indisputable heavyweight to have done the job. Some might make a claim for John Prescott, but in his case transport had to compete for his energy and questionable talents within a ludicrously bloated department that also included the environment and 'the regions'. For the Conservatives Nicholas Ridley (October '83 to May '86), Rifkind (November '90 to April '92) and possibly Brian Mawhinney (July '94 to July '95) might be reckoned to have risen above the run-of-the-mill.

The longest serving (October '59 to October '64) and probably best-known post-war transport minister was Ernest Marples. It was Marples who opened the M1 in December 1959 by declaring that a new era in road travel had begun 'in keeping with the bold, exciting and scientific age in which we live', and who prodded the fledgling motorway network into a steady creep across the countryside. It was unfortunate for Marples' reputation that his considerable achievements in government should have been overshadowed by subsequent dodgy business dealings. Fate also played him a mean trick in the shape of the slogan 'Marples Must Go', which began as a car sticker campaign against yellow lines and parking wardens. It achieved the status of legend as a graffito on a bridge over the M1 near Luton, where it survived well after Marples' death in 1978.

Marples belongs to a distant time, as do his equally dynamic predecessor, Harold Watkinson, and indeed Barbara Castle herself. But even those few among later transport ministers and secretaries who displayed a spark of initiative and drive were never allowed – or were never willing – to stay in the job long enough to develop worthwhile policies and see them through. No appointment – not even Northern Ireland – was more eagerly abandoned. Margaret Thatcher and John Major between them got through eleven transport secretaries in eighteen years – only Ridley, Norman Fowler (May '79 to September '81) and Paul Channon (June '87 to July '89) lasted longer than two years. After Tony Blair's election victory in 1997, Prescott floundered and blundered for a time until Stephen Byers became transport secretary. Byers was followed by Alistair Darling – at four years the longest tenure since that of Marples. After Darling came Douglas Alexander, Ruth Kelly and Geoff Hoon and finally Andrew Adonis, who at least had the advantage of not being John Prescott.

All of which may help explain the themes of incoherence, short-termism and extreme reluctance to take difficult decisions which have been the defining characteristics of the handling of transport issues by all governments during my automotive lifetime.*

One of the first reforms of Edward Heath's government in 1970 was the creation of the Department of the Environment, which absorbed several previously separate

---

* Adonis – now Lord Adonis – has since been followed by Philip Hammond (who lasted eighteen months), Justine Greening (ten months), Patrick McLoughlin (a remarkable three-and-a-half years) and the current incumbent, Chris Grayling (in the post since July 2016).

ministries, including transport. The following year the transport minister, John Peyton, issued a report to Parliament prosaically entitled *Roads in Britain*. The intention of its authors was that it should be imbued with the flavour of forward-looking dynamism that Heath had sought, with some success, to inject into his election campaign. Clapped-out socialism had been muscled aside by business-friendly conservatism. Railways were out, roads and motor cars were very much in.

Mr Peyton's plan promised 'a comprehensive network of strategic trunk routes to promote economic growth'. All cities with a population exceeding 250,000 would be connected by these routes. All towns with 80,000 or more people would be within ten miles of one. Existing motorway projects would be realised and exciting new ones would be put on the drawing-board – among them an extension of the M3 to Honiton. A pivotal component of the vibrant vision for Britain was a new airport for London, which would rise from the bird–infested mudflats on the coast of Essex (remember Foulness?) and would have a motorway all of its own.

Roads in Britain was bolstered by a thicket of forecasts. One in particular was designed to allay the recently raised suspicion that a hidden and undesirable function of new roads was to encourage more people to drive on them. 'The rate of increase in road traffic is expected to decline in the 1980s,' the report stated complacently. It did not reveal the statistical evidence for this prediction.

It was nothing new to be debating the place of the motor car in our lives, and its impact on town, suburbia and countryside. Over the previous half-century its allure had proved to be incredibly potent. It acted both as a symbol of freedom and individuality, and as the practical means of pursuing that freedom. As the magazine *Autocar* put it in 1929: 'Public transport, no matter how fast and comfortable, inflicts a sensation of serfdom which is intolerable to a free Briton.' The great motoring evangelist L. J. K. Setright celebrated the car's immortal power thus: 'It has enabled people to break out of their constraints, to attempt something they would never previously do, to venture somewhere they could never previously go, to support ideas and trends they could never previously endorse . . .'

But as with other freedoms, there was a cost. The best thing about the car was also its biggest flaw. Anyone who could afford it and drive it could have it. This drawback was spotted early on.

'Thirty years ago these people [the urban working class] never left the town except for perhaps one week in the year. Saturday night was spent in the gin-house and Sunday morning was spent sleeping it off. But such is the new democratic weekend, even if it is mainly devoted to covering decent sand with orange peel and cigarette cartons.' The words come from a book called *The Heart of England* published in 1935 and written by a well-known theatre critic and all-round journalist called Ivor Brown. He was one of a band of unashamedly elitist commentators who were appalled by the ease with which 'these people' were able to penetrate and ruin cherished beauty spots previously reserved for the privileged few. The popular philosopher C. E. M. Joad included the motorist among *The Horrors of the Countryside*, the title he gave to a pamphlet-length rant which he brought out in 1931: 'The faces are strained and angry; upon them is a look of tense expectancy and in the intervals between their spasmodic bursts of activity they glower at one another.' Elsewhere Joad likened cars to 'a regiment of soldiers who had begun to suffer simultaneously from flatulence', and the sound of their horns to 'a pack of fiends released from the nethermost pit'.

Others fell in love with the car. In a collection of travel pieces called *Along the Road*, Aldous Huxley rhapsodised about his 10 HP Citröen. 'The temptation of talking about cars when one has a car,' Huxley wrote, 'is quite irresistible. Before I bought a Citröen no subject had less interest for me; none, now, has more.' Virginia Woolf and her husband Leonard paid £275 for a second-hand Singer. 'The motor car is turning out the joy of our lives,' she wrote in her diary. 'Soon we will look back at our pre-motor days as we do now at our days in the caves. Nothing has ever changed so profoundly my material existence as the possession of a motor car.'

For the lucky few their possession permitted them to participate in the Golden Age of Motoring – even though its exact timing was a matter of dispute. In his autobiography, *Landscape with Machines*, Lionel Rolt – the biographer of Brunel, Telford and other great British engineers – wrote: 'By 1934 it had already become clear that the previous decade was the golden age . . . Though the roads had become dustless by then, they were still traffic-free. The term "the joy of the open road" was still literally true and carried no cynical overtones.' But W. A. Mackenzie, long-serving motoring correspondent of the *Daily Telegraph* in the post-war years, located it firmly in the 1930s – 'motoring was good . . . better than at any time before or since, because cars were more or less grown up but the volume of traffic hadn't grown up with them.'

Between 1930 and 1938 the number of cars on British roads more than doubled, to 2.5 million, and congestion was beginning to be recognised as a problem. Nevertheless motoring was still regarded as an exciting new pastime, and the ownership of a car as a passport to a new pleasure. The glitter of Hollywood stars fell upon the automobiles they favoured; Jean Harlow was pictured beside her Packard Roadster, Sir Guy Standing at the wheel of his Cadillac, Ginger Rogers leaning on a Pierce Arrow 12. Such creations were for gawping at, but increasingly the booming car industry was able to bring the motoring dream within reach of average middle-class families. In 1936 you could have bought a second-hand Morris Oxford from Charterhouse Motors in Great Portland Street, London, for £62. A new Morris two-seater was £118, a Hillman Minx £175, a 20 HP Alvis Crested Eagle saloon capable of 74 m.p.h. £800. *Autocar* magazine was full of articles enthusing about motoring holidays in France and Italy – even Palestine. The adventurous were urged to try Pretoria in South Africa to Salisbury in Rhodesia.

By the 1950s inquiring minds began to realise that the car presented a particular challenge to modern society. The democracy of car ownership was blossoming – by 1958 there were eight million cars on the roads. In that year the Scottish engineer and urban planner Colin Buchanan published a study of the motor car whose title – *Mixed Blessing* – indicated the Janus character of its subject. Buchanan believed that it was the state's duty rigorously to manage the growth of road traffic. He conjured a nightmare which he called Motopia, a place of 'death and injury, pain and bereavement, noise and smell . . . of vast winding trails of serious damage to urban and country amenities, with vulgarity, shoddiness, and the squalor of mud, dirt and litter . . . traffic like some destructive lava welling out from the towns, searing and scorching in long channels, ever ready to invade new areas.'

Buchanan's reputation as the country's foremost expert on road transport issues persuaded Ernest Marples to commission him to produce his famous study *Traffic in Towns*, which created such a stir that Penguin issued an abridged version as a popular paperback. Its prophetic tone was set in the foreword by the influential economist, Sir Geoffrey Crowther. 'We are nourishing a monster of great potential destructiveness,' Crowther wrote. 'The motor car is clearly a menace that can spoil our civilisation. But translated into the terms of the particular vehicle that stands outside our door, we regard it as one of our most treasured possessions or dearest ambitions, an immense convenience, an expander of the dimensions of life, a symbol of our modern age.'

Crowther and Buchanan put their fingers on an impossible dilemma. 'It is a difficult and dangerous thing in a democracy to prevent a substantial part of the population from doing something they do not regard as wrong,' Buchanan observed astutely. But traffic must somehow be restricted if our towns and cities were not to be made unbearable. Buchanan's answer was a complex balancing act, in which enhanced public transport, pedestrian precincts and concepts such as congestion charges and park-and-ride all had a place, but which still found room for the car. What happened, of course, was that the more radical suggestions – in particular for the redevelopment of urban centres on multiple levels, with roads soaring over the top – were never taken up because they were too expensive, contentious or imaginative. Instead, a new generation of town planners went to work wrecking town centres across the country in the name of modernisation and the promotion of commerce and business – a process in which the construction of ring roads, flyovers, inner distribution roads, multi-storey car parks and the like played a full part.

Outside urban centres the transport policies of successive governments from the 1960s onwards became concentrated on two parallel strands: running down the railways and building new roads. Long ago it had been the railway industry before which ministers genuflected, chequebooks in hand. Now the roads lobby held sway. No politician who wished to be identified with the cause of progress and prosperity could afford to question the philosophy behind road-building.

On the A303 the first significant stretch to be converted to dual carriageway extended west from the junction with the A34 to the eastern side of Andover, completed in 1962. Seven years later the Andover and Amesbury bypasses were opened. By then the M3 was eating its way from London to Basingstoke. In 1983 the link between the M3 at Popham and the A34 junction was rebuilt as dual carriageway and reclassified as A303 instead of A30. Two years after that the Weyhill bypass and a new section of dual carriageway at Thruxton were completed.

A bright future beckoned.

★ ★ ★

Had Mr Bob Brown looked behind him before or after cutting the tape to open the Andover bypass – as he may well have done – he would have seen a sizeable tract of woodland straddling the road and extending some distance either side. Had he asked the Mayor of Andover, Mrs Thorne, or any of the other dignitaries what it was, he would have been told that this was Harewood Forest, a part of the ancient royal forest of Chute. And had he taken a stroll along a path which cuts through the northern side roughly parallel to the A303 – which he probably didn't – he might have spotted, half-hidden among the trees, an unusual monument to a very dark deed.

Deadman's Plack

It consists of a cross above a granite pillar which rises from a granite plinth. The inscription is as follows:

About the year of Our Lord DCCCCLXIII upon this spot beyond the time of memory called Deadman's Plack tradition reports that Edgar, surnamed the Peaceable, King of England, in the ardour of youth, love and indignation, slew with his own hand his treacherous and ungrateful favourite Earl Aethelwold, owner of this forest of Harewood, in resentment of the Earl's having basely betrayed and perfidiously married his intended bride, beauteous Elfrida, daughter of Ordgar Earl of Devonshire, afterwards wife of Edgar and by him mother of King Ethelred II. Queen Elfrida, after Edgar's death, murdered his eldest son King Edward the Martyr and founded the nunnery of Wherwell.

Phew, what a story is that! Royalty, lust, treachery, betrayal, revenge, a brace of murders, a nunnery – across more than a millennium I could feel my journalistic taste-buds tingling.

The fullest version of the tale was compiled the best part of 200 years after the event by the chronicler known as William of Malmesbury. He told how Edgar, king of the West Saxons as well as Mercia and Northumbria, commissioned his friend Aethelwold to travel to the house of Ordgar to inspect the earl's daughter Elfrida with a view to offering marriage if the reports of her beauty were justified, which they were. Unfortunately for Aethelwold's long-term prospects he fell for her himself and married her, without informing her of Edgar's interest. To the king he reported that she was really nothing special, not worthy of his attention. Eventually Edgar became suspicious. He proposed a visit to his friend and his new bride. Aethelwold knew trouble when it was coming. He begged Elfrida to conceal her charms beneath her drabbest set of clothes. Poor sap.

In William's words: 'She adorned herself at the mirror and omitted nothing that could stimulate the desire of a young and powerful man.' Considerably stimulated and considerably angered, Edgar invited his old friend for a day's hunting in Harewood Forest, ran him through with a javelin and married his ungrieving widow.

But this was not the end of the saga. Elfrida had a son by Edgar, named Ethelred. After Edgar's sudden, early (but apparently natural) death in 975, he was succeeded by his son from a previous marriage, Edward. But not for long. The lad paid his stepmother Elfrida a visit at Corfe Castle and was pulled from his horse and stabbed to death by her thegns. Whether or not she actually ordered the murder is not clear, but her reputation was not helped by the prompt installation on the throne of young Ethelred. He, by the way, was blameless; he is said to have wept so violently at the news of Edward's murder that Elfrida was provoked to beat him with candles, traumatising the seven-year-old boy so severely that he could never bear to have candles near him again.

The finale, in the best traditions, has Elfrida repenting her crimes and endeavouring to expiate them. She founded one abbey at Amesbury and another at Wherwell, a couple of miles from where Aethelwold met his end. There she spent some years as abbess, 'beseeching Christ to grant her pardon', before falling into the Test one day and drowning.

By the volatile standards of the times, Edgar's fifteen-year reign was comparatively uneventful. Other sources – such as the *Anglo-Saxon Chronicle* – lay emphasis on his strength and good looks, his wisdom, the soundness of his judgement, his piety and support for the monastic orders. But history does not care for his virtues. It is the William of Malmesbury version, stitched together from various doubtful stories two centuries after the event, that has gradually acquired the status of accepted fact. Although William mentions Edgar's achievements, he prefers to dwell on the allegedly less savoury aspects of his character, in particular his 'inordinate lustfulness'. He includes an account of Edgar abducting a young woman called Wulfryth from a convent at Wilton near Salisbury, and having a daughter by her. The episode in Harewood Forest merely cements his reputation as a king unable to keep his urges under proper control.

In another age, one feels, William of Malmesbury would have been a highly paid feature-writer on a national newspaper or a spinner of best-selling historical fiction. His credentials as a historian did not impress Dr Edward Freeman, Regius Professor of History at Oxford in the 1880s. Freeman took a dim view of these old chronicles. In his view – which in his view was the only one that counted – they hardly qualified as sources at all.

He disapproved strongly of the weakness of these uneducated monks for including accounts of romantic or dramatic incidents without anything resembling corroboration. He would sternly instruct his students to reject these accounts, even if they fitted in with the known character of the subject. To illustrate his point, Freeman would cite what he regarded as the grossest example of tittle-tattle masquerading as history, the murder in Harewood Forest. He described it as 'a confused and rambling narrative' and rebuked later historians for having 'given credence to what was nothing more than a balladeer's invention'.

I like to imagine Dr Freeman spinning in his grave in the Protestant cemetery in Alicante (where he died of smallpox in 1892) in indignation at the longevity of William's myths. His own vast output – his *History of the Norman Conquest* in five volumes, his *History of Sicily* in three volumes, his *Growth of the English Constitution*, his two-volume *Historical Geography of Europe*, his six volumes of *Historical Essays* – have long since disappeared into the storehouses of the unread. William's *Deeds of the Kings of the English*, in contrast, has continued to bob buoyantly along the current of received knowledge, recycled countless times in guide books, local histories, tourist leaflets and on websites.

These days Deadman's Plack has a neglected air about it. The monument is crowded by saplings and branches, and the inscription on the plinth is hardly decipherable.

But it remains as lovely and lonely a spot as it was in Victorian times, when the great nature writer W. H. Hudson leaned his back against it to smoke a pipe and listen for the grasshoppers – although not quite as peaceful, with the A303 growling invisibly from a couple of hundred yards away.*

One minor mystery occurred to me as I stood before the cross. There is a secondary inscription recording that it was placed there by Colonel William Iremonger in 1825. But why? What was it about this ancient tale that inspired the local squire, as he was, to go to this trouble and expense? The Iremongers lived at Wherwell Priory, built in the eighteenth century where Elfrida's abbey had stood. The Colonel inherited the estate in 1806, two years before he took part in the Peninsular War as commander of the 2nd Regiment of Foot (subsequently the Queen's Royal Regiment). He left the army in 1811 to retire to Wherwell where – apart from Deadman's Plack – he seems to have made little mark.

I picture him as a whiskered veteran, living the quiet life of an English country squire, his mind stirred by memories of musket and cannon under the burning Spanish sun and the dreadful retreat to Corunna, and by the tale of Edgar and his friend and the irresistible Elfrida that had reached its murderous climax almost on his doorstep. All

* Hudson, incidentally, so disliked Freeman and his 'infernal cocksure arrogance' that he turned the story of Edgar, Elfrida and Aethelwold into a romance under the title *Deadman's Plack*.

supposition of course, but the impression made by the Harewood Forest murder was certainly deep. Apart from the monument, Iremonger named one of his sons Aethelwold and one of his daughters Elfrida.

A monument of a different kind has arisen on the other side of the A303, where it bypasses Weyhill on the west side of Andover. It is a rectangular grey building with an undulating pale green roof, and – unlike Deadman's Plack – you cannot possibly miss it. It stands out bold and brutal on what was once Andover Airfield, which was used by the RAF until deemed surplus to the nation's defensive needs in 1977. The size is the thing.

It is colossal, covering ten acres of ground, the equivalent of a dozen football pitches. It is a shed, a Great Shed. Its greatness is only the greatness of scale. It does not commemorate anything noble or splendid in the human spirit, merely our appetite for consumables.

It is a distribution centre for the Co-op, and it's an interesting thought, as you stand across from it trying to comprehend its scale, that it should have been very much bigger. The original plan, submitted on behalf of Tesco, was for a shed almost twice as large, to be accompanied in time by a hotel and conference centre, office blocks, a rash of smaller warehouses, and a lorry park capable of handling 1500 trucks a day. Subsequent events followed a path familiar to students of Tesco's imperial ambitions. Andover rebelled, and a 'Stop The Megashed' campaign rolled. Tesco offered blandishments: two thousand jobs, acoustic screening to keep the noise down, a new £5 million roundabout, a £200,000 'contribution to public art'. At first the members of Test Valley Borough Council resisted, then they gave in. Planning permission was granted in August 2009.

Great Shed

But there was an unusual twist. Tesco had second thoughts, and – for reasons never fully explained – pulled out. Into the breach stepped the Co-op. But the Co-op did not require such a monstrously Great Shed as Tesco, so a more modest project has been realised.

They are mysterious places, these distribution centres. Their blank walls are inscrutable. They reveal nothing of what goes on inside. Goods arrive from somewhere, goods depart for somewhere. Vegetables come from the fields of Lincolnshire, are sorted and dispatched – some of them back to Lincolnshire. According to the cultural analyst Joe

Moran, 'big sheds encapsulate the strange ethereality of the modern economy, the way it controls our lives while we have only the dimmest understanding of its workings.' As he points out, an essential element of the Great Shed is its impermanence. Implicit in the amazing speed with which it has risen from its concrete base is the assumption that it will not be there for long. It looks as if one good kick from a celestial colossus dispatched to earth to ask awkward questions about our habits would bring the Andover Great Shed crashing down. It is a temporary temple to our religion of shopping. But it will do nothing to help the archaeologists of two thousand years hence work out the kind of people we were, because it will leave no trace.

* * *

The road to Monxton leaves the new Great Shed round-about on the A303 and cuts through what is now the Headquarters of the British Army's Land Forces (known rather confusingly as Marlborough Lines, in tribute to the first Duke of Marlborough's great victories over the French at Blenheim and Ramillies). Monxton is one of a string of villages that lie along a little stream that used to be called the Ann (hence the Vale of Anna) but was long ago renamed the Pilhill Brook. Despite their proximity to ever-swelling Andover, these villages – East Cholderton, Amport, Monxton, Abbotts Ann and Little Ann – have managed to cling on to their rural character, significantly but not ruinously diluted by rashes of modern bungalows and 'executive-style' houses.

Monxton Church

Monxton has a pleasant green shaded by a big, spreading ash, which slopes down to the glass-clear Pilhill Brook. Next to the green is the pub, which stands in a row of pretty old cottages and houses, some red-brick, some flint, some with thatched roofs and cob walls. A turn down the lane to Amport leads over the brook to the church, a small flint and tiled affair with a sharp little steeple which was built in 1854 on the site of a much earlier and even more modest place of worship. Looking across at the church from the other side of the lane is the old rectory, a lovely, big, warm, eighteenth-century red-brick house surrounded by spacious gardens – just the kind of rectory, one feels, to suit one of Trollope's hunting parsons or one of Jane Austen's clubbable clerics.

The parish records of the early eighteenth century contain some curious snippets of news about Monxton's distant past. Henry Skeat, we learn, 'was not sick but thinking himself too full of blood was let blood and in four or five minutes after he was bled ten ounces expired, aged 25.' In 1730 there arrived a 'parsel of slaves from Turkey', and a shilling was offered from parish funds to help them. The following year another slave from Turkey – 'who had his tung cut out' – received a shilling.

In 1723 Thomas Rothwell, a choice specimen of English eccentricity, became Rector of Monxton. After his death twenty-five years later, another clergyman, a well-known antiquary and collector of historical scraps, William Cole, had occasion to visit Monxton, because his brother-in-law, Dr Apthorpe, was being invested as Rothwell's successor. Cole was not impressed by the place – 'the church, like most in this county, is very small and is a mean building' – nor by what he was told about the previous rector's way of life:

By the account even of his own children and neighbours he was a most whimsical and singular man. He sat all day long in a parlour by himself where he would dine and sup without any of his family, who were not suffered even to enter the room for fear of putting him out in his calculations. And there he used to amuse himself with figures and algebra to which study he was so devoted that for many of the last years of his life he stirred not out of his house, not even to the Church, but had a constant curate even though the Church is not a stone's throw from the rectory; and gave himself not to be shaved but let his beard grow till he was a spectacle . . . He brought himself into an ill habit of which he died, from which however he might have recovered even at the last, as his physician told him, if he would have taken moderate exercise, which he had taken into his head would kill him.

Regrettably William Cole failed to inquire closely into the nature of the Reverend Rothwell's algebraic calculations. The great challenge of the time – which foxed even Isaac Newton – was to ascertain a rule for working out the number of imaginary roots of an equation involving a negative (x squared minus 1 in its simplest form). The answer (which is not accessible to my understanding) was not provided until 1864, when the English mathematician James Joseph Sylvester published his catchily titled *Algebraical Researches Containing a Disquisition on Newton's Rule for the Discovery of Imaginary Roots and an Allied Rule Applicable to a Particular Class of Equations together with a Complete Invariative Determination of the Character of the Roots of the General Equation of the 5th Degree etc*. I particularly like the '*etc*'.

But is it not possible that Rothwell got there first? That

one day, in the parlour of Monxton Rectory, amid his accumulated mountains of calculations, he was transfixed by a shaft of the light of understanding? That he solved the conundrum that baffled Newton, Leibniz and Euler among others? And that his solution was lost, swept away when his family and servants came to clear up the mess he had left behind? It's possible; though more likely, on balance, that he went off his head in the attempt.

The next rector after William Cole's brother-in-law also made himself the object of unwelcome attention. George Bally had inclinations towards poetry and stronger ones towards drink. There were complaints about his behaviour at the communion table, and uproar when he publicly accused a local woman of being 'the whore of the parish' after she was found in a ditch with a young man who should have been helping with the hay harvest. Mr Bally composed his own eloquent epitaph:

> If just or virtuous to this tomb draw near,
> If knave or hypocrite shrink back in fear,
> He was a man when living did detest
> Alike the rogue conceal'd, the rogue confess'd,
> If he knew such should here presume to tread,
> This stone would be much heavier on his head.

5

BEASTS, BODY PARTS AND HORNS

The verge of the A303 is hostile terrain for humans. Walking along it is no fun at all. The ground is rough and uneven, and the incessant noise and blasts of displaced air from the traffic make it an uncomfortable place to be. Sometimes the ground is gouged by tyre tracks, serving as a reminder that passing vehicles do not always stay where they should and that being pulverised by one of them would be a bad way to go. But you do notice things.

The drivers, of course, notice nothing. They inhabit what the French philosopher Marc Augé defined, in a celebrated phrase, as a 'non-place', an environment where there is no sense of belonging. Other non-places include airports, shopping centres and motorway service areas. The car is a bubble, divorced from its surroundings. Its occupants can have no meaningful relationship with the landscape around or anyone in it. To drive a road such as the A303 is to enter what the sociologist John Urry calls 'a world of anonymised machines'. The machine moves too fast for the driver's eye to linger on anything or make contact with anyone. Most of the familiar components of everyday life – lights, sounds, smells, even temperatures – are missing. The experience of driving is reduced to the views through the windscreen, the rear window, and the wing-mirrors.

Having no need to take account of or even notice what is beside the road, the driver is able to adapt the vehicle into a movable extension of the home. The company of music, the radio, the audio-book helps reassure him that he hasn't really left his own territory at all. Increasingly, mobile phone, text and email facilities give him constant access to the communication stream. The rapid advance of so-called 'smart car technology' means that the machine itself requires less and less attention from its pilot to the business of driving, creating more opportunity for absorption in the world within the bubble.

Occasionally the motorist puts a foot on the brake and interrupts the hurtling progress along the highway to divert into the non-place that is the service area. The reason may be to obtain more fuel in order to resume progress as quickly as possible, to ease cramped muscles or to have a snooze, or to use the lavatory. Any one or all of these may be combined with entering a Little Chef which is the same in its essentials as all the other Little Chefs. Inside he or she picks up a generic menu and orders a generic plate of food. None of these activities makes a social or observational demand of any kind. There is no need to engage with anyone beyond the formalities of the commercial exchange. There is no need to know where you are.

The break in the driving routine is heavily ritualised, but remains voluntary. There is another situation, all too familiar, in which the driver is deprived of choice altogether. It occurs when too many others are trying to do what he is trying to do for the road to be able to cope. It is called congestion, and in theory it should offer an opportunity for the driver to connect with his or her surroundings. In practice, though, this rarely happens. Instead, the consciousness is flooded by the familiar feelings of frustration and weariness that are integral to the experience of being in a jam. These feelings are not conducive to appreciating the charms of the countryside. Even the marvellous view of Stonehenge that the A303 reveals as it rises then declines over the ridge west of Amesbury does little to comfort the westward-migrating horde of would-be holidaymakers crawling in an unbroken line of sealed social capsules towards campsites or rented cottages that seem almost unattainably distant.

I wouldn't say that those for whom the verges of the A303 are no more than a passing blur are missing too much in the way of beauty and interest. There is a passage in Joe Moran's *On Roads* which sets out considerable claims on the part of the neglected and overlooked margins of motorways to be regarded as the wildlife reserves of the high-speed age: havens for voles, moles, field mice, snakes, lizards, orchids, ferns, fungi, linnets, kestrels, hooded crows and a host of other flora and fauna. It may be so. Although motorways were necessarily built in sections they were planned as entities and great attention was paid to their setting. In the 1950s a distinguished committee of high-minded landscape architects, horticulturists and conservationists was formed to advise the government and its contractors on such matters as alignment, curvature, the avoidance of parallelism and ugly angularity, the interplay of light and shadow, and appropriate planting.

Bridges, the committee declared, should be designed to be as light and elegant as the use of pre-stressed concrete permitted, with slender supporting pillars and railings rather than parapets. The road should 'flow' through the landscape in long and harmonious arcs. The margins should be pleasingly embanked and planted with native species of tree like beech, oak and ash, and not with striking exotics, which would be too distracting. The arbiters of taste were particularly hostile to the idea of prettifying the verges and central reservations with flowering shrubs such as forsythia and pyracantha, on the grounds that they were much too fussy, ornamental, colourful and generally suburban.

Unlike the purpose-built motorways with their landscaped margins, trunk roads like the A303 tended to be stitched together episodically and haphazardly, using stretches of existing roads wherever possible. The detailed construction plans for the upgrading of the Hampshire section are on a scale of 1:2500, large enough for individual trees to be marked, and they reveal how the surveyors went about their laborious task. In between the major new sections, such as the Andover bypass and the Bullington Cross interchange, were the remnants of the old road that had to be incorporated and adapted into the whole. Sometimes it was just a matter of adding a carriageway to the existing road and tidying up the junctions. Sometimes long-standing awkward angles – a diversion that took the original turnpike around the local bigwig's estate or a dog-leg railway bridge – had to be smoothed away. These meant compulsory purchases – which could be of several hundred acres of farmland, or a row of cottages that needed to be demolished, or simply the corner of someone's garden. In some cases the deviation from the old A303 was limited to a hundred yards or so. In others – for instance between Thruxton and Cholderton – the old road was entirely superseded for several miles and relegated to the status of a country lane.

Key Plan, Andover bypass

Micheldever and other improvements

The result is that the A303 has an orphaned look. No one ever sat down – as the Advisory Committee on the Landscape Treatment of Trunk Roads did with the first motorways – and considered how to make it look good. The surveyors plotted the route, the engineers attended to the road, the designers doubtless did their best to make the bridges as inoffensive as possible. But no one addressed the holistic dimension, and it shows.

The A303's central reservation is a study in contempt for notions of pleasantness. Along most of it, grey safety barriers run in monotonous lines above concrete tufted with scalded weeds and rank grass. The one plant that seems to find a congenial roothold is ragwort. Numerous slender but flourishing colonies have established them-selves between Basingstoke and Amesbury, producing startlingly bright splashes of pale yellow during the April flowering season which darken over the summer to a shade somewhere between farmhouse butter and apricot.

Modern road – old hedge

Further east, near Micheldever, there is an extended length of unkempt, valiant hawthorn hedge along the reservation. When I first walked that way, I wondered briefly if it might represent an act of independence by some iconoclastic hedge enthusiast within the county surveyor's department. Then I realised that the trunks were thick and gnarled, and that it must have been planted long ago to stand beside the road in its single carriageway incarnation.

There are places where the A303 runs for a while beside or through handsome mature woodland – at Harewood Forest, for instance, or along the southern fringe of Stockton Wood, near Fonthill. There is also evidence of occasional efforts at tree-planting in the form of a cluster of green plastic tubes with spindly beech saplings within. But in general the provision of tree cover has been left to nature, and nature has responded with a thick, low scrub – chiefly hawthorn and the gleefully opportunist elder, with beeches, yews, apples and others appearing quite randomly.

The thicket is usually guarded by a barrier of brambles and nettles, which share the edgeland with the usual gang of floral chancers and trimmers: purple self-heal, rosebay willowherb, white dead-nettle, yellow wort, bindweed, cow parsley, mallow, thistles, clover, poppies. The grass is coarse and straggles in unsightly tresses across the stones and thin soil.

Apart from a once-a-year weedkiller treatment and the occasional foray with a chainsaw when a tree topples over or a branch is deemed to infringe on a sightline, no one interferes with these bands of wildwood. Their principal function, from the road's point of view, is to trap the rubbish thrown or blown from the passing traffic. Carrier bags, plastic wrappers, straps, bits of sheeting, the odd woolly hat – they fly from a window or a sloppily covered lorry load to be apprehended in the spiky brush where they flap and wave in the breezes until shredded or decomposed sufficiently to descend in stages to the ground.

Little effort is made by the authorities to keep the A303's edges tidy. The most it gets is a weekly or fortnightly visit from waste disposal operatives to empty the bins standing next to the 'Take Your Litter Home' signs in the lay-bys. And why should they do more? It would require an army of workers to clear the bags, coffee cups, chocolate wrappers, crisp packets, drinks cans, newspapers, tin foil, banana skins and the rest discarded by the don't-give-a-shit minority of litter louts among the road's users. And who would notice?

Apart from the litter, which is everywhere, I came across a wide variety of useless objects in the course of my wanderings, including trousers, gloves, empty purses (I checked) and a miscellany of windscreen wipers, hubcaps, petrol caps, mudguards and other vehicle bits. It was easy to imagine body parts being scattered into the under-growth from some horrendous high-speed smash and abandoned to decomposition. The fringes of the A303 would be excellent for hiding human corpses or the proceeds of crime. No one ever comes.

The body count among resident and passing wildlife along the fast dual-carriageway stretches is high. It's a well-known fact that more than a million mammals, chiefly rabbits, and ten times as many birds – the majority of them tame pheasants – perish on our roads each year. Society's view seems to be that the price is worth paying – an annual sub to the RSPB eases the guilt. In a random survey along four miles of the A303 either side of the Barton Stacey turnoff in Hampshire I identified one dead barn owl, one bat of unknown species, two badgers, a hedgehog, two rabbits, two pigeons and what I think was a greater spotted woodpecker. They were distributed along the verge. In addition there were numerous blotches on the surface of the road formed by tissue flattened so thoroughly into the texture of the asphalt that it was impossible to tell if it had once been bird, rodent, mammal or reptile.

Watch out – deer about

I am pretty sure, however, that there were no deer among them. The patches of tissue were not big enough. In fact in all my journeys up and down the 92 miles of the road, I came upon only two deer corpses – one a muntjac and the other a juvenile fallow. Yet the deer seems the one creature that the Highways Agency cares about. Along the A303, as well as motorways and main roads across southern England, the Agency has placed signs showing an abundantly antlered running stag. Frequently these signs also advise a specified length of road on which – presumably – the motorist may expect to encounter one of these animals. There is one on the westbound M4 which gives a distance of 37-and-a-half miles. Curiously the sign placed on the eastbound side at the far end has 33 miles on it – suggesting that there are four-and-a-half miles where a deer may appear on one side of the motorway but not on the other.

I am well aware that a large mammal, with or without antlers, capable of moving at 30 m.p.h. can pose a significant danger on the roads (although I do wonder if those Highways Agency signs actually serve much purpose in inducing heightened awareness of the threat). But it does seem slightly unfair that other species do not warrant any warning or protection. What about badgers, for instance? Judging from the number of dead badgers I saw, the casualty rate along the A303 must be enormous.* Does the Highways Agency not care about badgers? Or barn owls, bats, snakes, lizards, rabbits, foxes, hedgehogs, and domestic pets for that matter? Apart from anything else a variety of signs displaying other creatures at risk would alleviate the monotony of travel and provide interest for children.

* * *

Weyhill is a mile or so north of Monxton on the northern side of the A303, but has nothing of its neighbour's charm. It is a straggly, nondescript place which looks as if it lives with the fear of waking up one morning and finding that it has been swallowed by Andover. But there was a time

* Dark allegations swirl across the internet that many of the dead badgers found on roadsides are actually shot elsewhere by farmers anxious about TB, then dumped to conceal the crime. This seems highly improbable (why not hide them somewhere in the woods?) but perhaps the Highways Agency could arrange sample autopsies to clear up the matter.

when Andover counted for very little and the name of Weyhill was known across the land.

As so often, it was an accident of geography. Weyhill stood at the junction between two old, long-distance routes: the Harrow Way, and a north–south path extending to Christchurch on the Channel and known locally as the Gold Road, supposedly because it was used to transport gold from Ireland and Wales to the south coast for export to Europe. Weyhill occupied a prominent upland position accessible from several chalk ridges along which ran well-used tracks, and it had extensive grazing available on all sides. In short, it was an ideal location for the trading of livestock. In time, drovers' paths converged on it from most points of the compass, including Farnham, Winchester, Salisbury, Marlborough, Amesbury, Hungerford and Newbury.

Old path lives on

The fame of the Weyhill Fair spread and it found its way into the late-fourteenth-century epic, *Piers Plowman:*

To Wy and Wynchestre I went to the fayre
With many manere merchandise as my maistre me hiyte
Ne had the grace of guile ygo among my ware
It had be unsolde this seven yere, so me God helpe!*

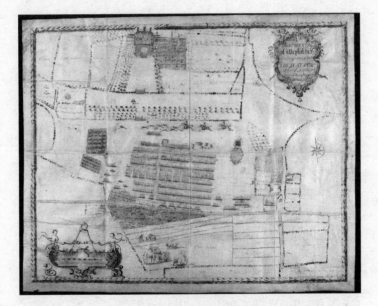

Old map of Weyhill Fayre

* 'At my master's bidding I went to the fairs at Weyhill and Winchester with a wide range of merchandise. If the grace of guile had not blessed my goods, God help me! they would have remained unsold these seven years!' (Translation by Stella Brook, Manchester Medieval Classics.)

By the time Daniel Defoe visited early in the eighteenth century it was 'the greatest fair for sheep that this nation can show'. Defoe says he was told by a local grazier that half a million sheep changed hands over the seven days of the fair in October. Even making allowances for local inflation, the numbers were enormous, and many of the animals were driven great distances, from as far away as Wales and Devon. The Welsh and West Country drovers tended to gather first at East Woodhay, on the Berkshire Downs near Newbury, where their sheep were fitted with little iron shoes to cope with the gravelled road to Weyhill itself.

Sheep was the main business of the fair, but by no means the only one. Horses, cattle, pigs and geese were also traded. Great stacks of Surrey hops, particularly from Farnham, were sold. The cheese fair was prodigious, and a regular excursion for the rector of the neighbouring parish of Kimpton, the Reverend Henry White, brother of Gilbert White of Selborne. Like his brother, Henry was an inveterate diarist, and he recorded all his cheese deals – among them the purchase of fifty-four on 10 October 1781 which cost him a total of thirty-three shillings and lasted for an average of four days each.

Other parts of the fair were reserved for general retailing. 'The booths,' wrote Defoe, 'were filled with the wares of goldsmiths and turners, of milliners, haberdashers and mercers, of pewterers and drapers and clothiers, with toys and books and medicines, and with the tables, benches, jugs and cups of the keepers of taverns, brandy-shops and cooks' shops, coffee-houses and eating rooms. Vast quantities of goods were sold and all the villages and small towns around were crowded and even barns and stables were turned into inns.'

One day was devoted to the Mop Fair, where labourers sought work for the coming year. They stood in line, advertising their specialities – a shepherd holding his crook or sporting a tuft of wool over his ear, the thresher with a flail or ear of corn, the carter with a knot of whipcord. Once a deal was done, the worker was given a coin to buy a ribbon which he would tie in his hat to show he was no longer for hire.

Business was amply spiced with fun. The pleasure fair was famous for its curious attractions. Henry White inspected 'an Oethiopian savage . . . a very wonderful but frightful resemblance of ye Human Form . . . by no means as gentle, docile or intelligent as monkeys of the smaller kind.' Colonel Hawker of Longparish, whose diaries were chiefly filled with records of his slaughter of tremendous numbers of trout from the Test and game birds from all over, was intrigued by 'a creature shown under the name of a Mermaid that was caught and brought alive from the Southampton Water'. A travelling circus advertised a lion and lioness from the zoo at the Tower of London, a laughing hyena ('disposition extremely ferocious'), a Hunting Tyger from Bengal ('the most beautiful of quadrupeds'), and a porcupine from Algiers ('not to be tamed by the most subtle art or courteous treatment of mankind').

Boozing, thieving, whoring and gambling were woven into the fabric of the Weyhill Fair, causing periodic outbursts of pious outrage from the local clergy. A hard day's buying and selling followed by a hard evening's drinking made for easy prey for the pickpockets and cutpurses who abounded. First-timers at the fair were expected to undergo an initiation ritual known as the Horning of the Colts. The initiate was fitted with a set of ram's horns on his head with a receptacle for a beer tankard on top, in which he capered around while the company roared out a song with the chorus:

> Horns, boys, horns, horns, boys, horns
> And drink to his daddy with a large pair of horns

For each drop of beer spilled, the lad or his daddy had to buy a gallon of beer. You get the picture.

The last Horning of the Colts was recorded in 1890, by which time the Weyhill Fair was on the slide. For many years a set of horns was on show at the Star public house (now an Indian restaurant called the Pink Olive, which does not have the same ring to it). They were lost – or possibly burned – but subsequently they or another set turned up, and may now be viewed in the Andover Museum.

The other Weyhill pub was the Sun, later renamed the Weyhill Fair,* which is still a pub and apparently doing

---

* No more. It closed suddenly in the late summer of 2018.

decent business. One wall of its upstairs room is covered by a striking mural illustrating scenes from the fair, which was executed by a previous landlord's brother. One of these scenes depicts the opening chapter of Hardy's *The Mayor of Casterbridge*, describing how Henchard (later the Mayor) sold his wife at the 'Weydon Priors' Fair to a sailor for five guineas.

Old days in Weyhill

By the late nineteenth century, farming ways had changed and droving had fallen out of fashion. The part of the fairground south of the Amesbury road was auctioned in 1919, and by 1930 fewer than 5000 sheep were offered for sale. The introduction of tests for TB soon after the Second World War was the final blow, and the auctions were abandoned in the 1950s. For a time, the site was used as a lorry depot, until the firm went bust. Later, the inevitable business park sprang up, although the quadrangle of booths by the road has survived, and has been turned into a craft and design centre where you can buy hand-made chocolates, stained-glass objects and bespoke pens, or even take tea and a bun at the café, deplorably named Ewe and I.

* * *

In 1973 I bought a bottle-green Saab 96 for £500 from a cousin who was leaving England for Australia. In my mind, it remains the only car I ever had that was more to me than a means of transport. At that time most of my friends drove Minis or 1300s or Triumph Heralds; or – if they had some money – a Capri or an MG. The Saab 96, with its snub-nosed front and weirdly distended sloping rear, was very different and very unBritish.* To own one, I discovered, was to join a club; other 96s used to flash their lights as they passed, as if to say, 'well done, nice motor, isn't she?'

The gears were on the steering column and there was a strange device on the floor, which when pushed down put the car into freewheel. But the most novel feature of the 96 was its reliability. Unlike all the cars I had owned before, reliable only in the frequency of malfunction, it was famously robust. The Saab 96 was the rally car of the time. You could drive it across Africa or the Arctic, and on my regular

---

* It was, of course, Swedish; the name is an acronym for Svenska Aeroplan Aktiebolaget, meaning Swedish Aeroplane Company.

journey from Windsor, where I lived, to Slough, where I worked as a reporter on the *Slough Observer*, I stopped worrying about imminent breakdown.

I clearly remember being rather proud of my 96's distinctiveness, and the relief that came with the confidence of being able to complete journeys. But I do not remember driving itself being particularly enjoyable, nor feeling liberated, let alone exhilarated, by the experience. By then, traffic was increasing rapidly. Already road building could not keep pace: the first motorways were cracking up under the weight of wheels, and traffic jams, roadworks and lines of cones had become regular features of the automotive life. I did not give the matter any thought at the time, but I had missed the best years of motoring by a wide margin.

Whether you follow Lionel Rolt in sighing for the golden age of the 1920s, or Mackenzie of the *Telegraph* in pining for the '30s, it is clear that by the 1950s a combination of increased traffic and inadequate roads was making driving a lot less fun than it used to be. However, the notion that buying your first car secured admission to a fellowship was still just about alive, and was energetically promoted by the AA. In 1955 it published a history of its first fifty years entitled *Golden Milestone*, which it dedicated to its members 'past and present, who by their support have enabled the Association to exceed the hopes and ambitions of its founders in the creation of an ideal of service'.

The patrolman was a crucial component of the AA's

self-image. Much was made of the rigour of his training. Like the police, they were ranked: the superintendent's uniform had gold bands on black at the sleeve, one wide and two narrow, whereas a mere chief inspector had one band fewer. Ten years' service was marked by a gold chevron on the collar, twenty by a gold badge. The patrolman protected the weak (meaning women drivers), advised the strong when their map-reading proved defective, and gave succour to the desperate in the form of a spark plug or puncture repair patch. At all times he lived up to and embodied the ideal of the fellowship of the road. The journalist and broadcaster Howard Marshall saw him as 'a man sure of himself, with an awareness of discipline . . . a conscientious man who never closes his eyes to an incident which can only mean more work for him.'

It's difficult to know if the chivalric code promoted by the AA ever really existed; and if it did, when it began to fall from favour. Certainly by the time I got my Saab 96 the innocent pleasure activity of 'going for a drive' had curdled into a much more troubled relationship between us and our vehicles, most notoriously depicted in the fantasies of death, violence and sexual obsession woven around the motorways and flyovers of London by J. G. Ballard in his novels *Crash* (1973) and *Concrete Island* (1974).

The German environmentalist and sociologist Wolfgang Sachs dated the souring of the love affair with the car to the 1970s, when 'the passions and utopias embodied in the automobile lost their buoyancy'. People were discovering that the more cars there were, the less joy there was in driving them. Other drivers' desires were getting in the way of their desires. Each additional car meant every minute was worth less in terms of distance travelled. The democratisation of car ownership was destroying its supreme advantage. Once, it had offered the ideal of travel guided by individual choice rather than by a man with a whistle. Now that everyone had access to the dream, it was revealed as an illusion.

But governments could not afford to grapple with this deep fissure within the relationship. The car industry was vital to all the developed economies; therefore the wisdom of encouraging mass ownership was not open to question. The only remedy was to build more roads.

6

MUTINY AND FLOWER POWER

A dreadful event took place on the night of 24 April 1920 on a stretch of the A303 west of Thruxton. It was sufficiently shocking to warrant headlines across the front pages of the national popular press, and to have Fleet Street's finest shouting for train timetables and maps of Hampshire. For the journalists on the local papers, the *Hampshire Chronicle* and the *Hampshire Observer*, it must have been the sensation of the decade. Their regular fare was strictly parochial: fluctuations in farm prices, the activities of women's institutes and the Andover Choral Society, an announcement of plans to tarmac roads, a heartening speech from the local MP about improving employment prospects. Crime was generally petty, and coverage was concentrated on the magistrates' courts which dealt with the thefts and drunken assaults committed by farm workers and soldiers from the several military camps in the area. They were not used to murder.

The headline in the *Hampshire Observer* read: 'Tragic

Discovery Near Andover'. The *Chronicle* reported that: 'An amazing "hold-up" tragedy in which the driver of a motor car was shot dead occurred on Saturday night near Andover.' A labourer identified tersely as 'Burridge' had discovered a body in a hedge on Thruxton Down 'which appeared to have been dragged a considerable distance across a field'. There was a bullet wound two inches from the victim's left ear.

The body had been identified as that of Sidney Spicer, a taxi driver from Salisbury. It seemed that Spicer had been engaged to take two men from Amesbury to the Bulford army camp a few miles away, and that while the hire was being arranged a soldier had intervened to try and secure Spicer's services. According to the *Hampshire Observer*, Spicer had returned from Bulford to Amesbury to pick up the soldier, who had subsequently shot him on a lonely stretch of the road where it rose over Thruxton Down. The taxi, a 12 HP Darracq, had been stolen, together with Spicer's money.

The man wanted by the police for the murder was named as Percy Toplis. The *Hampshire Observer* said he had posed as an RAF officer, while the *Chronicle* reported that he was a deserter from the Royal Army Service Corps and was wearing a blue serge suit and carrying a six-chamber revolver. One interesting detail was that he wore a monocle – blue, according to the *Chronicle,* gold-rimmed according to the *Observer.*

By the time the local papers were published, a week had elapsed since the killing, and the hunt for Percy Toplis had become a hot national story. The national press lingered long enough in Hampshire to attend a bizarre inquest convened in a barn near the scene of the crime at which the jury, seated on sacks of chaff, recorded a verdict of 'wilful murder' against Toplis – the first time in modern legal history that someone had been declared guilty of murder in their absence. By then Toplis was busy leading his pursuers an undignified dance. He spent a few days bouncing cheques and impersonating army officers in London before scarpering to Wales and then Scotland.

On 1 June, five weeks after the discovery of Spicer's body, Toplis was spotted in a bothy in the wilds of the Cairngorms, not far from Tomintoul. The village police constable, accompanied by a gamekeeper and a local tenant farmer, approached the bothy. Toplis opened fire, wounding two of the men, then rode off on his bicycle, allegedly singing the popular song 'Goodbyeee, don't sighee/There's a silver lining in the skyee/Bonjour old thing/ Cheerio, chin–chin/Napoo, toodle-oo, goodbyeee.'

He was traced first to Edinburgh, then Carlisle. On 6 June he set off to walk from Carlisle to Penrith wearing his military uniform. On the road between Low and High Hesket he stopped for a rest and sat on the grass outside a Wesleyan chapel to read the newspaper. He was still there when Constable Alfred Fulton chanced upon him. They chatted for a while and Toplis offered the constable his newspaper. PC Fulton then returned home, where his wife said she had seen a man pass the house who looked remarkably like the fugitive Toplis. Fulton hastened back to apprehend his acquaintance. 'If it's Toplis you want, I'm your man,' the soldier said, and levelled his gun at Fulton's head. The constable threw down his truncheon and handcuffs and legged it.

By the time he returned, armed and accompanied by two other armed officers, Toplis had reached the village of Plumpton and had changed into a brown suit. At this point the police contingent was joined by a demobbed army officer, Charles de Courcy-Parry, the son of Cumberland's chief constable, who was riding a motorcycle and brandishing a Belgian automatic pistol, a wartime souvenir. Without much ado the police opened fire. Allegedly it was de Courcy-Parry who fired the fatal bullet, although in later life – as a celebrated Cumbrian huntsman as well as a well-known sporting journalist – he always refused to confirm this.

Three days later Percy Topliss was buried in an unmarked grave in a cemetery on the north side of Penrith. The *Manchester Guardian*, sniffing an unseemly hurry, said it was a 'bad business'. The *Penrith Observer* disagreed. 'There are sentimental and perhaps soft-headed people who deplore the fact that Toplis was shot dead instead of being merely winged,' the local paper declared. 'Toplis went bad as a lad, gradually but rapidly went from bad to worse, and the world is well rid of a scoundrel of the most dangerous type.'

That should have been the end of it; certainly that was the intention of the authorities, who did their utmost to hush up the story of his end. But in the 1970s two journalists, William Allison and John Fairley, became intrigued by the story. In the main it was that of a singularly bad man whose criminal career began in boyhood in a Nottinghamshire mining village and encompassed attempted rape, innumerable cases of theft, fraud and blackmail, at least one murder and two attempted murders. Toplis's speciality was impersonating army officers and members of the upper classes. He preyed on women, cheated friends, ruthlessly exploited the good nature of others, and wherever he went left a trail of bounced cheques, forged papers, missing money and betrayed hearts.

Among his many exploits, Allison and Fairley discovered that while stationed at Bulford in 1920, Toplis had run a black-market operation in which army petrol was stolen and sold cheap to local taxi firms. Sidney Spicer had been the contact; the assumption was that Toplis murdered him either because of a dispute over the proceeds of the scam, or because he feared that Spicer was going to finger him. But the two journalists also had what they thought was a far more sensational revelation – a genuine scoop. They found evidence that Percy Toplis – conman, fraudster, blackmailer and thief – had played a crucial part in one of the infamous scandals of the First World War: the mutiny at Étaples.

Étaples was a training camp in northern France where Allied troops were toughened up by a regime of ferocious bullying to prepare them to be killed on the Western Front. In 1917 the arrest of a New Zealand gunner for desertion provoked a four-day revolt, after which one soldier was shot for mutiny, three others got ten years hard labour, and thirty more were sentenced to various punishments. The military authorities insisted at the time that all the ringleaders had been identified and dealt with. But according to Allison and Fairley, the actual organiser was Toplis, who subsequently managed his familiar trick of vanishing into thin air leaving others to pick up the pieces.

They called their book about him *The Monocled Mutineer*, a reference to his trademark toff's eyepiece. Several years after it was published, the BBC decided to commission the Liverpool writer Alan Bleasdale to dramatise it for TV. Bleasdale was hot property at the time, following the acclaim for his *Boys from the Blackstuff*, a series of television plays depicting the impact of unemployment and social deprivation in the economically ravaged north-west. Bleasdale apparently saw the Toplis story as an opportunity to explore class attitudes in a historical context. It was bad luck for him that the central premise in his source material – that Percy Toplis led the Etaples mutiny – turned out to be wrong (Toplis was almost certainly in, or on his way home from, India at the time). But the fatal mistake was made by someone at an advertising agency recently hired by the BBC, who labelled *The Monocled Mutineer* 'a real-life story'.

The row that it set off when it was shown in 1986 seems extraordinary from a distance of twenty-five years. But it's easy to forget the rancorous climate of that time and the vicious character of public debate after seven years of

Margaret Thatcher's Conservative government. An ugly alliance between the right-wing press and Tory back-benchers eager to suck up to their leader directed a firestorm of abuse at the series, its writer, and the hated BBC that had seen fit to spend public money on it. The assault was led by the *Daily Mail*, which branded it 'a tissue of lies' and portrayed it as yet more conclusive evidence of the socialist bias of the BBC. The *Mail* clamoured for a new chairman to be appointed to cleanse the Augean stables of the accumulated neo-Marxist filth. Its own choice was Lord King, Mrs Thatcher's favourite industrialist and the saviour of British Airways.

In the event King was considered too much of a bruiser by the Cabinet, and the job went to the one-legged but almost equally combative Marmaduke Hussey. One of Hussey's first moves was to force the resignation of the BBC's director-general, Alasdair Milne, a leading hate figure for right-wing columnists who appeared to hold him single-handedly responsible for the moral decline of the nation.

I watched *The Monocled Mutineer* again before writing this chapter. My first reaction was wonderment. What on earth was the fuss about? How could it have provoked such a baying frenzy of outrage? Then something of the flavour of the era came back to me: the ferocious polarisation between left and right that had characterised Thatcherite politics, the venom her sense of mission released, the belief that drove her and with which she infected her supporters that they were engaged in a mortal struggle with the forces of darkness. The BBC was a convenient target for this bile. It was extravagant, arrogant and riddled with left-wingery (as illustrated by the notorious *Maggie's Militant Tendency* Panorama programme). It was unpatriotic (interviewing the Sinn Fein leader Martin McGuinness for the *Real Lives* documentary about Northern Ireland). It was immoral (Dennis Potter's *The Singing Detective*). It was subversive (the *Secret Society* investigation into the Zircon spy satellite). No one laughed when the Prime Minister's husband called it 'a nest of reds', or when Norman Tebbit accused it of anti-American pro-Libyan bias in its coverage of the US air strikes on Tripoli in April 1986, or when the devotedly Thatcherite *Daily Mail* columnist Paul Johnson described *The Monocled Mutineer* as 'another bit of agitprop designed to inflame class hatred and denigrate Britain'.

It is nothing of the sort. It has its flaws, and occasionally it goes out of its way to make a tendentious political point. But overall it is drama of the highest order, powerful and rather beautiful. It is extremely well acted, outstandingly so by the young Paul McGann, who is unnervingly convincing as Percy Toplis. It is loving and convincing in its recreation of setting, costume and historical detail. It is touching, shocking and compelling, despite a pace that seems remarkably leisurely by the frenetic standards of today's TV drama. The depiction of class issues is in fact quite subtle; even Paul Johnson – assuming he took the trouble to watch it – might have noticed that the sadists and bullies at the Étaples training camp are the working-class NCOs, while the character of the upper-class commander (played by Timothy West) is drawn with considerable sympathy.

Far from inciting me to class hatred, *The Monocled Mutineer* filled me with nostalgia. It recalled vividly a time when the BBC regarded it as its duty to make elegant, serious drama for educated television watchers. It reminded me how swiftly and thoroughly things change. Nineteen eighty-six seems a very distant time and place.

Not as distant, however, as 1725, when a Church visitation to the village of Thruxton found that 152 people lived there, of whom but one – 'and she a poor woman without any family' – was a Papist, and none a Dissenter. Under the heading 'Gentry', the record notes: 'There is no person of note of either sex residing in the village.'

Nothing is said on the important subject of public houses, but we can be sure that Thruxton was not without. Almost 300 years later there are two. The one in the centre of the village is the George, which employs a man with a sandwich board advertising its attractions to plod up and down the eastbound carriageway of the A303 near the turnoff for Thruxton. The other is the White Horse, which has a sign on the A303 but would not, one feels, stoop to a sandwich board.*

---

* The George closed in 2017 and planning permission was given for it to be converted into a private house.

The White Horse is much the older of the two, fifteenth century in parts, or so they say. It is a pretty, whitewashed, thatched inn with low beams and ingle-nooks and fireplaces festooned with brass tongs and pokers and the like. It used to stand right on the A303, opposite the stone house where they took the tolls for the Andover–Amesbury turnpike road. Then the Highways Agency decided that as part of the dual-carriageway project, the section past Thruxton should be elevated, which was completed in the mid-1980s. This was good news for the village, which was protected from the worst of the racket. But it was not quite such good news for the White Horse, which found itself a little close to the elevated section for comfort. It rises like a sheer rock face immediately outside the front door, with the result that the traffic flashes by at the level of the thatched roof and hardly more than spitting distance away.

The atmosphere in the pub the night I stayed there might be described as subdued. The landlord was perfectly welcoming without being in the least bit genial. He revealed that he had previously managed what he called 'a gentleman's club' at Westminster. I had the impression he felt the move from the buzz of Queen Anne's Gate to the shadow of the A303 represented a coming down in the world. 'Put it like this,' he said when I asked him how it was going, 'it might not have been the best time to get into the pub business.' I overheard him telling the only other diners about the good days when the bar was thronged with horse-racing types from the stables at Kimpton Down and motor-racing fans attending events at Thruxton's own Formula Three circuit.

Pub and road

I slept in a room whose window looked out from beneath the thatch at the railings beside the A303. I went to sleep with the road in my ears and was awoken by its inexorable crescendo towards the morning peak-time. I lay listening to it, trying to locate a metaphor for the noise. It was harsh, like a sheet being torn, or waves breaking, but waves of wholly inconsistent size coming down at wildly fluctuating intervals – no comforting regularity, but restless, volatile, unsettling. A very different kind of sea.

Thruxton village is gathered together on the north side of the A303. But the parish of Thruxton extends in a slender strip the best part of six miles from Weyhill in the east almost to the Hampshire–Wiltshire border in the west. Travellers heading that way may well be momentarily distracted by the appearance over to the left of Quarley Hill, which is shaped rather like a flying saucer and is the site of an Iron Age hillfort assiduously dug over by students of prehistoric ditch systems, palisading, middens and allied matters. But they are likely to be recalled to the present by a green sign welcoming them to Wiltshire. It would be nice if there was another one saying 'And Hampshire Bids You Farewell' or words to that effect, or – even better – if the two councils could collaborate on a sign expressing both sentiments.

But Hampshire doesn't?

The odd thing is that there is no welcome to Hampshire for those motoring east on the other side of the A303.

I did wonder if there might be an obscure and ancient dis-agreement between the two counties over the exact position of the border, which does wander whimsically here-abouts. The absence of a sign is all the more peculiar as elsewhere Hampshire is keen – some might say excessively so – to announce itself as 'Hampshire – the Jane Austen County'.

I'd like to know where this business of identifying a county with literary celebrities began. Was it with Warwickshire (Shakespeare County), Yorkshire (Brontë County) or Dorset (Hardy County)? In fairness, if it was Warwickshire, the choice of notable scribe was pretty limited, although George Eliot was born and brought up near Nuneaton. But why should Hampshire be just Jane Austen County? Why not Dickens (born Portsmouth), Izaak Walton (died Winchester) or Gilbert White (*The Natural History of Selborne*) County as well? And why doesn't Somerset market itself as T. S. Eliot (buried East Coker) or Samuel Taylor Coleridge (born Ottery St Mary, lived Nether Stowey) County? Wiltshire could call itself Trollope County or go the whole hog and change its name to Barsetshire, since Anthony had the idea for the sequence while wandering around Salisbury.

Come to think of it, why shouldn't trunk roads brighten their image with some literary associations? The A303 could be the Tennyson Road (Guinevere died in Amesbury and Alfred immortalised her in his *Idylls of the King*). The A4 at Reading could be the Wilde Road (Oscar jailed there for gross indecency) or the Austen Road (Jane went to school there), then become the Sassoon Road at Marlborough (where Siegfried went to school), and the Chaucer Road at Bath (the Wife). The possibilities for the A40, which goes through Oxford, or the A10 to Cambridge, or the A1 between London and Edinburgh, are mind-boggling.

★ ★ ★

They don't grow beans there any more; oil-seed rape and barley, more likely. But the field is still there, where a heap of dreams and ideals came a cropper amid a welter of truncheon blows and kicks from big black boots on a summer's day in 1985. It was known as the Battle of the Beanfield.

I was travelling to Scotland by train in September 2010 when I read in the paper that Sid Rawle was dead. The photograph with the obituary brought him back: the shoulder-length hair thinning on top and tucked behind tall, straight ears; the slight body encased in denim; the patchy beard, the lazy, smiling eyes, the smile itself proclaiming delight in the comedy of life and his part in it. 'King of the Hippies', the headline called him. 'He fought for love, peace and land', said his obituary. He'd died of a heart attack sitting by the campfire at his 'Superspirit' summer festival in the Forest of Dean.

I doubt if the name meant a great deal to later generations of *Guardian* readers, but it struck a deep chime with me. In 1972 – when I was in my green Saab 96 phase – Rawle and his followers, who called themselves the

Diggers, helped stage the first People's Free Festival on Crown land in Windsor Great Park. The idea belonged to Bill 'Ubi' Dwyer – William Ubique in full – the Irish-born prophet of LSD-induced psychedelia. Dwyer said it came to him in the course of an acid trip, and he informed sceptics: 'I personally have God's permission for the festival.' He was too wild and Irish to make much sense for the benefit of the media, whereas Sid Rawle – who did not take drugs and preferred to devote his energies to the pursuit of young women – was more than ready to deploy his soft Exmoor accent to expound the doctrine of free love and land for all.

Rawle was already a familiar figure to longer-serving journalists in Slough when I joined the *Slough Observer*. He had lived there with his mother, working for a time as a park attendant, and he was fondly remembered for having organised a 'love-in' in the meticulously maintained public gardens opposite Slough Town Hall, which provided many hundreds of juicy column inches for the newspaper.

Windsor Great Park was well out of our patch, so I never covered the free festival. But for the reporters based in Windsor the story of the conflict between the solid, bourgeois citizens of the town (backed, it was said, by the Duke of Edinburgh himself) and the counter-culture imported by Rawle and Dwyer and their kind was irresist-ible. By the summer of 1974 Windsor had had enough. Daily editions of the *Windsor Freek Press* distributed among the 15,000 festival-goers – and eagerly seized upon by the local hacks – chart the progress towards the final confrontation. Much of the advice concerns drugs. Acid came in brown, green, pink and orange microdots. People were cautioned against something called 'S.T.P.', allegedly developed from nerve gas, morphine ('anyone who sells this shit deserves everything that's come to them'), and 'garbage hash' mixed with patchouli oil.

The pigs – as the men in blue from Thames Valley Police were invariably known – were becoming an increasing problem. Anyone 'busted' or 'pulled' was urged to stay cool. At the same time pigs were to be urged to 'fuck off the site'. One editorial begged people to 'shit and piss in the bogs . . . Don't shit in any old place.' On the Thursday after the August Bank Holiday 600 officers of Thames Valley Police invaded the site and cleared it. The following year Dwyer and Rawle were both imprisoned for breaching an injunction banning them from promoting a 1975 festival. A cartoon in the very alternative *International Times* showed the female holder of the flame of justice crying 'BURN KILL BUGGER PILLAGE MANGLE MAIM RAPE FUCK FLAGELLATE', which made some kind of point.

Windsor '74 may have been, as one journalist called it, 'the last stand of the psychedelic underground'. But the hunger it represented – for the freedom to take drugs, have unlimited casual sex, not to have a job or a mortgage, to lie around in the open listening to eardrum-battering rock music – did not go away. At no time did it involve more than a minute sliver of the population. But the counterculture of which the free festival movement was a basic element developed to a point at which it came to represent – or seemed to – a genuine threat to the established social order. And the establishment reacted as the establishment must.

Ten years after Windsor died, an estimated 100,000 people gathered for the free festival at Stonehenge, held over nine days around the summer solstice. Access to the monument was unhindered – one photograph shows Sid Rawle within the circle of the stones, naked to the waist, holding his arms out to the sun while the tom-toms beat. The event passed off peacefully, but by the time it ended the forces of reaction were building. The political climate had changed radically since Labour's reforming Home Secretary, Roy Jenkins, had in effect sanctioned a free festival at Watchfield in Oxfordshire in 1975. Under Margaret Thatcher the principle was established that disorder or anything resembling it or threatening to turn into it should be met with force. The treatment of the miners in 1984 showed a government entirely comfortable with the proposition that the police should be used as a weapon against dissent. Mrs Thatcher was no more inclined to look kindly at a rabble of travellers, squatters, druggies, hippies, anarchists, diggers, levellers, bikers, layabouts and free-lovers than at the sooty cokemen of Orgreave.

So when a group of Wiltshire landowners approached the police after the 1984 Stonehenge Festival to say that they no longer wished to have their property invaded, their fences trampled down, their copses felled for fire-wood, their livestock alarmed and their meadows dug up to make impromptu latrines and left shin-deep in rubbish, they got a sympathetic hearing. Lord Montagu of Beaulieu – chairman of English Heritage, the quango that had taken charge of Stonehenge in 1983 – obtained injunctions banning eighty-three named people from coming within two miles of the monument.

At the end of May the permanent core of the festival movement, the self-styled Peace Convoy, was parked among the beeches of Savernake Forest in north Wiltshire. The solstice was approaching, and the pull of the stones was on them. Canny Sid Rawle, one of the banned as well as the beautiful people, was aware that trouble was coming. He urged the others to delay leaving Savernake until rein-forcements arrived. Rawle believed that their only chance of beating the forces waiting for them would be with weight of numbers. But others did not share his acute appreciation of how the battle lines were drawn. On 1 June the bulk of the Convoy, 140 cheerfully painted buses, caravans, trucks and cars, trundled down the A338 Marlborough–Salisbury road towards its junction with the A303 at Cholderton, where they would turn right for Stonehenge. Flags were waving. Bob Marley boomed from ghetto blasters.

Just short of the junction – more than four miles outside the exclusion zone secured by the Wiltshire land-owners – the A338 had been blocked by a mound of gravel. As the Peace Convoy came to a halt, a version of war broke out. Police in riot equipment came down the line of vehicles smashing windscreens and windows and dragging out the occupants and arresting them. Most of the Convoy then broke through a hedge into a field of beans in the shape of a triangle with the A338 and the A303 forming two of its sides.

Several hundred police officers followed them. They were led by Wiltshire's acting Deputy Chief Constable, Lionel Grundy, who informed the travellers that they were being stopped because of their clear intention to break the Stonehenge exclusion zone. He refused to let them turn around and go back to Savernake, saying that they would have to abandon their vehicles, which for many of them were their homes. A lengthy stand-off ended with the police being ordered to arrest everyone. Buses and caravans were wrecked; members of the Convoy were chased, beaten and dragged around by the hair. One of the very few journalists present, Nick Davies of the *Observer*, said afterwards: 'Over the years I had seen all kinds of frightening and horrible things and always managed to grin and write it. But as I left the Beanfield, for the first time I felt sick enough to cry.' An ITN reporter, Kim Sabido, described the assault as 'the most brutal police treatment of people that I've witnessed in my entire career' – although, mysteriously, both his voice and the footage of the worst of the savagery were missing from the report broadcast that night.

Unfortunately for Mr Grundy, there was a witness to the

events in the beanfield who was neither a journalist nor an unwashed hippy but secretary of the Marlborough Conservative Association. Lord Cardigan had become acquainted with the Peace Convoy because his father, the Marquess of Ailesbury, owned the part of Savernake Forest where they had parked. He decided to follow them towards Stonehenge on his motorbike and saw what happened. He publicly described the behaviour of the police as brutal, and when challenged by one of his fellow Wiltshire landowners, he replied: 'If I see a policeman truncheoning a woman I feel I'm entitled to say it's not a good thing.'

Largely because of his testimony, the charges against more than 400 Peace Convoy members arrested during the Battle of the Beanfield had to be dropped. Cardigan himself, having been widely denounced as a class traitor, successfully sued *The Times*, the *Daily Telegraph*, the *Daily Mail*, the *Daily Express* and the *Daily Mirror* for libel (*The Times* called him 'barking mad', a condition it attributed to his notorious ancestor at the Charge of the Light Brigade). Six years later, twenty-four of those charged by Wiltshire Police won an action for wrongful arrest.

No matter. These were minor setbacks to the Thatcher government's offensive against the free festival move-ment and its highly subversive message. The year after the Battle of the Beanfield, the Public Order Act came into force, redefining what the state regarded as disorder and giving the police enormously enhanced powers to control, ban and disperse assemblies. The era of free love, free music, free festivals, of the Wallies and hippies and Hengists, of the Tibetan Ukrainian Mountain Troupe and the Mystic Wankers, the Albionists and the Freaks and all the rest was over.

So too, by coincidence, was Britain's time as a world leader in making motor cars. In 1960 we were the second-biggest car manufacturing nation. By 1974 we had slipped to sixth place, and the slide continued. In November 1979 Derek Robinson, known as 'Red Robbo', the Amalgamated Union of Engineering Workers' convener at British Leyland's Longbridge plant, was sacked for publicly criticising the plan proposed by the new chairman, Sir Michael Edwardes, to save the company from collapse. The BBC credited Robinson with having instigated more than 500 industrial disputes over the previous two and a half years. BL, by then the last wholly British volume car producer left, became a terminal victim of what became known around the world as 'the British disease', namely industrial anarchy. In 1986 the Japanese car maker Nissan – where such problems were unknown – opened its first European plant. The location it chose was Sunderland.

As for me, the green Saab 96 marked a decisive break with my own country's automotive heritage. It was followed by another 96, orange and not so appealing. After that came two Volvo estates and a successions of Peugeots. I never owned a truly British car again.

7

ANCESTRAL VOICES

The road rises steadily from the Beanfield over the south end of a long ridge that reaches towards the Berkshire Downs to the north. Up to this point the environs of the A303 have been pleasant enough (when not despoiled by the Great Shed) but nothing special. But suddenly, as it crests the ridge, it is as if a curtain had been whipped away.

The view south from Beacon Hill

To get the best of what is revealed, you need to stop somewhere and ascend the chalky path on the north side of the road. It leads to the top of Beacon Hill, so named for the same reason that Popham Beacons is called Popham Beacons. The top is a rounded knoll of rabbit-nibbled rough grass dotted with gorse bushes and wind-battered little thorn trees, and populated at certain times of year by a large number of snails. There is a tapered GPS marker stone and, close by, a bristling radio mast defended by a formidable fence with signs warning of terrible consequences for trespassers. This installation detracts somewhat from the charm of the place, as does the thunder from the road below. But on a clear day nothing can diminish the wonder of the panorama.

The land drops away steeply on three sides. To the north Beacon Hill becomes Dunch Hill then Sidbury Hill, with its Iron Age fort. Far beyond is the blue line of the Marlborough Downs and Tan Hill, another prehistoric fortified settlement. West is the valley of the Avon, the trees along the river making it look as if a fat finger had been dipped in green paint and dragged down the middle of Salisbury Plain. Either side is spread the Plain itself, a rolling plateau of tawny grass. Somewhere far away are the artillery ranges of Larkhill and Westdown, and the army's training grounds reach as far as Warminster, although the distances cover all the details in a dun-coloured haze. Closer, you can see the tank and transport tracks snaking across the bare terrain, almost white against the grass. The Old Marlborough

Road, originally a droving way and for a long time the main route to Salisbury, cuts a pale, empty line due north.

Bulford, the first of the military camps, is at the foot of Beacon Hill. Due west is Amesbury, hidden by trees, and beyond it Stonehenge, sufficiently straight ahead for the line between it and Beacon Hill to be listed in the web of routes radiating from the monument that have been identified over the centuries by stargazers, Druids, ley hunters, ufologists and other seekers after spiritual illumination – some visible, many invisible, all regarded as being of immense importance. Salisbury is away to the south, the spire of its cathedral showing like a dart when the air is clear; and the great oval mound of Roman Sorviodunum, Old Sarum. Most of this southern tract of country is arable land, dotted with woods and copses. The eye that roams across it is likely to be held by two unmissable military sites with dark associations: Boscombe Down and Porton Down.

I cycled in and around them both one blustery summer's day and came back to tell the tale. Boscombe, the aircraft testing station, is spread over the high ground to the southeast of Amesbury, its two enormous runways forming a cramped L-shape with its apex close to the town. It appeared to be entirely deserted when I pedalled past, apart from the occasional MoD jeep glimpsed far inside the perimeter fence. There was no one to say 'good morning' to or to ask about the various hush-hush activities that bring a glitter to the eye of the conspiracy theorists – in particular the alleged accident involving an alleged hypersonic spy plane that allegedly happened in September 1994. There weren't even any guard dogs, just a long, long barrier of wire fencing hung at intervals with signs stating: 'Prohibited Place Under The Official Secrets Act'. Inside the fence, half buried in the ground and grassed over (presumably to make them invisible from the air), were bunkers with green nodules like hose connectors on top. Was there anyone inside, looking out?

Porton Down is a couple of miles south-east of Boscombe Down. The name is indelibly associated with the experimental station established by the War Office nearly a hundred years ago to test chemical weapons. Since then scientists have developed and researched a host of horrible agents of death, disease and paralysis, from mustard gas and phosgene to anthrax and botulinum to LSD and sarin. In the process a mushroom cloud of rumour concerning hideous experiments on unsuspecting victims has settled over the Porton Down labs; and other tales have been told, of alien organisms retrieved from the scene of UFO collisions with earth being analysed and producing results too terrifying ever to be mentioned again.

But to botanists and nature lovers, Porton Down means something else entirely. Its appropriation in the cause of inflicting death and suffering meant the abrupt end of farming. Since 1916 the down itself has been untouched by plough, fertiliser, herbicide or pesticide. As a result of this accidental return to nature, it is now acknowledged as the most important large (3500 acres) expanse of pristine chalk grassland in Europe. Amid the sheep's fescue and meadow oat-grass, rare orchids brush against toadflax, milkwort, fleawort, squinancywort, viper's bugloss, horse-shoe vetch and other curiously named flowers. More than forty species of butterfly and moth shimmer between the clumps of spiky, black-berried juniper. Skylarks soar and the stone curlews flute their sad cry. An estimated thirty billion ants occupy the three million anthills that resemble an outbreak of green measles. And none but a very few authorised humans may go there.

I cycled somewhat nervously down the long avenue into the Porton Down Science Campus, unable entirely to suppress the thought that, if apprehended, I might be liable for use for experiments by mad virologists. I kept going briskly past an enormous complex of buildings, including the Defence, Science and Technology Laboratory where thousands of mice, pigs, ferrets, rats and monkeys experience horrible (though possibly useful) deaths each year; and the Health Protection Agency's Emergency Centre for Preparedness and Response, where men and women in white coats work out what should be done in the event of a bio-terrorist attack or the arrival of plague. A notice stated that the current response level – I was unclear what to – was 'heightened'. Back on the road I paused briefly opposite a closed gate beyond which a dead-straight, clearly very private indeed way rose steeply to a cluster of low buildings where – it seemed to me – ANYTHING MIGHT HAPPEN. I urged my bicycle back to the village of Porton.

It is probably the least interesting of a string of villages along the lower part of the River Bourne, which is a tiny chalkstream that wriggles south through the eastern sector of Salisbury Plain and eventually joins the Avon in Salisbury itself (its theoretical source is far away towards Marlborough but in these thirsty times much of its course is dry for much of the year). Idmiston is the next village upstream from Porton, where there is a very beautiful old flint church. The vicar there in the late eighteenth century was the Reverend John Bowle, known by his friends (who included Doctor Johnson) as 'Don' Bowle on account of his great accomplishments in Spanish. He edited *Don Quixote* and wrote a *Life of Cervantes* in Spanish; the *Dictionary of National Biography* calls him 'an ingenious scholar of great erudition and varied research in obscure and ancient literature', which is a nice thing to have said about you. 'Don' Bowle loved his dog Pedro, and wrote these lines to him: 'My dog, the trustiest of his kind/With gratitude inflames my mind.' After Pedro's death his owner had his skin used to bind a few favourite books so that he might continue to pat him in the absence of his animating spirit.

A couple of big loops further up the Bourne is Boscombe, huddled below the western runway of the airfield. Another cleric of great learning, Richard Hooker, was rector here in the 1590s, when he was writing his epic treatise on church governance, *Of the Laws of Ecclesiastical Politie*. Hooker is pretty much forgotten now but was revered after his death for his simple piety and erudite theology.

Izaak Walton wrote an admiring biography of him, in which he attributed Hooker's domestic troubles to poor choice of wife. She nagged him incessantly, on one occasion – according to Walton – rousing him stridently from his study of Horace to get him to rock the baby's cradle. Walton alleged that he only married her because he was bashful and had poor eyesight.

Edward Hutton, in his marvellous *Highways and Byways in Wiltshire*, speculated that there must have been something that inspired scholarship in the 'thin and pure and musical air' that wafted over these downs. At the same time that Hooker was toiling over his *Ecclesiastical Politie* in Boscombe, Nicholas Fuller, the Rector of Allington – not much more than a mile away – was up to his ears in the studies that would eventually, in 1612, bear fruit in the publication of his *Miscellaneorum Theologicorum*, a great brantub (written in Latin) of reflections on the relationship between languages and religion.

A further mile upriver is Newton Tony, another appealing little place. That tireless traveller on the atrocious pre-turnpike roads, Celia Fiennes, came from there.* The Fiennes had the big house in Newton Tony. After they were gone, a bigger one was built by a rich landowner, William Benson, who was celebrated for his passionate love for the poetry of Milton. He paid for the

---

* Motivated largely by curiosity, she travelled much of the country between 1684 and 1703; her memoirs were eventually published in 1888 under the title *Through England on a Side Saddle*.

marble monument to him in Poets' Corner in Westminster Abbey, and forked out the amazing sum of £1000 to have *Paradise Lost* translated into Latin hexameters. It was not obvious to Benson's contemporaries why anyone should wish to read it in someone else's Latin rather than Milton's English; but it was still a considerable act of homage.

From Newton Tony I took an old droving track called the Green Way to Cholderton, the last village before the A303 crosses the Bourne. It was dark, hemmed in by beech and oak trees, worn into a rounded dip by sheep hooves long ago but firm and flinty beneath my wheels. It was very quiet and I did not meet a soul. When I emerged into open country, I immediately heard the buzzing of the A303 ahead.

★ ★ ★

From Beacon Hill the road slopes down to Amesbury. I came across some verses about the place that appealed to me. They were dated 1946 and were composed by 'G.E.G.', a modest poet. Part of the poem goes as follows:

> In crook of wandering Avon's elbow do I lie
> At peace secure . . .
>
> Vespasian's legions from the wooded camp above
> My reedy vale have marched my ancient straeds
> The centuries have passed and poets sang of love
> Within the confines of my peaceful Abbey glades.
> I lack not fame . . .

Deep in my heart I hold romantic story
Age-old my tales of armour and the men,
Illustrious knights who honour England's glory
Frequent my downs that come within my ken
And Amesbury is my name.

They don't make poetry like that any more. ('Straeds', by the way, is Old English for 'streets', which doesn't rhyme with 'glades'.)

Amesbury's history is immensely ancient. It leads back to the bluestones of Stonehenge, shipped from Wales and unloaded in the crook of the river's elbow. It holds the legend of Guinevere's end and Launcelot's final act of devotion. Vespasian himself may or may not have come by, but the Roman legions certainly did so. Amesbury Abbey was a renowned religious house until Thomas Cromwell had it despoiled. To Edward Hutton, writing at the time of the 1914–18 war, it was 'not only the chief but the oldest place in the upper valley of the Avon . . . nor is there any town or village in Wiltshire more to be loved . . . it is delicious, deeply embosomed in woods in all the loveliness of that fair vale.'

I fear that Hutton would howl if he could see it now. Most of the loveliness has been erased in the course of contemporary Amesbury's search to establish a new identity and function for itself. Its rebranding is summed up by a 160-acre gash in the chalk on its eastern fringe, predictably named Solstice Park. The way in from the A303 passes the main southern distribution centre for Robert Wiseman Dairies, a group of grey steel hangars guarded by rows of milk lorries in black-and-white livery. Across Equinox Drive from Robert Wiseman stretches a bleached wasteland of weeds and chalk and heaps of shattered tarmac, still empty several years after clearing. The far boundary is Sunrise Way, on the other side of which stands a trio of office blocks in smoky glass and tubular steel called The Crescent. You may agree with its developer that it is spectacular, inspirational, innovative and high-profile; certainly it looks rather lonely perched on the edge of a white, thistly emptiness.*

The Ordnance Survey map reveals a rich abundance of ancient sites either side of the A303 as it heads west past Amesbury. The land is littered with long barrows, round barrows, disc barrows, burial grounds of every kind. Many have been flattened by ploughing or have disappeared under buildings. But many survive, a visible graveyard left by our invisible forbears, the Neolithic people and the Bronze Age people after them.

You can meet one of them, in a manner of speaking, as you turn into Solstice Park from the A303. In fact you can hardly miss him. Even though he is kneeling, The Ancestor – as he is known – is more than twenty feet high. Welded from bits of dark steel that glitter like newly cut coal, he

* Much of the thistly emptiness has subsequently been filled up, most notably by a distribution centre operated by T.J. Morris/Home Bargains, which dwarfs the Robert Wiseman centre (now Muller Wiseman) and is more than twice as big as the Co-Op's Great Shed at Andover

faces east from a patch of land in front of the Holiday Inn, arms outstretched, gazing skywards. His brow protrudes, his eyes are sunken, his nose is wide and flat. In spring and summer he wears a spiky copper-coloured head-dress of leaves and corn stalks and balls of wire. His sculptors have supplied a text to explain what he represents: 'Ancient man on his knees, head thrown back, arms open wide. Reaching up to the sky, spreading out like a mighty oak, straining towards the sun on the longest day, rooted into the moon, protected by three magical hares. The sun and the moon with life in between. THE CIRCLE OF LIFE.'

The Ancestor

There is a message, too: 'The Ancestor means many things to many different people. This is what he means to us. WE HAVE FORGOTTEN TO BE GRATEFUL.'

It's lucky for him that he looks east towards Beacon Hill. If he faced west instead, the first thing he would see (be grateful for?) would be the Holiday Inn, an example – according to its designers – of 'Neolithic chic . . . very boutiquey, very contemporary and modern, appealing to the techno-savvy.' If he rose from his knees and walked past the Neolithic chic and the Co-Op service station next door, he would come to the Harvester Inn, built in no discernible style at all, where he could grab an Earlybird breakfast or a combo meal-deal. Beyond are Pizza Hut and KFC, with drifts of discarded packaging in front and another tract of weed-infested waste ground behind.

If The Ancestor lumbered on towards town along what used to be the A303 until the bypass came, he would find Lidl on the left, followed by a spanking-new Tesco with angled blue-and-white funnels on its flat roof. Should he be grateful for Lidl and Tesco? If, instead of taking the road into town, he turned left and went past the innovative, inspirational and high-profile Crescent and the entrance to Boscombe Airfield, he would come to the great swathe of new houses that now covers the high, sloping ground on Amesbury's southern flank. The development is called Archer's Gate, in honour of a real-life ancestor, whose skeleton was uncovered when they were clearing the area for the builders to move in. Buried there about 2300 BC, he was immediately dubbed The Amesbury Archer because of the arrowheads and bowman's wristguard found with him. His mortal remains and possessions – including minute gold hair ornaments, the oldest gold objects ever found in this country – are now in Salisbury Museum, which would be a bit of a hike for The Ancestor. But if the two of them – Archer and Ancestor – could talk, what a tale they might tell!

Somewhere on his tour, The Ancestor might well be invited to pick up a leaflet from the tourist board which makes the bold claim that Amesbury's ten-fold growth into a town of 30,000 people has not lessened its charm. He might scratch his head-dress at that; might even forget to be grateful.

The charm that survives, such as it is, is to be found by the river. After coming under the bypass, the Avon executes two big meanders, an extravagant 'S'. With protective high ground to the south and west, it made for an ideal place to set up home. It was evidently a place of some importance at the time of the Archer, who came there all the way from the Alps with his bow and arrows and tools. More than a thousand years later an Iron Age hillfort looked down on the river, later still incorporated into a Roman military base.

It was to Amesbury that Guinevere stole away after the death of Arthur and the knights. In Malory's version, 'there she let make herself a nun and wore white clothes and black, and great penance she took, as ever did sinful lady in this land, and never creature could make her merry.' Launcelot came after her, and she commanded that 'thou never see me more in this visage'. And he, honourable knight that he was, went away to Glastonbury where he did his own penance, until he learned in a vision that she was dead. Then he marched with eight of his fellows to Amesbury, to be told that the Queen had died half-an-hour before. 'And there was ordained a horse bier, and so with a hundred torches ever burning about the corpse of the Queen and ever Sir Launcelot with his eight fellows went about the horse bier singing and reading many a holy orison . . . Thus Sir Launcelot and his eight fellows went on foot from Amesbury to Glastonbury . . . and after she was put in a web of lead and then in a coffin of marble, and when she was put in the earth he swooned.'

The charm of Amesbury

Maybe there never was a Guinevere nor a love-lorn Launcelot nor a sword in the stone. But the historians believe there may well have been a religious house of some kind in Amesbury in the murky period before the Saxon invasion of Salisbury Plain in the mid-sixth century AD. And it is certain that in 979 or thereabouts Elfrida – the cause of all the trouble in Harewood Forest – founded a convent there. That unreliable chronicler William of Malmesbury says she did so from remorse over her part in the murder of the stepson Edward, but it's just as likely that it was no more than a conventional act of piety. In time, Elfrida drowned in the Test, her son Ethelred made a hash of things, the Danes came and went, the Normans came and didn't go. Under Henry II a whiff of scandal emanating from Amesbury became strong enough to reach the nostrils of first the King, and then the Pope, Alexander III. There were rumours of riotous living and lax morals; the abbess herself was said to have given birth to three children. The Pope sent two worthy bishops to investigate. They deposed the abbess, expelled the bad nuns, and dispersed the rest to other convents. Henry II himself – in acute need of restoring some credit on earth and in heaven following the infamous murder of Becket in Canterbury Cathedral – refounded the convent by importing two dozen presumably extremely chaste and pious nuns from Fontevrault, in his French dominion of Anjou.

A fine new abbey rose a little distance from the three or four streets of medieval Amesbury. After a while some monks came too, with a prior, but the prioress had ascendancy over the prior and the nuns over the monks – in accordance with Henry II's command that 'the authority which Christ gave to Mary on the Cross should be the model of the relation between the women and men of his congregation.'

Over the succeeding centuries Amesbury Abbey's importance and usefulness were never seriously challenged, until the arrival in 1539 of Thomas Cromwell's visitors signalled the end. The nuns and monks were sent packing, and the monastery with its twelve acres of gardens, orchards and fishponds was snapped up by the lordly and rapacious Edward Seymour, then Earl of Hertford, subsequently Duke of Somerset and for a time Lord Protector of England. By Somerset's order the lead was stripped from the church, the chapel, the cloister, the dormitories, the chapter-house, the kitchens, the prioress's lodging, the buttery and the infirmary. Everything that could not be recycled for use in his various mansions or sold was left to decay. Edward Hutton damned Somerset as 'this great rogue' and gloated that he eventually 'met the end he so richly deserved on Tower Hill'.

Every vestige of the Abbey has long since vanished. Since the 1840s the site has been occupied by an imposing porticoed stone mansion which is now a nursing home. It is surrounded by spacious parkland, with the willow-shaded Avon curling around its edge. There is a private − but not too private − road that leads from the parish church through lawns and past stately oaks to the front of the house, then bends away to rejoin the official road beside a bridge with a dark pool beneath. I cycled absent-mindedly through, reflecting on Guinevere and Elfrida and lustful nuns and tyrannical lead-stripping earls, until I came out by the gatehouse. Traffic noise filled the air, banishing the past.

8

OLD STONES, BIG BIRDS

Maybe it's fanciful to suggest that the great sweep of land that reveals itself west of Beacon Hill could somehow 'feel' ancient, could in some subliminal way transmit a sense of belonging to the deep past. At the same time, however, even the most severe rationalist would have to accept that a great weight and depth of old history is spread across it. In addition to the prehistoric burial sites, there are earthworks, ditches, fortifications, lynchets, Celtic field systems, Romano-British villages, Roman roads, medieval droving paths – a wealth of footprints from the past still visible along the ridges, over the downs, in the valleys.

The archaeologists tell us that six-and-a-half thousand years ago Salisbury Plain was mostly covered by forests of ash, elm, lime, hazel and alder, which were hunted by isolated bands of men with bone axes and tools fashioned from antler. Fifteen hundred years later, extensive areas had been cleared for crops and grazing, and communities were sufficiently settled for them to consign their important people to burial chambers. By the second millennium BC society was organised into extended family units mostly gathered into hilltop enclosures defended by ditches and ramparts, with grazing and arable land close by. By 100 BC permanent settlements of considerable size had been long established, still concentrated on hillforts, with land boundaries defined and marked, if not always respected.

Then the Romans came with their roads and towns, and history proper began.

At the heart of this old, old world, on a rise of ground a little way to the west of the crook in Avon's elbow, is a circle of upright stones that look as if they might have been left behind from some celestial building game.

But first you have to get there.

On a quiet traffic day the cars and lorries skim along easily enough from the beginning of the A303 almost to Amesbury. The first intimation of the impediments and irritations that lie ahead is a 'Queues Likely' sign near the turn-off to Solstice Park. At unquiet times the driver will not need to be told about the likelihood of queues as he or she will already be in one. At peak times the sign assumes the function of a satirical comment for the solid line of traffic extending back to Beacon Hill and beyond.

It should not have been like this.

Although the A303 was labelled the London–Penzance Trunk Road, there was never a systematic plan to make it so. In fits and starts the road got bigger and faster. But two ugly and intractable complications hovered on the horizon. The lesser was how to extend it from its existing end, short of Honiton, to Exeter, which had to happen if the vision of a through-route to Cornwall was to be realised. The other was what to do about Stonehenge.

As the upgrades proceeded, so the traffic anxious to take advantage of them multiplied. Like so many of our roads, the A303 became a victim of its own expansion far more swiftly than the gloomiest forecaster could have predicted. There was never time when motorists were grateful to their leaders for the far-sighted investment in it. Instead it became a byword for jams. The assumption among road builders and surveyors was that the pressure from hauliers, motoring organisations, lobbying groups and the increasing (and increasingly irate) army of A303 users would eventually compel central government to summon the resolve and the cash to deal with the intractable complications.

The first big obstacle to the A303's progress west was the Countess roundabout just north of Amesbury. The great scheme for the London–Penzance Trunk Road envisaged this being effortlessly surmounted by a flyover on which the road would soar over the roundabout on stilts of concrete and sweep gloriously forward along whichever route had finally been agreed on to take it away from Stonehenge. But the flyover never happened. The glorious new route away from Stonehenge never happened. The joining up of all the pieces never happened. The dream remained just that.

A few hundred yards beyond the Countess roundabout is another visual warning of bad things to come: a two-pronged upside-down fork, meaning that two lanes are about to become one. It is this fatal constriction that is responsible for the queue, rather than the roundabout itself, where traffic signals have now been installed to try to control the flow more equitably. But what do the queuers care for the finer points of traffic dynamics? All that matters to them is that they are stuck in it, imprisoned, enslaved. Theirs are the faces of queues everywhere: patient, resigned, weary. Their expressions acknowledge the reality – this is the way it is, lump it and don't bleat. If you ever believed them when they told you they would make it better, more fool you. Now you know otherwise.

Somewhere along the road the ideal of automotive freedom died. Sitting in the queue waiting to get onto the roundabout is as good a place and time as any to reflect on how this happened.

It was rooted in the notion of the 'open road', of cars as liberators of the spirit. To have one was to possess the key to new worlds and experiences. Public transport looked pitiful beside the motor car; waiting for the bus was for losers. With the car you could go where you wanted when you wanted, taking with you whatever you needed. Cars were affordable, democratic, individual. They were at the same time conveniences, and symbols of status and aspiration.

But the ideal was intrinsically and fatally flawed by its

interior contradictions, or 'antagonisms', as the sociologists call them. The first was that for the freedom to exist at all, it must be limited. To avoid chaos and anarchy there must be rules governing basics like which side of the road to drive on, how to behave at junctions, speed and so on, and there must be sanctions for those who infringe the rules. As car ownership increased, further antagonisms revealed themselves. Too much mobility resulted in general immobility, otherwise known as congestion. Cars despoiled the environment and polluted the air. They killed and maimed, bringing misery to the families and friends of victims.

In the end the alliance of liberty and mobility – call it automobility – collapsed inwards on itself, undone by its fundamental conceptual disharmony. But it took time for this failure to sink in. The car meets too many needs and fulfils too many desires for us to forsake it lightly. It remains an article of faith for the car industry, the haulage industry, the motoring organisations, the road builders and for many drivers that the concept of automobility is strong and good. To make it work, all that is required is access to unlimited fuel (to be guaranteed by military action if need be), for society to accept that a certain level of road deaths and injuries is a price worth paying, and for governments to find the funds to build the necessary roads and the will to stand up to the eco-bleaters.

Some years ago, before he became Mayor of London, the effervescent, straw-thatched Boris Johnson produced a book called *Life in the Fast Lane* which set forth the fruits of his deep thinking on this subject. It comprised columns he had written earlier for the *Daily Telegraph* in the persona of a Woosterish throwback to the glory days of the open road, all goggles-and-capes and jolly japes and thumbing a nose at the traffic bobbies with their beastly speed cameras. 'It has always seemed obvious to me,' boomed Johnson, 'that the car has not only made our modern landscape, it has been the biggest revolution since print, and the spread of the car, like the spread of literacy, has been a fantastic and unstoppable force for liberty and democracy. It has done more for human freedom than the aeroplane, penicillin, the telephone and the contraceptive pill put together.'

The great bugbear for Johnson and other four-wheeled libertarian crusaders was not congestion or pollution. It was the interference of the state, as represented by the seat-belt law, the drink-drive law, speed bumps, 'calming schemes', and above all by the loathed remote speed cameras. 'The more widespread a liberty becomes,' Johnson lamented, 'the more necessary it seems for governments to regulate, trammel and constrain it.' He wondered if the state would finally annihilate 'the joy of the car' – 'or will science come to the aid of freedom, as she has so often in the past?'

Regrettably Johnson did not pursue the question of how science might solve a problem that to lesser minds might seem insoluble, namely how to coax a pint of liquid into a half-pint pot. These days Boris Johnson is more often to be seen on a bicycle rather than at the wheel of a Ferrari or a supercharged Merc. It is possibly significant that one of his first actions after becoming London Mayor was to endorse the principle of the congestion charges imposed by his predecessor to the accompaniment of bellows of protest from the motoring lobby. It may even be that Johnson found the realities that came with his new job more unyielding than he had suspected.

The flame of automotive liberty has not, of course, been extinguished. There are plenty of websites maintained by dedicated (overwhelmingly male) enthusiasts and filled with correspondence about which stretch of which road can still offer the thrill of unimpeded high-speed passage. But these bands of brothers are like steam-train clubs, their passion fuelled by a nostalgia for a lost past. The freedom of the road is no longer a true freedom if you need special-ised information and an appointed time to find it.

Much easier, therefore, to experience it through TV – hence the phenomenal popularity of the BBC programme *Top Gear*, in which three overgrown schoolboys (no girls, please!) giggled and whooped their way through daredevil escapades and high-speed jinks inconceivable on our twenty-first-century road network. This was the automo-tive dream world, presided over by a tall man in tight jeans with curly hair and a loud upper-class voice. Jeremy Clarkson's secret was to combine two irresistible types in one: the boy prankster raising two fingers to school rules, and a latterday Mondeo Man, bolshy, individualistic, single-minded in the pursuit of his pleasure, anti-socialist, anti-union, anti-state, anti-eco. Clarkson was loved not for his personality, but for his powers. He was a kind of god, endowed with magic or divine attributes that enabled him to enjoy on a weekly basis experiences that to mere mortals remained unattainable fantasies.

★ ★ ★

Great bustard – larger than life

I kept hoping to bump into the world's heaviest flying bird, but I never did. It's not so surprising, as there are fewer than twenty distributed across the 320 square miles of Salisbury Plain, and they are notoriously leery of human company. On the other hand, most of the reported sightings do come from motorists stuck on the A303. It's possible I might have had better luck if I could have whistled to them in Russian, since their birthplace is the flatlands of Saratov Oblast, down by the Volga.

'Once the pride of our Wiltshire downs,' lamented the Reverend Alfred Smith in his definitive *The Birds of Wiltshire*, '. . . now alas! driven out from among us by the march of civilisation.' Even in 1887, when Mr Smith's book was first published, the great bustard was little more than a memory among a few old shepherds and once keen-eyed slaughterers of game. Until the middle of the eighteenth century it was reasonably abundant across the brecks of Norfolk and Suffolk as well as the rolling downs of Hampshire, Dorset and Wiltshire. Its decline was rapid – sufficiently so for Gilbert White of Selborne to think it worth recording in his diary in 1775 that he had heard a carter from Andover tell of seeing a flock of a dozen or so birds twelve years before.

Many were shot and eaten, and the gathering pace of enclosure and the disturbance of the plough converting grazing land to arable hastened the bustard's demise. By the turn of the nineteenth century it was scarce enough for an encounter with a single bird to be an incident worth reporting. In 1801 a man travelling on horseback to Tilshead, north of Amesbury, was attacked by one. He managed to capture it, and presented it to a Mr Bartley of Tilshead. He kept it as a pet for a while, feeding it a mixed diet of live mice and sparrows – which it swallowed whole – and clumps of charlock and rape, before selling it to Lord Temple for the princely sum of thirty guineas.

Human interference and persecution were certainly major factors in the bustard's destruction. But it might also be said that the bird's physiology and habits made it an unlikely candidate for survival in a changing world. It is very big – the males are up to three-and-a-half feet tall and more than thirty pounds in weight – and very cumbersome. Its mating rituals are elaborate and impressive, but the consequence of them does the bustard few favours. It lays no more than three large eggs on the ground, which makes both the eggs and the mothers incubating them irresistibly vulnerable to predators, particularly foxes. The only circumstances in which the bustard can survive in the wild are where – as is the case beside the Volga and in isolated parts of Spain and Portugal – there is a resident population large enough to sustain an infant mortality rate of 80 per cent. The tipping point for such defenceless and unadaptable creatures is easily reached. In other words, our world is not for them.

But that kind of callous Darwinism makes us uneasy. We suffer from an absurd guilt over the indifference shown by past generations of our species to other species. We are revolted by the Victorian enthusiasm for killing scarce creatures and displaying them in glass cases. We like to feel that we are enlightened enough to make redress for the crimes of our ancestors by tenderly bringing these lost treasures back into our lives, where we can at least watch them on television. It can work – there have been successful campaigns to re-introduce red kites and white-tailed sea eagles, and to build up numbers of golden eagles and ospreys. But tinkering with the natural balance – whether by accident or design – can have unforeseen consequences. American signal crayfish now swarm over the beds of most of our rivers, causing untold damage to native fauna. Muntjac deer nibble their way through the woodlands of southern England. The despised but highly successful grey squirrel scuttles and skips across gardens everywhere. At the same time there is a tendency – witness the recent reintroduction of beavers in the Scottish Highlands, and periodic calls for wolves and bears to be once more numbered among our wildlife – for quixotic nostalgia to obscure common sense.

In 2003 the government's Department of the Environment, Food and Rural Affairs granted a ten-year licence to permit a band of volunteers called the Great Bustard Group to release birds obtained from Russia on one of the military training areas on Salisbury Plain. The group, established by an ex-policeman and his wife, subsequently secured a grant of £2.2 million from the EU to fund its project. It employs seven staff, who are backed by a team of twenty regular helpers. I am forbidden to disclose the exact location of their base, but it is located on the edge of an enormous area of unimproved chalk grassland which – apart from army exercises and some low-intensity livestock grazing – is left to its own devices.

I visited it in September 2010. I was told that over the previous six years a total of 104 great bustards imported from Saratov Oblast had been released, of which it was estimated that fifteen to twenty were still alive. The remains of the majority of those that had not survived had been recovered. Almost all of them had been killed by foxes. There had been a number of instances of the birds mating successfully after release. None of the eggs had hatched. Almost all of them had also been eaten by foxes. Although foxes were periodically shot, the size of the Plain (as big as the Isle of Wight) and the nature of the terrain made it impossible to control their numbers. With a great deal of human support and money, the bustards were clinging on. The foxes, without any help, were doing very nicely.

Everyone at the Great Bustard Group was very friendly to me. They brimmed with enthusiasm for the big, brown, ungainly, improbable birds and clearly believed they were engaged on conservation work of the utmost importance. The brochure they gave me described the project as 'a flagship for conservation' and asserted that 'the foundation for a new British population has been laid'. I did not have the heart to say that it struck me as a pipe dream; nor that I thought the money and effort would be very much better deployed on something else.*

---

* In 2014, the group switched from Russian to Spanish chicks for release. By 2017 it was talking about a 'self-sustaining population' before long.

I smiled and nodded and took a last look at the pens where the bustards are kept in preparation for release. I watched them pecking away and looking nervy in these fortified fox-exclusion zones, and wondered how long they would last in the big, bad world outside.

But at least the bustard crusaders have something to show for all their hard work. Pity those who tried to save poor Stonehenge!

'The solitude of Stonehenge should be restored to ensure that posterity will see it against the sky in lonely majesty' – Stanley Baldwin, Prime Minister, 1928.

'If there is one thing I am going to do as chairman it is to sort out Stonehenge' – Sir Jocelyn Stevens, chairman of English Heritage, 1992.

'The status quo is not an option . . . that is the circle we have to square' – Chris Smith, Secretary of State for Culture, Media and Sport, 1997.

'It is clear that the current situation is completely intolerable. Something needs to be done to ease the traffic burden . . . yet maintain Stonehenge's presence as a national monument. I would like to state that sorting this problem out is very high on my list of priorities' – Margaret Hodge, Minister for Culture and Tourism, 2007.

The A303 rises gently and steadily from the Countess roundabout at Amesbury. In the soft-fruit season there is a booth in the lay-by where you can buy strawberries and cherries; the sign advertising its presence lingers on in the depths of winter, perhaps as a reminder that summer will come again one day. Past the lay-by the road becomes single carriageway and flattens over a ridge. Beyond, the country opens out: rolling downs to the south, Larkhill Camp and pale grasslands to the north. Below is the circle of stones. From that distance they always seem small, surprisingly so; and the space they occupy is modest. But because of the emptiness around they are unmissable.

Stonehenge and the emptiness around

This, in its essentials, is the view the Amesbury Archer and The Ancestor's ancestors would have had. And at all but the quiet times, you are likely to have ample time to drink it in as you wait your turn to pass. The road descends to a junction just east of the monument. The right fork is the A344 to Shrewton and Devizes. The left is the A303, which proceeds west to its next obstacle, the roundabout junction with the A360 known as Longbarrow Crossroads.

The essentials may be timeless but the detail is, of course, somewhat different. One of the details is that on an average day between 20,000 and 30,000 vehicles pass one way or the other. Stonehenge is caught between the prongs of the fork, as if in an insoluble dilemma.

The Stonehenge road saga is a revealing commentary on the way we do things – or do not do them – in this country. It is difficult to imagine such a study in futility occurring in, say, France or Germany. Over a period of a little more than twenty years around £40 million of public money has been spent drawing up, proposing, publicising, discussing and dumping various schemes to protect the monument from the noise and disturbance caused by passing traffic. There was the northern route, which would have taken the A303 away from the Countess roundabout in a loop below Larkhill and Shrewton and north of Winterbourne Stoke to rejoin the existing path far to the west. There was the southern route across Normanton Down. There was the noble Parker Plan (named after a local military man, Colonel Graham Parker) to divert south from Beacon Hill in a majestic arc down to Old Sarum and up the Wylye Valley past Stapleford and Berwick St James.

And then there was the answer that finally emerged as the least bad option from all the exhibitions and consultation exercises and interminable public inquiries: to send the A303 over the Countess roundabout, to widen it into dual carriageway, to bury it in a tunnel past Stonehenge, to send it north around Winterbourne Stoke, and to bring it back to its old route somewhere near Yarnbury Castle. The corollary was that the stretch of the A344 to the north of the monument would be erased from the map altogether.

It was a fine scheme, a good scheme, with elements of grandeur to it. Its weak point was the tunnel. To build a wider, faster, busier, noisier A303 without the tunnel would be to defeat the purpose of the exercise. Everything swung on the tunnel. Its cost in 2002 was estimated at £180 million. Then the engineers looked again at the chalk they would have to dig through. It turned out to be 'the wrong type', and by 2005 the estimate had risen to £470 million. At this point the government did what governments always do when something is getting out of hand, and ordered a review. The then Transport Minister, Dr Stephen Ladyman, said he hoped it would enable him to decide on an 'affordable, realistic and deliverable option'. The review put the likely cost at over £500 million, and in December 2007 another Transport Minister, Mr Tom Harris, announced that the affordable, realistic and deliverable option was to cancel the tunnel altogether.

Since all other aspects of the scheme – the flyover, the dualling, the bypasses around the Longbarrow roundabout and the village of Winterbourne Stoke – were contingent on the tunnel, they all fell in a heap as well. The rumour that the money that would have been spent on the A303 was diverted to widening the M25 did nothing to console those who had invested so much time, effort and hope. The upshot is that, now as before, the motorist has plenty of opportunity between reaching the queue before Amesbury and accelerating along the next available stretch of dual carriageway well beyond Winterbourne Stoke, to contemplate the vagaries of our bureaucratic processes and – when the moment comes – to enjoy the sight of a 5000-year-old jumble of stone.*

The fate of the road has been mirrored in its futility by that of the notorious Stonehenge visitor facilities. These consist of a car and coach park; a collection of small green prefabs where you buy a ticket and can, if need be, get a cup of tea and a sandwich and go to the loo; and a

---

* But for how much longer? The government has revived the vision of the Stonehenge tunnel, and at the time of writing – March 2019 – Highways England has completed the public consultation and submitted the scheme to the Planning Inspectorate with a view to starting work in 2021. The £1.6 billion project is, in effect, a modified version of the one discarded in 2007. English Heritage, the National Trust and Historic England are all in favour in principle, on the grounds that covering the road will 'reunite' the ancient landscape. The Stonehenge Alliance of environmentalists and archaeologists says it will do the opposite, and wreck it. I once said on Radio 4 that the tunnel would never happen, and I acknowledge that I may have to eat my words. But I continue to believe that this is basically an unwarrantably costly vanity project that will merely shift the A303's chronic congestion issues further west to the next stretch of single carriageway beyond Wylye.

pedestrian route under the A344 to the stones themselves. No one could pretend that the visitor centre is sumptuous or elegant. It is tatty and tacky. But it does have the great merit of being unobtrusive and convenient. It is also very modest, and one suspects that it is this modesty, above all, that sticks in the throat of English Heritage, the many-splendoured quango that has charge of Stonehenge.

A million people a year come to see it

A million people a year come to look at Stonehenge, making it the second biggest visitor attraction in the country outside London. But the average length of stay is twenty minutes. You, in your ignorance, might think twenty minutes sufficient to view from several angles a number of rather similar blocks of stone without any pretence to being works of art. English Heritage knows better. Stonehenge is too important, too extraordinary, too damned old to be treated thus. Visitors need to be detained, for their own good. There must be exhibitions to explain context, a lecture hall to hear experts, a shop with Stonehenge chocolate and pencils and all the usual heritage stuff. There must be a café selling highly sustainable, organic locally sourced dishes.

Successive chairmen of English Heritage wrestled with the challenge of dignifying Stonehenge. Lord Montagu commissioned plans for a new visitor centre at Larkhill, and Salisbury District Council threw them out. Sir Jocelyn Stevens had a grander vision, for an £80 million complex complete with 'virtual' Stonehenge a mile and a half away from the monument to the north of the Countess roundabout. Under Sir Neil Cossons this metamorphosed into a £67.5 million centre with a train to the stones instead of Sir Jocelyn's bus. Perversely, local opinion turned against the idea of carriages chugging across a World Heritage site; at any rate, the plan sank with the tunnel.

Nothing daunted, English Heritage came back with a new plan and a new location. They proposed a pavilion with an undulating roof comprising a transparent pod containing the shop and café and a pod clad in local chestnut for exhibitions, to be sited at Airman's Corner, a mile up the A344. Access would be by a 'low-key transport system', which turns out to be a bus that looks like a train. The A344, the horrible old visitor centre and the car parks would all be grassed over. Cost: a modest £27 million, with the government putting up a third. After the 2010 election the coalition promptly cancelled its contribution, whereupon the Heritage Lottery Fund stepped into the breach.*

* All this has now come to pass. The new centre opened in 2017, and for a mere £19.50 – £50.70 for a family ticket – you can be transported to the Stones, stare at the Stones, and experience the 'Stonehenge Collection' exhibition. And, of course, for nothing you may – for the time being – still see them as you crawl past on the A303.

9

MEN IN WHITE ROBES

The earliest resident Stonehenge guide was a local carpenter known as 'Gaffer' Hunt, who had a hut against one of the northern stones and a cellar dug beneath another, where he kept provisions and drink. Gaffer readily dispensed his wisdom to visitors, one of whom was John Wood, the great architect of Georgian Bath. Wood came away from Stonehenge in 1740 with his head stuffed with nonsense which he solemnly wrote down in a book called *Choire Gaure, Vulgarly Called Stonehenge, Described, Explored and Explained*. Wood was in no doubt that it was a Druid centre of sun and moon worship. But his claim that it had been built in 100 BC by the entirely mythical King Bladud (also, by a happy coincidence, the founder of Bath) enraged the other eminent Stonehenge expert of the time, Dr William Stukeley. Stukeley, a Lincolnshire-born physician, parson and antiquarian who called himself Chyndonax in honour of a French Druid prince, assigned a date of 480

BC to the creation of Stonehenge. He denounced the 'crack imaginations' of John Wood's 'fabulous whimsys'.

Fabulous whimsies were the stock-in-trade of Stonehenge guides. Henry Browne installed himself there in the 1820s, describing himself as 'the first custodian of Stonehenge'. At around that time Amesbury Abbey and the Amesbury estate – including Stonehenge – were bought by Sir Edmund Antrobus, the Antrobuses being a Cheshire family. Henry Browne dismissed the Druid connection promoted by Dr Stukeley. He was an unswerving Catastrophist, assuring anyone who would give him a hearing that Stonehenge and the other great stone circle at Avebury were built before Noah's Flood by Adam himself. After his death in 1839, his job and his antediluvian narrative were inherited by his son Joseph. Over the next forty years Joseph became as familiar a feature of the landscape as his father had been, wheeling around a Stonehenge peepshow on a vehicle like a wheelbarrow and selling copies of his father's guide at a shilling each.

After Joseph Browne, Stonehenge entered the photographic age. Visitors would have their picture taken in front of or on the stone of their choice by William Judd, the 'attending illustrator', whose photographic van was pulled up to the monument each day by a white horse. By then, under first one Sir Edmund Antrobus and then the next, the character of the estate had greatly changed. Much of the old sheep-grazed downland was ploughed up and turned to arable. Although the railway did not reach

Amesbury until the early twentieth century, access to Stonehenge by wagonette from Salisbury was regular and easy and it became a favourite destination for trippers. Parties picnicked, clambered over the stones, inscribed names and messages, chipped off pieces for souvenirs, and scattered bottles, chicken bones and wrappings on the ground. Some even complained when they found that hammers and chisels were not provided.

All approaches to the Antrobuses from archaeologists reputable and disreputable to be allowed to dig at Stonehenge were abruptly rebuffed. But without putting fortifications around it, they could do little to prevent the progressive trashing of the site by an ever-increasing stream of visitors. The situation worsened after the Army began moving in strength onto Salisbury Plain from the 1890s onwards. Soldiers proved to be even more brazen than civilians in treating the monument as a recreation facility and helping themselves to bits and pieces that took their fancy.

The Royal Artillery took up residence at Larkhill, and in 1910 the War Office decided that an airfield should be constructed there for the use of the new Royal Flying Corps. In the course of the 1914–18 war, hangars sprouted around the northern and western side of Stonehenge. The Larkhill camp spread down to the edge of the Cursus, the great embanked earthwork to the north of the monument. A light railway reached across the downs to Winterbourne Stoke. All day heavy military traffic ground along the roads, and the stones trembled with the bursts of artillery fire and the detonations of mines. The end of the war left a vast area disfigured by redundant installations. For a time parts of the aerodrome reverted to being a pig farm. The monument itself came into the care of the Office of Works, which authorised the building of a café just across the Shrewton road and even considered allowing a modest development of bungalows.

March past Stonehenge, 1915

In 1928 Clough Williams-Ellis, the architect of Portmeirion and crusader against the forces of philistinism, raged against the treatment of Stonehenge. 'Never were venerable remains less venerated,' he wrote. 'Stonehenge is intolerable . . . Hemmed in by iron railings, guarded by a turnstile and a post-card kiosk, glowered at by the derelict aerodrome and smirked at by café and bungalow, this sacred place is indeed painful beyond bearing . . . Stonehenge is a mockery and a wounding of the spirit.'

A303 turn left

Periodically the philosophical/cultural debate about who owns Stonehenge splutters back into life, usually after Wiltshire Police have been summoned to defend it against a peaceful invasion by sun and moon worshippers, pagans, Wiccans, Druids and solstice enthusiasts. *Who Owns Stonehenge?* was the title of a book edited by Christopher Chippindale (author of the indispensable and richly entertaining *Stonehenge Complete*) which attempted to reconcile the differing perspectives of archaeology, astronomy, Druidism and so forth.

Had the question been asked of any of the Sir Edmund Antrobuses of Amesbury Abbey, the answer would have been simple: 'I do.' In 1883 General Augustus Henry Lane-Fox Pitt Rivers, Britain's most eminent field archaeologist and the first Inspector of Ancient Monuments, wrote to the third Sir Edmund offering to assume responsibility for Stonehenge. Sir Edmund declined the offer. Ten years later the General tried again, arguing that the leaning and unstable stones must be raised and fixed in concrete and that a permanent custodian needed to be appointed. He was told to mind his own business.

Five years later the third Sir Edmund died and was succeeded by his nephew, the fourth Sir Edmund. He offered to sell Stonehenge and 1300 acres of downland to the nation for £125,000. The Chancellor of the Exchequer, Sir Michael Hicks-Beach, decided the nation could not afford it. Sir Edmund responded by putting a fence around it, blocking the several tracks with tree trunks, and charging a shilling for entrance. The ensuing rumpus eventually reached the High Court, where Mr Justice Farwell ruled decisively in favour of the rights of the landowner and admonished the fledgling National Trust for daring to bring an action in the first place.

A shilling to get in

Whatever the rights and wrongs of the case, later archae-ologists agree that the intransigence of successive Antrobuses did Stonehenge a priceless favour by defending it from the Victorian enthusiasm for ham-fisted excava-tions and restorations. Major work was limited to raising stone 56 upright, and fixing it in concrete. It was super-vised by Professor William Gowland of the School of Mines, who also carried out a limited and careful excava-tion of other stones which showed how they had been trimmed and shaped and put in place.

Within six weeks of the outbreak of war in 1914, Sir Edmund Antrobus's son and heir – who would have been the fifth Sir Edmund – was killed in Belgium. A few months later his father died, and the Amesbury estate was put on the market. Lot 15 – 'Stonehenge, with about 30 acres, 2 rods, 37 perches of surrounding downland' – was knocked down for £6600 to Cecil Chubb, the made-good son of a Shrewton saddler.* The purchase was a spur-of-the-moment decision; appar-ently Chubb was worried that the monument might fall into the grasp of an American showman with ambitions to turn it into a vulgar tourist attraction. In 1918 he handed it over to the Ministry of Works, acting on behalf of the nation, with the proviso that there should be free admission for the people of Shrewton, Netheravon

---

* He became Sir Cecil Chubb and subsequently devoted himself to running Fisherton House in Salisbury, at that time the largest private lunatic asylum in Europe.

(where his father was born), Durrington (his mother's birthplace), and Amesbury.

Since then Stonehenge has been, in the sonorous but woolly phrase, 'held in trust for the nation'. Thus we all own it, and have some kind of ill-defined right to make a claim on it. Throughout Stonehenge's 'modern' history – dating, for the sake of convenience, from 1620, when James I sent Inigo Jones to survey it and report back on its likely provenance – claims of ownership have been lodged. A multitude of antiquaries, historians, archaeologists, visionaries, prophets and crackpots have studied it, speculated on its origins, and promoted their accounts of its meaning and purpose. Inigo Jones identified it as a Roman temple, and Henry Browne attributed it to Adam himself. But the most persistent claimants to Stonehenge and its truths have been the Druids. It was Dr Stukeley who first argued the Druid case. His Druids were a gentle lot, proto-Christians really. The Romantics who came afterwards preferred theirs more savage:

> It is the sacrificial altar, fed
> With living men – how deep the groans

wrote Wordsworth in *The Prelude* with lip-smacking relish.

One way or another, Druids have made a habit of causing a nuisance at Stonehenge – none more so than the once-celebrated socialist mystic and ranter George Watson MacGregor Reid, Chief Druid of the Universal Bond of the Sons of Men. This outstandingly brazen example of the spiritual adventurer was born in Skye in the 1860s or, quite possibly, somewhere else at some other time. He claimed to have served in both the Royal and the Merchant navies, and to have spent some years fomenting union agitation in the docks at Hull and San Francisco. He had a Zoroastrian phase, during which he began to style himself as a Buddhist mystic named Ayn Subadra, before settling down to militant Druidism.

Reid's first recorded visit to Stonehenge was in 1912. An article in the *Salisbury Journal* headlined 'Sun Worship at Stonehenge' noted the attendance of Ayn Subadra ('the messenger from Tibet') and various followers including Kelkusbru Turnbull ('A Persian gentleman'). The following year Reid – now additionally styled Dastur Tuatha de Dinaan – arrived with an enlarged Druid contingent for the summer solstice, only to find access barred on the orders of Sir Edmund Antrobus. He responded as a Dastur is inclined to, with a curse, and within eighteen months both Sir Edmund and his son were dead. Cecil Chubb prudently permitted Reid and the Universal Bond to resume their rites. For some time after Chubb's gift to the nation, the Ministry of Works continued to raise no objection to the Druids and their ceremonies. They were even given permission to bury their dead beneath the stones, at which point archaeologists set up a clamour of protest. The permission was withdrawn, provoking a mass invasion of the monument at the summer solstice in 1926 and the pronouncement of a curse against the hated custodian, who died the following year.

Eventually Reid decided to withdraw from Stonehenge in protest at the way the Universal Bond had been treated, and against the sacrilege of allowing archaeologists to excavate at the site. He took his Druids off to Normanton Down, on the other side of the A303, where he planned to erect a replica Stonehenge, until the landowner took fright and kicked him out. In time, after the old fraud's death in 1946, his son Robert MacGregor Reid brought the Universal Bond back to Stonehenge, opening the way for a more general influx of pagans and Wiccans and assorted occultists and psychedelists to annex it in the noble cause of the Free Festival.

The Universal Bond faded away, but the banner of Druidism has been kept aloft for many years by the Battle Chieftain of the Council of British Druids, King Arthur Pendragon. The former soldier in the Royal Hampshire Regiment (under his less fanciful given name John Rothwell) has engineered a long series of largely successful publicity stunts designed to make English Heritage look foolish. These have included his arrest for possession of an offensive weapon in the shape of his sword, Excalibur, and chaining up the doors of English Heritage's offices in London. Subsequently, he pressed, unsuccessfully, for a judicial review of the decision to allow archaeologists to remove human remains from Stonehenge and use radio-carbon techniques to find out how old they were. For many years, King Arthur's flowing white locks and beard were a familiar sight in the old car park, where he handed out leaflets calling for the return of the remains of dead Druids. In terms of nuisance value, he has shown himself a worthy successor to George Watson MacGregor Reid. Although his dilapidated caravan is no longer parked on the potholed byway leading from the A303 to Larkhill, he continues to campaign inside the courts and outside for the restoration of ancient rights – under the banner Your Temple Your Stones (see www.warband.org.uk).

* * *

Christopher Chippindale, in *Stonehenge Complete*, describes the established and undisputed data about the monument as 'technical and mundane', and the accumulated finds of chips of bluestone and sarsen and fragments of pottery as 'a dismal collection'. Since the 2004 edition of his book,* the Stonehenge Riverside project organised by a team of archaeologists from Sheffield University has revealed strong evidence of an abiding relationship between Stonehenge and the Neolithic timber circle known as Woodhenge, on the

---

* A new revision was published in March 2012

Avon at Durrington, two miles to the east. Even so, the headline conclusion – that Stonehenge was a funeral and burial site to honour the dead, and Woodhenge and other connected henges were used and inhabited by the living – is no more than plausible supposition. The fact is that there are almost no facts about Stonehenge.

The result is that any theory, however barking, can obtain a hearing. The silence of the stones excuses every kind of jabbering nonsense. We may titter condescendingly at Geoffrey of Monmouth's version, which has Merlin deploying his magic powers to fly the stones over from Ireland, and at Stukeley's Druidic fantasising. But there are plenty of contemporary accounts just as batty – without the excuse of ignorance. Many of these depend heavily on astronomical deductions, even though – as Chippindale points out – there is no evidence of astronomical alignments apart from the solar orientation of the axis. But in the half-lit world of the truth-seekers, that deficiency merely serves to fuel the business of speculation. For thirty years until his death in 1999, Donald L. Cyr, an American aeronautical engineer, produced *Stonehenge Viewpoint*, a journal in which he developed a theory originally propounded by a Quaker teacher named Isaac Vail that the earth was surrounded by a canopy of ice crystals left behind after the final glaciation. This canopy, undetectable by scientific instruments, created mystic haloes visible only at certain times and from certain sacred places, of which Stonehenge was the principal.

Just stones

The stone circle is imperfect in other respects. For sure, it is a striking sight; sometimes – under certain conditions of light and season, and when the swarms of visitors are absent – very beautifully so. But it was built to serve a function and we do not know what that function was. The stones are just that: stones, with their colours of blue and orange-brown rendered grey by a mantle of lichens. They were put up a very long time ago by people of whom we know almost nothing. Furthermore the circle as it stands now is a very meagre affair compared with the original. Half the sarsens and bluestones are missing, and those that remain have been subjected to all kinds of indignities over the centuries. Twenty minutes is about right to take it in close up; even if a lifetime is not enough to consider the possibilities of its past and wander the paths of make-believe.

Stonehenge actually works best from a distance. One good way to see it is to walk or cycle from Woodhenge – where there is really not much other than modern repro – and cut down from Larkhill to the eastern end of the Cursus. I pedalled west along its edge, the epic nature of the design as clear as day. The turf was short-cropped beneath my wheels by the sheep which hardly bothered to glance at me before resuming the eternal nibbling. I saw the stones over to my left, circled by spectators. I took a diagonal over to the car park, had a poke around the miserable visitors' centre and wondered what all the fuss was about, then followed the byway past King Arthur Pendragon's caravan (no one home) to the A303. I stood by the road and looked back at Stonehenge and beyond. Beacon Hill rose in the east, the A303 a narrow band beside it. From that distance the road – so insistent and overbearing close at hand – looked remarkably insignificant in that great, wide landscape.

Another slow, satisfactory route is to follow the old pre-bypass A303 through Amesbury, over the river, and up the western side of the Abbey grounds. The Avenue – which may have been used to transport the bluestones from the

Avon as well as having an unknown ceremonial function – diverts off to the right, crosses the A303 and loops left to pick up its solstice alignment towards the monument itself. But it is hard to follow; better to take the track to the left past Normanton Farm and along the edge of Normanton Down. The way takes you through a Neolithic and Bronze Age graveyard; burial grounds are on all sides. The mounds are easy to spot, like outsize grassed-over molehills. There is a line of them stretching up the A303 and beyond. From there Stonehenge appears, with more barrows beside the Cursus and to west and east. The feeling of looking out across the vestiges of some system of worship or reverence, dimly understood but engineered with enormous care, is very strong.

The third way to see Stonehenge in its landscape – English Heritage will not thank me for this – is from the A303 itself. From the west the view is good, from the east it is magnificent. I have seen it a hundred times, at speed when the road is empty, at leisure when crawling along. It does not fail to lift the heart and magnetise the senses.

10

DIGGING DEEP

The road rises easily past Stonehenge in a narrow straight line to the roundabout at Longbarrow Crossroads, where it nods a greeting to the Salisbury-Devizes A360. When I passed this way in August 2010 the land on the south side of the A303 up to the roundabout was occupied by pigs. It was a kingdom of the pig: the ground denuded, broken and trampled by snout and trotter. There were neat roofed shelters in the shadow of which immense, prone backsides could be glimpsed. At strategic points, round feed dispensers had been placed where the porkers gathered at important times. Great flocks of rooks swarmed around, landing to harvest the worms exposed by the animals; then all of a sudden, for no obvious reason, taking off with a harsh chorus of croaks and violent flapping of wings to circle and come down somewhere else.

Kingdom of the pig

There is something very restful in watching pigs. Their feeding does not have the same urgency that impels the unceasing nibbling of sheep and the strenuous chomping of cattle. Sheep rarely lie down and rest, as if worried that if they stop eating they might forget how to do it. Cows do lie down, but with their heads up, watchful. But the repose of pigs is splendidly abandoned. After a period of thrusting their flat noses through the mud and earth, their absurdly curly tails twitching, they flop onto their sides, their great pink and grey flanks still, their eyes hidden beneath flap-like ears. You imagine them dreaming of a well-filled, well-seasoned swill bucket, or the pleasure of suckling their piglets. And when they resume the food business their progress is unhurried. They give them-selves time to pause and look around, as if ready for a grunt-chat about pork prices and the chances of a shower later in the day.

At that time the pig kingdom stretched far into the distance and along the road. It was the early days of the coalition government, and there were signs along the A303 imploring Mr Cameron and his colleagues not to wreck the countryside with cuts. When I walked by a couple of months later cuts of a different kind seemed to have been implemented. The signs had gone, as had most of the pigs. The kingdom had been reduced to a distant corner, and all the rest had been sown for winter barley.

★　★　★

On a fine September day in 1808 a man of striking features left a lodging house in Amesbury and rode over to Normanton Down. There he met a father and son, John and Stephen Parker, who – like him – lived in Heytesbury, a village on the Wylye twelve miles away to the west. The ridge where they gathered was littered with ancient burial sites: three long barrows and almost forty round barrows of different types. Under the direction of the man with the singular face, the Parkers began to dig into a round mound which had been given the name of Bush Barrow by a previous visitor, the druidical Dr Stukeley, because it had stunted trees growing on it.

First they cut a trench across it. Then they dug a pit in the middle, using spades. They had already made one attempt on the barrow, two months before, but had found nothing. This time they were more thorough. They found a skeleton on its side, in a crouching position. They were encouraged but not excited. They had been excavating barrows for ten years and had uncovered skeletons before.

Casting their spades aside they proceeded more cautiously, using slender trowels. Eighteen inches from the skull they uncovered a quantity of bronze rivets, a bronze axe head, decayed fragments of wood, and the remains of a bronze dagger with studded hilt. Near the shoulders was a bronze chisel, and next to the right arm were two more daggers, a gold belt-hook, and a decorated lozenge of sheet gold. On the skeleton's right side lay another gold lozenge and a stone mace-head. The handle of one of the daggers was ornamented with a chevron design made up of tiny gold pins – 'but unfortunately John Parker with his trowel had scattered them in every direction before I had time to examine them with a glass.'*

These words – which still cause archaeologists to shudder – were written by William Cunnington, a Heytesbury wool merchant and shop owner. A lithograph shows him as a man with an exceptionally dark and promi-nent brow and a massive chin. Christopher Chippindale

---

* Scarcely credibly, there were 140,000 of them, each the width of a human hair, each individually set into the hilt. In the 1960s the surviving pins were removed to Cardiff University for examination by the leading Stonehenge expert of the time, Professor Richard Atkinson. After his death they were put in a drawer where they were eventually found forty years later. They have now been reunited with the other finds from the Bush Barrow at the Wiltshire Heritage Museum in Devizes.

speculates that he may have suffered from acromegaly, a condition caused by excessive production of growth hormones from the pituitary at puberty that can result in a bulging or protruding forehead, enlarged cheekbones, and a lengthening and widening of the jawbone. The associated tumour often compresses brain tissue, causing severe headaches, sleeplessness and periodic bouts of depression – all of which afflicted Cunnington.*

In general acromegaly does not reveal itself fully until middle age. These days the condition is successfully treated by surgery to the pituitary. But when William Cunnington began to exhibit symptoms in the 1790s the only advice his doctor could give him was 'ride out or die'. Early in 1797 he rode over from Heytesbury to Stonehenge after hearing that two of the biggest uprights, with their lintel, had fallen outwards causing a thud that was felt by ploughmen half a mile away. Cunnington had already undertaken some amateurish excavations on the downs above Heytesbury, recovering bits of pottery and beads which he had tentatively identified as Roman.

At Stonehenge he dug with a stick into the shallow depressions left by the fallen stones and found 'several pieces of black pottery'. They seemed to him remarkably

* Other sufferers have included Abraham Lincoln, Richard Kiel – who played Jaws in the James Bond films *Moonraker* and *The Spy Who Loved Me* – the Italian heavyweight boxer Primo Carnera, dubbed the Ambling Alp by American sports writers, and the puppet figure Pulcinella or Mr Punch.

similar to those he had found near Heytesbury. He communicated his findings to John Britton, a hot-tempered and impulsive former attorney's clerk then engaged on writing a projected three-volume work to be called *The Beauties of Wiltshire*. Unfortunately Britton's impressionable mind was already buzzing with wild theories about the dim past. He had been much influenced by the work of a well-known Welsh philologist, William Owen Pughe, who had toiled for many years on a Welsh dictionary and had recently branched out into Bardic fantasising.

No one could doubt Pughe's dedication or capacity for hard work, but his judgement was another matter. His belief that Welsh was derived from some primitive mother tongue caused him to twist himself into knots with word derivations and spellings. His reputation was not helped when he declared himself a believer in the prophecies of Joanna Southcott, a religious lunatic from Devon who announced herself as the woman spoken of in the book of Revelation 'clothed with the sun and the moon under her feet and upon her head a crown of twelve stars' who would give birth to the new Messiah (she died in 1814 at the age of sixty-four, after causing a sensation with the news that she was pregnant with the harbinger of the Second Coming).

Pughe asserted that Stonehenge had been constructed in the fifth century AD on a site previously used by the Romans. John Britton seized upon Cunnington's discovery of supposedly Roman fragments at Stonehenge as proof positive of Pughe's eccentric chronology and the accompanying Druidic make-believe. Cunnington soon repented of his association with Britton. But as he widened and systematised his exploration of the Wiltshire barrows, he could do little to restrain the reckless speculations of those intent on running their own historical hares. The Wiltshire MP, Henry Wyndham, convinced himself and some others that the big barrows contained hundreds of victims of battle interred by the victors after slaughter that left the ground soaked in blood. Thomas Leman, a learned antiquary and expert on Roman roads, argued loudly for a Roman dating. William Coxe, the Rector of Stourton, had in mind elbowing the irritating Mr Britton out of the way and writing his own history of Wiltshire's antiquities.

What all these men had in common – apart from a fondness for airborne castles – was a disinclination to engage in the time-consuming and often thankless business of opening the barrows. They were content to leave the dirty work to Cunnington and his assistants, and to use the results to promote their versions of the past. To their disappointment, these findings were generally rather meagre and confusing, and in time they all lost interest. This was a fortunate development, as the responsibility for funding and recording Cunnington's work then passed to someone much more suitable. This was Sir Richard Colt Hoare, the owner of Stourhead, the fabulous garden paradise created just beyond the western edge of Salisbury Plain by his grandfather, Henry Hoare.

The Hoare family business was banking. But Richard

Colt Hoare's reflective, melancholic temperament did not suit him to money-dealing, instead inclining him to lengthy travels, drawing, and history. He and Cunnington became close colleagues, despite their very different backgrounds. Colt Hoare never interfered with the excavations, and rarely even attended them. He depended wholly on Cunnington's meticulous record-keeping when he got down to compiling his monumental *Ancient History of North and South Wiltshire*. His contribution to the partnership was an open-handed liberality with his money and what the *Dictionary of National Biography* characterised as 'the extraordinary zeal' which he expended on the eventual printed record.

'Our object is truth,' he wrote to Cunnington. 'In this curious investigation we must form no previous system about Britons, Romans or Saxons.' But the more Cunnington and the Parkers excavated, the more elusive the truth became. Cunnington learned from his earlier indiscretions. He wrote: 'The only conclusion we can draw from finding Roman pottery on this ground [Stonehenge] is that this work was in existence at the period when that earthenware was made use of.' Both he and Colt Hoare mocked the deluded William Owen Pughe for deducing that fragments of marked bone found in a barrow south of Stonehenge 'were used in casting lots . . . Under the druidical system many important decisions were taken this way.' 'The poor man is bit by the Prophetess Southcott,' Colt Hoare observed.

In ten years' digging Cunnington and his team opened around six hundred barrows, a third of them around Stonehenge. Often they dealt with two or three in a day, and only those supporting mature trees or under crops were spared. Most of the time the influence of Colt Hoare and the other sponsors was enough to secure the required permission, although on one occasion, when they were searching for a barrow above Fonthill they were threatened with prosecution by the farmer, 'young Candy, who took us all for poachers'.

William Cunnington died on the last day of 1810 at the age of fifty-six, having survived long enough to see the first part of his friend's *Ancient History* published. Hoare dedicated it to him; the engraving used as the frontispiece shows Cunnington holding a drawing of Stonehenge. 'How grand! How wonderful! How incomprehensible!' was Hoare's verdict on the monument that had preoccupied them for so long. In the end, the more they found, the less they knew, and they were forced to give up the great endeavour of establishing a chronology for prehistory. Unusually for the time, they were humble enough to realise that the subject was too much for them. They had glimpsed an appalling truth: that the span of time involved was simply beyond their understanding.

By the standards of modern archaeology, Cunnington's methods appear dreadfully crude. The casual reference to John Parker scattering the gold pins unearthed in the Bush Barrow was a cause of agony to the painstaking professionals who went to work in the twentieth century with their tiny brushes and abundant university funding. One of the kingpins of Stonehenge scholarship, Professor Stuart Piggott, declared sternly that 'the excavations and their record fail lamentably to satisfy even the most moderate demands of modern archaeologists'. But Piggott's sense of historical perspective was defective. What struck him and his contemporaries as a blundering clumsiness almost too painful to contemplate amounted to a species of rare restraint in its own time, when grave raiding was standard practice.

A later generation of archaeologists has been kinder to Cunnington. In the case of the famous Bush Barrow – the richest of all the finds – the care with which Cunnington recorded and described the skeleton and the objects with it has enabled a team led by Stuart Needham, formerly the British Museum's Keeper of Bronze Age Artefacts, to reconstruct the deposition with remarkable exactness.

'They had the audacity,' wrote Needham and his colleagues of Cunnington and Hoare, 'to believe that more could be learned about the ancient past of Britain by the excavation of ancient monuments than by assuming that the literature of "the ancients" (i.e. the legends of Merlin and mythical kings) was relevant and faithful. They had the perseverance to conduct many such excava-tions . . . despite the fact that the majority of sites did not yield results that were either exciting or interpretable within the prevailing climate of knowledge. Most unusually they realised the importance of individual context . . . to the extent that they recorded each burial site in its own right and ensured the correlation of relevant finds in perpetuity.'

It's a generous tribute to a pair of long-departed and much-abused pioneers. Having offered it, Needham and his fellow archaeologists proceed to some informed guess-work of their own. Their starting point is the extreme rarity of rich treasure such as that interred in the Bush Barrow. They like the idea that 'exceptional grave goods connote something exceptional about the person interred'. They hypothesise that the position of the barrows on Normanton Down – looking down on Stonehenge – was reserved for the cream of society, possibly the masters of the ceremonies, the rulers of the time. It's a persuasive account, but no more. Like William Cunnington and Richard Colt Hoare, we can never know.

★ ★ ★

Nineteen seventy-three was the year of the oil crisis.

On 17 October the energy ministers of seven Arab countries as well as Iran, Indonesia, Venezuela, Ecuador and Nigeria, collectively known as the Organisation of Petroleum Exporting Countries, agreed to impose a complete embargo on exports of oil to the United States. Shipments to America's Western allies, including Britain, were to be severely curtailed, and the price doubled. The immediate trigger for the OPEC decision was the American support for Israel in the Yom Kippur war. Long-term the oil producers had determined to end the era of cheap fuel. The Shah of Iran expressed the sentiment thus: 'It's only fair that you should pay more. Let's say ten times more.'

It was bad luck for Edward Heath and his Conservative government in Britain that they should have had to deal with the oil embargo at the same time as becoming involved in a trial of strength with the National Union of Mineworkers under its combative new leader, Arthur Scargill. The first effect of the squeeze on fuel imports was to set off panic buying at petrol stations across the country, where the queues recalled conditions in eastern Europe, and police were on hand to quell the rage of motorists limited to one or two gallons at most. The government ordered petrol ration books and coupons to be printed, imposed a 50 m.p.h. speed limit, and even considered banning motoring altogether on Sundays. Heath himself vetoed a suggestion from the Queen that she should call for national unity in her Christmas broadcast. Viewers were treated instead to footage of the Royal tour of Canada and the marriage of Princess Anne to Captain Mark Phillips, which did little to quell the sense of crisis.

On 13 December Heath announced in the Commons that from 1 January 1974, factories and commercial premises would be limited to three working days a week. In February the leaders of the miners rejected a 16.5 per cent pay offer and ordered a national strike. Heath called an election under the slogan 'Who Governs Britain?' By

March he no longer did. Labour were back in power, if not in control.

One of the short-term casualties of the energy crisis was Britain's road-building programme. This had travelled far since Alfred Barnes's timid undertaking to improve the roads 'subject to the means available'. Little by little the Conservative administrations of the 1950s had realised that the car had become integral to modern life, and that owning one figured at or near the top of the average family's list of aspirations. People wanted cars and decent roads to drive them on; furthermore, it was obvious to even the dimmest minister that improving the road network was essential if the country were to modernise and maintain progress towards ever-greater affluence.

'There are votes in roads' – Harold Watkinson's rallying call to his Cabinet colleagues in 1957 – rapidly evolved into the dominant transport orthodoxy. Spending rose to £60 million a year under Watkinson, more than doubled under his successor, Ernest Marples, and continued on its upward trajectory after Harold Wilson's Labour government came to power in 1964. Wilson's transport minister, Barbara Castle, could not drive, but she was susceptible to the evangelical lobbying of Lancashire's County Surveyor and Bridgemaster, James Drake, the driving force behind Britain's first stretch of motorway, the Preston bypass. 'A gloriously unpolished Northerner of blunt speech in a broad Lancashire accent, obsessed with roads and a real go-getter', was Castle's assessment of Drake. In her two and a half years in charge, annual spending rose from £209 million to £273 million. In 1970 Labour produced a White Paper entitled *Roads for the Future*, proposing the construction of 1000 miles of motorway over the next fifteen years at a cost of £4 billion. After the Tories regained power that year, the Ministry of Transport was swallowed into the mighty new Department of the Environment under Peter Walker, who talked chirpily of a ten-year programme to built 2000 miles of motorway and 1500 miles of 'high quality strategic routes'.

It was an article of faith that new roads would mean a better, more prosperous Britain. No one of any importance questioned the assumptions, and hardly anyone objected to the schemes themselves. Before building the M1, Sir Owen Williams, head of the construction firm of the same name, personally visited every affected landowner to explain the virtues of motorways. Two minor objections were lodged and accommodated.

The economic crisis precipitated by the 1973 oil embargo and the subsequent capitulation of the new Labour government before the might of Arthur Scargill's NUM served to demolish any surviving belief that Britain could ever match its overseas competitors, as well as slamming the brakes on the road-building programme. The Heath government slashed spending by a fifth. Under Labour it was cut again, and in 1976 a six-month freeze on all new starts was announced.

The climate of acquiescence was also changing. 1972 saw a novel co-operative venture between the rail unions, the newborn Friends of the Earth environmental pressure group, the Council for the Protection of Rural England, the National Trust and the Civic Trust. It was called Transport 2000, and its mission was to campaign against further reductions in the rail network and for a more sceptical attitude towards road-building. At the same time a new generation of militant environmental campaigners identified a way to challenge what the most notorious of them – a Sheffield Polytechnic lecturer, John Tyme – referred to as 'the consummate evil' of the motorway programme.

The arena was the public inquiry. During the 1960s these were very low-key affairs, because the objections were few and muted. But they offered anti-roads fundamentalists tremendous opportunities for disruptive action and glorious publicity. In 1974 John Tyme repeatedly held up the inquiry into the proposed extension of the M16 (later annexed into the M25) through Epping Forest. His argument was given some weight by Dr John Adams, a geography don at University College, London, who produced the first detailed statistical critique of the traffic forecasts used to justify new motorways. Two years later an improbable alliance was formed between the loquacious Tyme and the somewhat liberal and trendy headmaster of Winchester College, John Thorn, to oppose plans to slap a twelve-mile stretch of the M3 across Winchester's historic water meadows. The repeated ejection of the two men from the proceedings reinforced a general impression of chaos bordering on anarchy.

By 1978 the average length of time for a major road scheme to proceed from conception to realisation had grown to fifteen years (in 1957 it was four, in 1969 seven, in 1973 ten). Roads were still being commissioned and built, but the process had become hugely costly in terms of money, time and effort, and hugely contentious. There may still have been votes in roads, but they were counterbalanced by the appalling publicity generated by the feeling against them. Government commitment to the concept of the strategic network was quietly dropped, as spending fell from nearly 8 per cent of the overall Department of the Environment budget in 1973 to less than 5 per cent in 1978.

Onto this scene of faltering faith in the motor car strode Margaret Thatcher. She disdained rail travel, and would no more have been seen on a bicycle than galloping naked on a white stallion. Proclaiming Britain to be 'the great car economy', Mrs Thatcher appointed Nicholas Ridley as her Environment Secretary, a heavy smoker not noted for sensitivity to environmental concerns. Ridley was followed by Paul Channon, a devout believer in the doctrine that the only way to tackle congestion was to build more roads. He was largely responsible for the notorious White Paper of 1989 provocatively entitled *Roads for Prosperity*. Rather foolishly described by Channon as 'the biggest road-building programme since the Romans', this proposed a 50 per cent increase in spending to £6 billion.

But wonderful as she may have been, the Thatcherite model – pro-business, pro-Mondeo Man, indifferent to public transport, contemptuous of tree-hugging eco-types – found itself increasingly undermined by awkward realities and alternative propositions. An influential report from the Oxford-based Transport Studies Unit entitled *Transport: The New Realism* challenged the Channon orthodoxy that road-building should keep pace with demand, and called for much greater investment in rail and bus services. The so-called Earth Summit in Rio de Janeiro in 1992 added the phrase 'sustainable development' to the political lexicon and raised awareness of the pollution of the planet by vehicle emissions.

By then the lady herself – like Mr Marples long before – had gone. John Major's Transport Secretary, John MacGregor, initially declared himself for 'roads, roads, roads'. But the spectacle of mass protests against the section of the M3 through Twyford Down in Hampshire and the inevitable police backlash did nothing for the cause. MacGregor himself was compelled, through gritted teeth, to acknowledge that even Tories must think in terms of making 'better use of the existing road system . . . and reducing people's need to travel without restricting their freedom to do so, and making them aware of the real cost of travel.'

'The real cost' was a deadly phrase, wherein lay a revolution in attitude. In that same year, 1994, a Royal Commission report on environmental pollution recommended that the road-building programme should be cut by half and the price of fuel doubled. Even more crucially, the government's own Standing Advisory Committee on Trunk Roads woke up to a truth that had dawned long before on everyone other than the wholly dim-witted: that building roads encouraged people to use them; or, as the committee vividly expressed it, 'induced traffic can and does occur quite extensively'.

In the context of transport policy, this was the equivalent of Luther rejecting the doctrine of transubstantiation. For forty years the building of roads had been regarded as essential to the pursuit of ever greater prosperity and efficiency. Bigger, faster roads were the answer to inadequate transport links. Now we had finally noticed that roads were part of the problem. The more you built, the more people wanted to drive on them. The provision of new roads would never and could never keep up with the desire to use them.

The prophet of the new government approach was MacGregor's successor, Brian Mawhinney. With his immensely high forehead, gleaming teeth, and quiet, reflective Ulster voice, Mawhinney demonstrated that being a fervent Protestant and coming from Belfast did not necessarily inspire a fanatical urge to consign the Pope to the fires of hell. He was an expert on radiation, and arrived at the Ministry of Transport determined to tackle what he saw as the damage caused by vehicle emissions to the nation's health. He rejected Margaret Thatcher's 'great car

economy' line, urged the road lobby to talk to environmentalists, pledged to minimise the impact of new trunk
roads on the countryside, and announced a review of all
the 270 road schemes he had inherited.

Mawhinney had the nerve to announce in Parliament
that he considered the trunk road network 'broadly
complete'. Paradoxically his last act before his promotion
to party chairman was to approve one of the most contentious road schemes of all, the A34 Newbury bypass, which
also took some balls. The construction led to a civil insur-
rection in the woodland along the route, and the temporary
deification of a local lad, Daniel Hooper, under the *nom-
de-guerre* Swampy. Much later Mawhinney looked back at
the battles among the tree-houses and reflected on the
dilemma he had faced:

'Yes, I still remember the beautiful countryside around
Newbury which is no more, and how much I enjoyed
walking through it as a preliminary to making my decision
– even as I know that tens of thousands of people live
better lives as a result of that decision.'

Myself, I think that Mawhinney got it about right. I
drive that section of the A34 fairly often on my way to
join the A303 to go fishing near Amesbury, and I bless the
convenience of it. For Newbury it was more salvation
than convenience – the town had been identified forty
years before by Colin Buchanan as an extreme illustration
of the damage and misery caused when a market town
high street becomes a major arterial trunk route. The

problem with our apprehension of big road schemes is that it tends to be governed by familiar visual images of violation: bulldozers tearing open woodland and fields, mountains of spoil, slicks of mud, buildings tottering before the wrecking-ball. Unless we live in the town or village ravaged by the queues of traffic, we cannot imagine the relief of quiet. Nor at the time of outrage can we visualise the road as it will become, the way the land heals and takes the road into it.

* * *

Newbury could count itself lucky. It got its bypass in the nick of time, just as society turned decisively against that kind of grand engineering project. Since then the big roads rhetoric has been periodically reheated by ministers to appease the roads lobby and foster an impression of boldness and tough thinking in the pursuit of the dynamic economy. But the roads themselves have generally been left where they started, on drawing-boards.

Winterbourne Stoke, two-and-a-half miles or so west of Stonehenge, was not as fortunate as Newbury. No one disputed the case for Winterbourne Stoke to have the same relief as a string of other towns and villages along the A303, starting with Andover and Amesbury in 1969, and ending with Bourton and Zeals, whose bypass opened in July 1992. The route, looping through empty farmland around the north of the village, was accepted, even embraced, by all. The curse was Stonehenge. While the wrangling over the tunnel continued, Winterbourne Stoke waited patiently. Then it dawned on its people that their curse would not be lifted. Not now; probably not ever.*

The village lies at the bottom of a dip in the downs, beside a little stream of erratic flow. There are roughly eighty houses spread along both sides of the A303 and over land to the south. Apart from the handsome brick-and-flint Church of St Peter there is one notable building, Manor Farm, a splendid and lovely mainly seventeenth-century gabled house in pale stone and flint at the western edge of the village. Otherwise there is a smattering of pleasant old cottages and a preponderance of less pleasant modern houses. It could be any unexceptional, non-descript rural settlement – if it were not for the road.

Instead, Winterbourne Stoke is a place bruised, battered and traumatised by noise and movement. There is no peace there, except when some horrendous crash blocks the A303 and police divert the traffic elsewhere (it was shut for four hours once, and in the silence that descended on Winterbourne Stoke, someone suggested holding a street party). At peak times more than 30,000 vehicles pass through each day; the year-round average is 22,000. The noise is pretty much continuous. When the traffic is flowing freely it is a high-volume rasp thickened by the roar of lorry engines and punctuated by the clang of wheels

* Of course, if – I emphasise if – the scheme for the Stonehenge tunnel does proceed, the curse will be lifted and the northern bypass will finally bring relief.

on drain covers. When the queue is solid, the sound is heavy, more threatening, dissonant with the hiss of brakes, the crunch of gear change, the swell of acceleration.

Some residents are more philosophical than others. I bumped into Charlie Vince the day before he retired from running the village garage and shop. He said there were plenty of places worse than Winterbourne Stoke; and he must have meant it, because he was retiring no further than his cottage on the other side of the A303. He regaled me with well-used stories of apocalyptic collisions and gruesome deaths in his forty years looking out on to the road. One of his elderly customers, Charlie told me, was too slow to be confident of getting across in one piece, so he would wait on the other side until Charlie came out to throw his daily packet of fags across to him. Just next to the garage is a comparatively new pedestrian crossing with traffic lights; it is common practice, apparently, for people to press the button to cross, then dash back to their cars in order to get out onto the road.

I was shown a quartet of old postcards of the village, dating – I would guess – from the 1930s. The road is amazingly narrow, wandering this way and that around the walls of the buildings. The bridge over the stream – which was replaced in 1939 – looks just wide enough for a single stream of traffic. In all but one of the pictures the road is empty.

There was peace then in Winterbourne Stoke.

11

WILTSHIRE HORN

Winterbourne Stoke's stream is called the Till. Both stream and name come from Tilshead, an isolated village a few miles over the downs to the north. It seems that the place-name – said to be a contraction of 'Theodwulf's hide' – came first, which is not usually the case with rivers and the settlements beside them.

Stop on the bridge in Winterbourne Stoke in spring or early summer after a winter of decent rainfall, and you will see a pretty little stream of water as clear as glass beneath. But, generally speaking, by July or August the flow has faltered. The little tresses of green water crowfoot wilt and vanish. The gravel is exposed, and any trout that ventured up in search of extra rations will have fled back down-stream. Through autumn and early winter it remains a forlorn sight. Then, as the rain clouds sweep over the empty downland, the chalk aquifers are recharged; and quite suddenly the stream is reborn.

A stream but no water

These days – because of abstraction from the aquifers and generally lower rainfall – the rebirth is a hit-and-miss affair.* But in times past the yearly cycle was reliable enough to sustain a method of land use that was crucial to the economy of Winterbourne Stoke, and of a host of communities across Hampshire, Wiltshire, Berkshire and Dorset.

Vestiges of the system can just be made out in the meadows beside the Till upstream of the bridge at Winterbourne Stoke, like an old, faint footprint. There is a pattern of connected miniature ridges and depressions. Here and there a slab of cut stone shows through the rough grass, which

* Curiously it did not dry up at any point during the dry, hot summer of 2018, owing to the exceptional rainfall and aquifer recharge in the late winter.

once formed part of a tiny culvert or supported the top end of a channel or ditch. There are the remains of a Lilliputian aqueduct. Someone, a long time ago, went to a deal of trouble to engineer these meadows to a very particular end. There are plenty of other more or less detectable traces of the uses to which this landscape has been put over the ages: the thatched roofs and cob walls of the old cottages, the flints that give the churches their grainy pallor, the hedges marking boundaries recorded in Domesday, the terracing still visible on downland slopes indicating field systems that go back to the Bronze Age.

Roughly half of the A303 runs across the great chalk stratum of which Salisbury Plain forms the western sector. The chalk downland ends a little way west of Fonthill, roughly where the A350 Blandford–Bath road cuts at right angles across the A303. Beyond that point the traces of the distant past are generally sparser and more hidden, if not wholly erased. But across the wide, rolling uplands of the Plain, and on the slopes of the valleys and in the meadows by the streams, the long, long story of how our species sought to manage this landscape and exploit its peculiar qualities is quite clearly written.

Go back six thousand years. The process of clearing the primeval upland forest is in hand. Tools of antler and bone are in use. Flint blades and stone axes are being developed. Mesolithic gives way to Neolithic. By 3000 BC emmer wheat, einkorn and barley are being ground in stone querns to make flatbread. Decorated pottery is in circulation.

Prominent ancestors are laid to rest in collective burial chambers. The earth bank and ditch around Stonehenge are constructed, and the first circle of bluestones put in place. As Neolithic gives way to Bronze Age, deforestation accelerates. Permanent settlements are established. Burial chambers for individual leaders are excavated.

By 1500 BC Stonehenge in its mature form was already a thousand years old. Over the next thousand years the hilltop settlements grew in size, and were surrounded by substantial earthworks. Quarley Hill, Yarnbury Castle and Cadbury Castle are three notable examples close to or next to the A303. The prominent dead were cremated and their remains placed in urns for burial. The emphasis of agriculture was arable, but sheep and especially cattle were established components of the economy. In the period up to Roman occupation the land was divided between different communities and marked by visible boundaries. Wheat and barley were the main crops, but rye and oats were also grown.

In terms of land use, not a huge amount changed over the next millennium and a half, except that settlements generally migrated into the valleys or rivers and streams, and sheep grazing tended to elbow out the Celtic field systems. Invading armies – Romans, Saxons, Danes, finally the Normans – swept through, spilling blood and spreading destruction. Occasional periods of peace and good order – for instance under Alfred's kingship – were preceded and followed by longer periods of violence and political flux.

As far as they were able, the ordinary folk went about their ordinary business, which was extracting the means to live from the land they occupied. The relative stability that the Normans brought was reflected in the development of the rural economy. Mills were installed along rivers and streams to grind corn for bread and to treat cloth. The lands of the Salisbury Plain plateau were parcelled out between manors. Sheep ruled the upper pastures, the lower slopes were dedicated to crops.

It was the sheep and the shepherds that caught the eye. The animals roamed and nibbled in vast numbers. Their teeth kept the downland grasses, clovers, herbs and flowers close cropped, giving the turf what the great nature writer W. H. Hudson called 'the smooth elastic character which makes it better to walk on than the most perfect lawn'. The celebrated seventeeth-century antiquary, John Aubrey, described how the standard shepherd wore a long white cloak of wool with a deep cape and carried crook, sling, scrip (wallet), tar-box and flute, with a dog at his heels. Shepherds were freelances, employed by a co-operative of farmers attached to each manor to manage the flocks. Traditionally they were difficult, obstinate and unbiddable. But they were also irreplaceable, and the owners of the animals would go to great lengths to avoid offending them.

Shepherds could also be of service to travellers. Daniel Defoe, writing early in the eighteenth century, referred to the 'certain, never-failing assistance' they rendered in a landscape where 'there is neither house nor town in view and the road which often lyes very broad and branches off insensibly might easily cause a traveller to loose his way . . .'

Sheep defined the Plain, but they were not its core business. It was corn that sustained the rural economy of Wiltshire and Hampshire. The role of sheep, although crucial, was entirely subsidiary.

The sheep of the downland was the Wiltshire Horn. Unusually, both males and females were horned: hence the name. It had a big, uncouth, round-nosed face, long body, and thick legs. Its meat was edible but distinctly mediocre, its wool serviceable for cloaks and rough garments but too coarse and sparse to be valued by the textile industry. The worth of the Wiltshire Horn lay in its strength and stamina, and in its digestive system. It was regarded primarily as a dung machine, and its duty was to fertilise the arable fields.

The pattern of their day hardly varied. From morning to afternoon or evening – depending on the season – they roamed the grazing land filling their bellies with herbage. Before light faded they were driven down from the pastures to the arable fields and confined within hurdled pens for the night. There, tightly packed together – the recommended density was a thousand sheep to the acre – they defecated for their living. At daylight they were driven off again to the uplands. The wattle hurdles were dismantled, moved along, and reassembled so that the next acre of ground could be manured the following night. Only in the bitterest winter weather were the sheep allowed into shelters; then the dung was collected and carried to the field.

The corn that grew in that rich ground made the money that kept the farmers of Wiltshire and Hampshire afloat. Some was sold in small local markets at Salisbury and Amesbury. The famous Weyhill Fair and the annual fair which was held within the big prehistoric hillfort known as Yarnbury Castle both saw large-scale trading in corn and sheep. But the regular outlets were the markets at Hindon, south of the A303 near Fonthill, and Warminster. William Camden, visiting Warminster in the time of Queen Elizabeth I, described the quantities of corn sold there as 'scarcely credible', while John Aubrey's bailiff counted 'twelve or fourteen score loads of corn' arriving there for market day.

The system was an early version of the collective later embraced by Stalinist social planners across Russia and eastern Europe. It was held together by dependence. The grazing was common land, and crops were grown in strips across big, open fields – generally one for winter wheat, one for spring barley, and one left fallow. The great majority of farmers participated in the common sheepfold; if they didn't, they had no entitlement to the precious dung. Their reciprocal duties including paying towards winter fodder when it was needed, and contributing hurdles for the fold.

During the seventeeth century a radical new technology gave a tremendous boost to the chalkland rural economy. Historically, the chief restraint on the numbers of sheep that could be kept – and therefore the amount of manure available – was the so-called 'hungry gap', the late winter period when reserves of hay were exhausted and the grass had not yet started growing. To fill that gap, the practice developed of 'floating the water meadows', as it became known. It involved taking water from the nearest stream and, by means of an intricate grid of channels and carriers, spreading it across the meadows. The flooding took place in November, and the effect was to protect the grass from winter frosts, thereby encouraging early growth, which was further promoted – though no one realised it at the time – by the exceptional nutrient-load of chalkstream water. Ideally the depth was no more than an inch or two, and towards the end of February the water was drained off the land, which was then given a couple of weeks to dry off a touch and get its grass going. Come March the hungry ewes and lambs were unleashed into the rich, emerald pasture for the day, and driven off to the arable fields for the night.

Towards the end of April the grazing of the water-meadows generally ceased, as the grass began to grow on the uplands. The meadows were flooded again, and the grass left for the July hay crop. This could amount to two tons an acre, and in a good summer there was often time for a second crop to be grown and cut. After that cattle were allowed to graze for a time, before the whole network was cleaned and refurbished in time for the winter flooding.

The method may well have originated in northern France in the medieval period, possibly at the great Cistercian abbey at Clairvaux. Having migrated across the Channel, it seems to have been first adopted on a commercial scale in Dorset, on the rivers Piddle and Frome. It worked best on chalkstreams, where water levels did not vary much and serious floods were very unusual, where gradients were gentle, and where drainage into the soil and chalk was swift. Adapting the meadows was laborious and expensive. It could take two or three years to dig the main carrier and the host of little channels feeding off it, to construct the levees between them, and to install the weirs and hatches needed to control water levels. Usually the main carrier fed more than one meadow, and over time the network spread downstream. One scheme on the Avon south of Salisbury involved excavating a carrier two-and-a-half miles long, and building a new weir as well as several bridges and hatches – all of which cost the vast sum of more than £2000.

Upkeep did not come cheap, either. The accounts kept by Richard Osgood – who farmed between Normanton and Wilsford in the 1680s – record payments to repair weirs, hatches and channels on the Avon, and the proposed replacement of a wooden hatch with a stone one costing eight pounds and six shillings – an investment discussed at length in an alehouse called the Chopping Knife in Amesbury. But the dividends could be heart-warmingly large. It was reckoned that converting to water meadow increased yield per acre at least three-fold, and doubled the sale value of the land. By the end of the eighteenth century 20,000 acres in Wiltshire were regularly watered, with about the same in Hampshire, and around 6000 acres in Dorset.

The lynchpin of the operation was a figure of intimidating toughness and independence of spirit, known as the Drowner. It was his task to maintain the system and organise the movement of water to produce a uniform growth of grass across the whole meadow or series of meadows. It required fine judgement to get the timing and volumes right. As the water spread down from the main carrier, the drowner would be on hand, ready to make a series of swift decisions and adjustments – raising or lowering a sluice here, opening a channel there, switching the flow by placing sods of earth at critical points.

The drowner's busiest time was after Michaelmas, when the whole grid had to be cleaned and restored in time for the flooding to begin in November, so that the grass would be showing by Christmas. Throughout the winter months he was out in all weathers, wading through freezing water for hours at a time in nothing more waterproof than leather breeches and boots. He exercised absolute power over his meadows. His status was equal to that of the miller, with whom he would have long-standing agreements regulating the 'stems', the times when water could be impounded to fill the mill leat, and when it was available for irrigation. The drowner decided when the sheep were allowed on, and while they were grazing he took control of them from the shepherd. It was by his order that grazing ceased, and he also supervised the hay crop.

Co-operative farming fostered tightly knit, distinctive communities. Typically an average farmer would have a house with yard, paddock, barn and garden, eight to ten strips scattered around the open arable fields, rights to graze a prescribed number of cattle, pigs and geese on common land, a proportion of the sheep flock and an entitlement to cut turf and wood. The shepherds and drowners might proclaim their independence but the truth was that everyone depended on everyone else. Neighbour helped neighbour, and the mutual dependence extended beyond the collective. All the other trades and services – carpenters, blacksmiths, weavers, cordwainers, bootmakers, tanners, butchers, shopkeepers, builders and the rest – relied on the success of farming. Everyone knew everyone and did everything together, with the church acting as binding agent.

England's agrarian revolution arrived late on the chalk downland, held at bay by the powerful interests vested in the collective model. But by the 1750s the old shared field system was steadily on its way out. New crops – clover, oil-seed rape, turnips, cabbages – were introduced, with new patterns of rotation and new breeds of livestock. All this required a new system of tenure. The common land was divided up according to the ancient tithes, but previously scattered holdings were consolidated together. This was obviously far more efficient for those with reasonably extensive entitlements. But for the wretched peasant at the bottom of the scale it represented disaster. Previously he could scrape by with as little as two acres because of his common rights. Now he had forfeited those, and most were forced in time to sell to better-off neighbours and join the swelling ranks of labourers for hire.

The outward and visible sign of the enclosure movement were the hedges. These were generally planted as hawthorn, known as 'quickset'. In our sentimental fashion, we tend to think of hedges as ancient and comforting symbols of the old rustic ways. It's worth remembering that their function was entirely hard-headed: to show who owned what, and to keep out those who owned nothing.

One of the casualties of the revolution was the Wiltshire Horn. The 'walking dung-cart', as it was characterised by the agricultural historian Eric Kerridge, suited the old ways. Farmers forgave it its meagre fleece and indifferent mutton for its strength and digestive properties. The new generation of landowners was less indulgent. With demand for corn on the up because of the growing population, they were intent, where possible, on converting pasture to arable. Where they retained sheep, they wanted something fleecier and meatier than the Wiltshire Horn. These virtues achieved ideal sheep form in the cross-bred Hampshire Down, which so thoroughly displaced the Wiltshire Horn that by 1840 there was but one flock of the old dung-spreaders left on Salisbury Plain.

For a time the new order flourished. Farmers on the small and medium scale held their own; the big land-owners got rich; the dispossessed ended up hoeing someone else's earth or else on poor relief or in the work-house. But during the 1870s imports of cheaper corn from the United States and of refrigerated meat from Australia and Argentina began to undermine the domestic market. Arable farmers struggled, while sheep farmers went out of business. The slump lasted until the 1914–18 war and beyond; although in Wiltshire and Hampshire the worst of the economic effects were offset by the establishment of large military camps on Salisbury Plain and elsewhere. During the 1920s and 1930s much of the chalk downland was simply abandoned. Without the sheep it was colo-nised by scrub, coarse grass and thistles, and left to the rabbits.

★ ★ ★

In 1946 Rob Turner's grandfather came to farm at Winterbourne Stoke. He bought Manor Farm and with it the manor house, which looks like a rather grand mansion but is actually pretty homely inside.

Grandfather Turner had considerable ambitions. The lend-lease project introduced by President Roosevelt in 1941 enabled British farmers to lay their hands on new tractors and other advanced agricultural machinery. The development of chemical fertilisers made it worthwhile to plough up the long-neglected downland and either turn it to arable or to grazing rich enough for cattle. The use of mobile milking parlours made it possible to keep the cows out all year, and for a while good profits were made from milk.

Eventually, however, arable farming – assisted by bountiful grants for fertilisers, pesticides and herbicides – came to hold sway. Grandfather Turner was a restless soul, and soon went elsewhere, handing over Manor Farm to his son. By the mid-1970s wheat and barley ruled the landscape. The Turners held most of the triangle formed by the A303 between Stonehenge and Winterbourne Stoke, the B3083 from Winterbourne Stoke to Shrewton, and the A344/A360 between Shrewton and the stones. Right up to the boundaries of the monument, the fields were ploughed for corn.

Then the climate of opinion changed and the pendulum began to swing back again, as we became aware of the impact of modern agribusiness. Thanks to chemicals and subsidies, arable farming more than paid its way for the farmers. But the land had fallen silent. The birds and mammals and insects had been banished. The cereal mono-culture had drained the diversity and richness from what was increasingly being seen as part of the nation's heritage rather than an economic asset. In 2003 the National Trust decided that its land around Stonehenge should revert to grassland. Chemicals were banned and the fields were sown with a brush-harvested mixture of wild fescue and bent grasses and wildflowers such as devil's bit scabious, wild thyme, bird's foot trefoil, harebells and bellflowers. Rob Turner, who had succeeded his father at Manor Farm, reached agreement with the Trust to rent their land for light grazing of beef cattle.

Turner fulfils most notions of what a farmer should look and sound like. He is ruddy-faced and powerfully built. He moves slowly and deliberately and speaks in the same way, with a hint of country burr. He is friendly and informative, with a deep knowledge of the land and aware-ness of his duty of care. He works tremendously hard and I would guess that he is a good neighbour. I know he is a good friend to the little River Till.

As Rob drove me through his meadows and past his ploughed fields he spoke with quiet pride of his steward-ship of his land. Altogether he owns and rents 2200 acres, slightly more than half of which is arable – mainly oil-seed rape, wheat and barley – and the rest grazing for his 400 beef cattle. He is, I would say, a man of the soil in the best sense, steeped in traditions of husbandry and in the land-scape of which his holding forms part. The past is important to Turner, but it is the present that fills his life and time: the ceaseless round of jobs that comprise a farmer's day. Plough, fertilise, seed, spray, harvest, buy cattle, sell cattle, move cattle, check cattle, mend fences, replace gates – these and all the other tasks measure out the year and afford little time for looking around, let alone looking back.

Nostalgia is for writers, naturalists and local historians – those whose love for this austere, often desolate landscape is bound up with an ache of awareness for what is lost. For W. H. Hudson – who roamed far and wide across the Plain – the sense of loss was focused on the disappearance of sheep and the way of life that went with them, and on the arrival of the Army. Hudson harboured a fierce distaste for urban life and a feeling akin to hatred for the military and the potential for violence implicit in their khaki uniforms. In 1910, in *The Shepherd's Life* – a minutely observed and loving celebration of the old simplicity – he wrote:

'To the lover of Salisbury Plain as it was, the sight of military camps with white tents or zinc huts, and of bodies of men marching and drilling, and the sound of guns, now informs him that he is in a district which has lost its attraction, where nature has been dispossessed.'

The paradox that escaped Hudson in his melancholy was that the annexation of so much of the Plain by the military was to be its salvation. By sealing off the remote parts and either preventing farming altogether or permitting no more than restricted grazing, the MoD, quite unwittingly, gave protection from the worst effects of modern agricultural methods. While huge areas of arable land were being rendered lifeless by the application of fertilisers, weedkillers and pesticides, the artillery ranges and exercise grounds provided a sanctuary for birds and beasts, once they got used to the boom of guns and the grinding of tanks.

Hudson's spiritual successor was Ralph Whitlock, who was born in a village between Salisbury and Amesbury just before the outbreak of the 1914–18 war and spent his whole life on Salisbury Plain. Whitlock wrote scores of books and hundreds of newspaper and magazine articles about the history and geography of the Plain, its flora and fauna and its village society. For Whitlock – the son of a shepherd-turned-Methodist preacher – the tragedy of the chalk downland was precipitated by the arrival of agribusiness. In a lecture to the Amesbury Society in 1979 he quoted John Aubrey's description of the texture of Salisbury Plain – 'the turfe is of short, sweete grasse, good for the sheep, delightful to the eye, for its smoothness is like a bowling green.'

'That is how I remember it,' Whitlock told his audience. He lingered on the little flowers he knew so well: milkwort, eyebright, squinancywort, rock-rose, viper's bugloss, lady's finger, tormentil, thyme, sheep's bit scabious, carline thistle, harebell, rest-harrow, autumn gentian – 'their names are as fragrant as the flowers,' he said. Over them flitted the butterflies – 'now rare but then abundant' – chalkhill blues, small coppers, Adonis blues, marbled whites, skippers, green hairstreaks, fritillaries, burnet moths. From the butterflies he moved to the birds: wheat-ears ('now only a bird of passage') and the stone curlew. 'I have seen as many as seventy collecting on the downs for migration,' Whitlock said, 'and have heard the haunting carolling across the twilit downs.' The whole piece is like a hymn or chant to a lost world.

At length the passing of the Wiltshire Horn sheep was followed by that of the water meadows. They limped on into the twentieth century, but in general the system was too labour-intensive and expensive to remain viable in the agricultural depression that lasted until the outbreak of war in 1939. The drowner was relegated to folk memory, and his armoury of long-handled spades and trenching tools to the display cabinets of various regional museums.

In a few places the drowner and his art clung on a little longer. In his classic book *Keeper of the Stream*, Frank Sawyer – who for more than fifty years was in charge of the Services Association trout fishing on the Avon upstream from Amesbury – recalled conversations with Seth, the old drowner who had worked the meadows since the 1890s. As old-timers do, Seth harked back to a golden age; he was particularly antagonistic to the proliferation of willows and alders along the stream banks, calling them 'thirsty varmints . . . idle critters' and accusing them of sucking the river dry in summer.

Sawyer mourned the disappearance of the multitude of tiny waterways that made up the grand design. 'These grass-fringed runnels, ditches and carriers remain vivid in my memory,' he wrote. 'Everywhere were masses of

crawling caddis and snails, every stone or loose turf shel-
tered a horde of shrimps and small fly larvae, while
thousands of minnows scattered in panic as great trout and
eels sped along the carriers to safety in the deep pools at
the hatchways. When the meadows were drained, all this
wealth of fish and food was washed back to enrich the
main river. Moreover the main drains, kept clean of silt by
the drowner, provided first-class spawning for trout on the
bright, golden gravel and the chalk.'

All are long gone now, almost all, anyway: ridges flattened and ploughed, drains filled in, the ground trampled
by cattle, hatches left to rot, brick arches collapsed,
carriers filled with mud and choked with rushes. The
imprint of this rather beautiful and intricate technology
can be seen everywhere along the south-country chalkstreams – for instance along the back road that connects
the village of Wylye with its three sweetly named neighbours, Hanging Langford, Steeple Langford and Little
Langford, where the River Wylye winds quietly through
rough meadows. Many of the old carriers are maintained
to provide fishing for trout anglers, and in the pools
beneath the hatch-gates the trout and grayling sway in
the current, picking off hatching insects just as their
forbears did in the days of the drowners.

12

GROSSLY DISORDERED

An improvised flagpole stands at the eastern end of a lay-by a little way out of Winterbourne Stoke. When I first stopped there it was flying a weather-seasoned Cross of St George, later replaced by a bright new Union Flag which flew bravely for a time before being blown away by a gale. The last time I passed it the old flag was on guard again. The lay-by is one of the few on the A303 big enough to take several trucks at one time, with a substantial island between it and the road. Apart from a bin for rubbish, the authorities provide no amenities. Its only attraction is a modest example of A303 private enterprise in the form of a stumpy little caravan that stands on the verge across from the flag. The name on the caravan is Joseph's.

The name of the man inside who wields the spatula and smiles his welcome across the hot-plate is Fatih. But after his arrival in this country from Turkey, an employer said customers would be unsettled by Fatih, and renamed him

Joseph; and he has stuck with that. His clientele comprises truck drivers, squaddies from the military camps, and motorists inclined to a bacon sandwich and a mug of hot tea in preference to an Olympic breakfast in the more formal setting of Little Chef. Joseph is there seven days a week, all the year round except when he returns to his home in southern Turkey to see his family. He has a room at the farm-cum-B&B down the road, where he keeps his caravan at night.

He told me – and I don't think he said it because he thought it would please me to hear it – that he liked it in England. In fact he preferred it to Turkey. People here do not bother you, he said. In Turkey everyone wants to know your business. He enjoyed chatting with his customers, many of whom stopped regularly to chew the fat and a sandwich. Sometimes his cousin came over from Salisbury to keep him company and give a hand cutting the bread (mainly white, but he does offer brown), flipping the eggs and the sizzling bacon off the hot-plate.

I asked him about the flag. It was there because the Highways Agency, which has charge of the lay-by, did not object to it. For some obscure reason probably arising from a pettifogging regulation concerning visual distraction or sightlines, the Agency will not permit Joseph to have a sign advertising his first-rate sandwiches and revitalising mugs of tea. I am therefore happy to urge readers of this book who happen to be on the A303 anywhere near Winterbourne Stoke to stop at Joseph's. In warm weather he puts out a plastic table and chairs for the benefit of those who want to take their time and take in the view of the road and the fields beyond. Otherwise you either have to take your sustenance standing in front of the hatch or hasten back to your vehicle with your bacon sandwich warming your hand through its wrapping.

★ ★ ★

The first of my several encounters with Joseph and his butties occurred when I was walking back to Winterbourne Stoke from Yarnbury Castle, the enormous hillfort spread over the crown of the next hill along the road. It was my second attempt to find and explore the site. On a previous occasion I had cycled from Shrewton on what began as a well-marked bridle-path, only to lose my way and bearings completely. Had I been Daniel Defoe, I could have summoned a rough-hewn shepherd to put me right. As it was, the landscape of huge fields of corn was utterly devoid of human life. I eventually found myself on the wrong side of a rectangle of golden barley so immense that one end was out of sight. Beyond it I could see the tops of the lorries grinding along the A303, but there was high, tight barbed wire between me and the barley, so I went around it – the long way, as it turned out.

Having completed a three-quarters circumnavigation of this one field, my interest in Yarnbury Castle was waning fast. Had I known it, I was at the time equally close to Parsonage Down, a nature reserve comprising 5000 acres of pristine grassland covered in hundreds of ancient anthills and home to a prodigious abundance of wildflowers, including Europe's biggest population of the rare burnt tip orchid. But I was getting to the state of sweaty irritation in which I couldn't have cared much about that either. I found my way to the road blocked by another barrier of twangingly tight barbed wire. By now more than a little desperate, I propelled my bicycle over it and followed it, tearing the skin on my left palm and a large rip in my trousers.

Finally reunited with the A303, I dragged myself and my machine along the verge for a couple of hundred yards, whereupon Yarnbury Castle revealed itself to my right. By then it was 1.30 p.m., and had it been the Sphinx itself rearing from the Wiltshire countryside, I would not have stopped to inspect it. There was a pub in Wylye at the bottom of the hill ahead, which I suspected would stop doing food at 2 p.m. – food that I needed even more than I needed beer. I therefore rode my bike along the verge. Fortunately it was downhill all the way and I managed to get up to nine or ten miles an hour, which still made being overtaken by pantechnicons travelling at 80 m.p.h. distinctly unnerving. I made it to the Bell in the nick of time.

Yarnbury Castle, I reflected, could wait for another day. After all it had been there for almost two-and-a-half thousand years.

Position is everything for a hillfort. No good picking a spot where your enemies can creep up on you unseen and stick a dagger in your back or apply a mace to your skull. The first priority is the view, then clearing the trees so you can see who is coming, preferably for several miles. After that you may start feeling secure.

The hill on which Yarnbury Castle was first constructed around 300 BC is 500 feet high, which isn't a lot. But the configuration of the landscape gives it an impressive command. To the east a look-out could easily make out Beacon Hill, well beyond Stonehenge. To the south-west the land drops down into the valley of the Wylye, then rises again to Great Ridge Wood. Further round to the south is a long, even ridge, covered in the ancient woodlands of Grovely. North, the chalkland rolls away, concealing no secrets. Friend or foe would have given plenty of warning that they were coming.

So they got down to the digging. 'Yarnbury Castle,' wrote Sir Richard Colt Hoare, 'presents a very fine specimen of ancient castramentation.' Indeed it does. It is a mile around the outer ditch, and the total extent is close to thirty acres. The entrance on the eastern side was between two parallel banks of earth, with an additional mound shaped rather like a kidney to protect the mouth. Two banks separated by a deep ditch surrounded the fort. Within was a level enclosure, presumably the main living area. At some stage a third outer embankment was added, and later still a Roman garrison constructed a V-shaped extension on the west side with a wooden gate as entrance.

Colt Hoare hazarded the guess that Yarnbury was

originally occupied by 'Britons', then Romans, then Saxons. He was not far off, if we take Britons to mean the pre-Roman Iron Age residents. The main excavation at Yarnbury was carried out in the 1930s by the archaeologist Maud Cunnington, by a neat coincidence the wife of William Cunnington's great-grandson Ben. She found the usual shattered pottery and human bones – nothing exciting and nothing to suggest a particular history for Yarnbury beyond the familiar stuff: growing crops, grazing beasts, making tools, obscure death rites, obscure social hierarchy, probably some killing, probably some plague and pestilence.

The Saxons came down from the hill to the valley. Yarnbury had served its purpose and was left to the sheep and the rabbits (after the Normans introduced them): a huge, brooding, silent commentary on a life that had run its useful course. People continued to come by; there was a well-used trackway along the eastern flank and another on the west side. There was also, very likely, a route of some kind to the south, more or less coinciding with that of the A303, although its status is unclear. The famous atlas created by Charles II's 'Cosmographer and Geographick Printer', John Ogilby, shows the road from Andover and Amesbury forking left at Stonehenge for 'Stoke', i.e. Winterbourne Stoke. But there is no indication from Ogilby that it amounted to a through route to anywhere else, and he recommends the right fork leading to Shrewton and Warminster. It was not until the turnpike age of the second half of the eighteenth century that what we now know as the A303 developed into a more coherent road at least as far west as Mere.

At some point – certainly by the eighteenth century, possibly much earlier – Yarnbury Castle became the venue for an important annual sheep fair. It was held early in October, giving farmers and dealers time to drive newly acquired or unsold animals across the downs to Weyhill Fair, which took place a week later. The Yarnbury Fair was evidently a big date in the local calendar. Caleb Bawcombe, the shepherd in Hudson's *A Shepherd's Life*, recalled that the Ellerbys of Doveton Farm – for whom he worked for many years – sent sheep there over an unbroken period of eighty-eight years. Ella Noyes, who lived up the Wylye valley at Sutton Veny, described how the earth-works were packed with penned sheep, ponies and carthorses. In her book *Salisbury Plain*, published in 1913, she recorded that 'up to within the memory of people still living, the fair was followed by horse-races next day and sports of all kind. But now the pleasure part of the meeting has been abandoned; the folk disperse quietly . . . leaving Yarnbury to the silent occupation of prehistoric ghosts for another year.' Three years later the last fair was held, after which the military put the Castle out of bounds.

It is still out of bounds, surrounded by barbed wire, without even one of those reassuring English Heritage noticeboards to tell passers-by how old and important it is. You may do as I did, and climb the wire and hope that the minions of the landowner are somewhere else. But that is hardly conducive to communication with Miss Noyes' prehistoric ghosts.

★ ★ ★

Just east of Yarnbury Castle, the A303 becomes dual carriageway again. The effect on westbound traffic is wondrous to behold. Drivers trapped in the long crawl from the ridge before Stonehenge explode like sprinters off the blocks. Waves of outrage envelop any truck that pulls out first to heave itself past some panting hay-trailer or combine harvester. The grassy earthworks of Yarnbury Castle are a blur as the cars flash downhill past Wylye and over its river.

In 1997 John Major and his feuding Tories were finally booted out by an electorate grown weary of Thatcherism and its smoking fag-ends. Tony Blair stormed into Downing Street, a bright-eyed zealot bursting with vigour and promising – well, what did he not promise? One of his first exciting initiatives was to put John Prescott at the helm of the gargantuan new Department of the Environment, Transport and the Regions, a vessel whose size and manoeuvrability may have reminded its skipper of his days as a steward on cross-Channel ferries.

Three years later, to usher in the new millennium, Prescott presented a Ten Year Transport Plan – 'a route map', he called it in the jargon of the time. It was stuffed with platitudes and commitments to 'vigorous innovation ... radical reform ... integrated solutions [and] strategic approaches'. Road congestion would be cut by 3 per cent by 'smarter network management' and better 'real-time management of traffic'. Roads would be 'smart', motorways 'electronic'. A Network Traffic Control Centre would be established to 'drive through' the new smartness. All road schemes would be assessed according to the New Approach to Appraisal (NATA), which would balance the 'economic, environmental, safety, accessibility and integration applications'. Over the ten years, £21 billion would go to 'strategic roads', out of a total transport budget of £180 billion.

After Prescott, lesser, greyer figures were invited to take the transport helm: first Stephen Byers, then Alistair Darling, who held on to the job between May 2002 and May 2006, making him the longest-serving transport minister or secretary since Ernest Marples. Throughout this period the consultations over what to do about the A303 and Stonehenge ground agonisingly on. In December 2002, Darling announced that the 7.7-mile stretch between the Countess roundabout at Amesbury and the start of the Wylye bypass at Yarnbury Castle would be upgraded to dual carriageway, with 1.3 of those miles disappearing into a tunnel past Stonehenge. The fine words floated off over Salisbury Plain, while someone – Darling, Blair, or someone else – decided that a Ten Year Plan was too modest, and that what was really needed was a Thirty Year Plan.

Tony Blair himself provided a foreword to this prophetic document, which appeared in 2004. He described the challenge ahead as 'a tough one'. It would, he said, admit of 'no quick fix'. Like its predecessor, the new plan made much of 'smart solutions'. The smart solution to the A303/Stonehenge scheme turned out to be cancellation.

Lucky Wylye had got its bypass long before, in 1975, in retrospect a golden age for the road-builders. Before then the A303 had cut through the western part of the village, crossing the river on a tight, dog-leg bridge which was the cause of much loathing among holidaymakers and truck drivers. Now it sweeps past over the river and under the A36 Salisbury–Warminster road, with which it shares a complex junction requiring close attention. You can find the 'old' A303 just out of Wylye, on the western side of the railway line. The original bridge has been removed, leaving an abrupt termination high in the air above a murky pond. A pile of railway sleepers and a rusted red plough have been abandoned among the bushes that have forced their way through the fractured tarmac. The amputated old road creeps along beside the new for a mile-and-a-half, separated from it by an embankment and a line of scrubby thorn trees. It is narrow and forsaken, its cat's eyes gouged out and removed, its surface broken and weed-infested. Here and there a splash of its white line can be made out, like a murmur of its past, when it went somewhere and counted for something.

Old and new, side by side

Historically, Wylye stood guard beside the main ford on the upper section of the river from which it got its name. It was the most important of a string of villages between Salisbury and Warminster. The political firebrand and social commentator William Cobbett counted thirty-one; W. H. Hudson made it between twenty-five and thirty – the number, he said, seemed to change each time he walked or cycled the valley. It was a valley beloved by those who knew it. Edward Hutton, in his *Highways and Byways in Wiltshire*, called it 'an epitome of all the valleys of the Plain . . . fruitful and very quiet, but not dumb; in it the heart of England still laughs and sings, serene and steadfast under the great downs that compass it with their strength on every side.' Hudson wrote of the stream showing 'like a bright serpent' in the meadows, then disappearing into the trees that hid the villages so completely 'that at some points, looking down from the hills, you may not even catch a glimpse of one and may imagine it to be a valley where no man dwells'.

The villages are still there. They all have their charms, and some – I think of Stockton, Boyton and Upton Lovell – are so pretty as to seem almost unreal; in Hudson's words, 'of the old, quiet, now almost obsolete type of village, so unobtrusive as to affect the mind soothingly, like the sight of trees and flowery banks and grazing cattle'. There are plenty of the crooked old cottages he loved – 'weathered and coloured by sun and wind and rain . . . mostly thatched, but some have tiled roofs, their deep, dark red clouded and stained by lichen and moss . . . they stand among and are wrapped in flowers as a garment – rose and vine and creeper and clematis.'

Mostly they have been tarted up, of course, and frequently tarnished by tactless extensions. Often, too, the spaces between them have been filled with specimens of contemporary housing: machine-cut bricks in deadly beige or dog-shit brown placed in dead-straight lines of spirit-choking regularity, complete with concrete tiles, dismal brown window-frames, and built-in garages with corrugated doors. The unwitting effect of the intruders has been to endow their elderly neighbours, with their roofs of thatch or wandering tiles and walls of soft grey stone and chequered flint or bulging cob, with an ethereal and poignant loveliness.

But it is not the lamentable quality of modern house-building that has robbed the Wylye Valley and its villages of the magic that entranced Hudson, Hutton and others. It is a road, a bully of a road – not my A303, but the A36. This is essentially a country road doomed by geographical bad luck – it is the only feasible way from Southampton and Salisbury in the south to Warminster and eventually Bristol to the north-west – to serve as a major arterial route. It is narrow, it twists and turns, it rises and falls with every fold in the land. Everyone hates it: car drivers because it is difficult and hazardous to overtake, truckers because of the constant gear-changing and wheel-turning, locals because of the risks involved in turning onto it and the horrible grinding racket with which it fills their days.

I have spent many happy hours on the Wylye between Stockton and Heytesbury. It is a lovable stream: a pleasure to look at, but a double delight if you are in it, wading the firm gravel bottom, pushing up beside beds of thick, waving weed, ducking between trailing willow branches, searching ahead for the rings on the water that betray feeding trout and grayling. I have promised no fishing, and I will keep my promise, but I could not pass this jewel of a chalkstream without paying my respects. It has given me joy and will, I am sure, give me more. The happy hours would have been happier still if they had been free of the pestilential roar of the A36.

★ ★ ★

A mile west out of Wylye the bypass ends and the A303 reverts to single carriageway. To the left is Wylye Down, the terracing of a Celtic field system clearly visible on the grassy slope. Ahead, nudging against the road, is a sweep of woodland known collectively as Great Ridge Wood; although it is composed of lesser woods with their own names, of which the most intriguing is Snail-Creep Hanging. The ridge of Great Ridge Wood continues to the south of the road in another great swathe of trees. This is Grovely Wood, which looks down over the lower Wylye almost to its junction with the Nadder.

Since time immemorial the people of two villages in the shadow of Grovely – Great Wishford on the Wylye and Barford St Martin on the Nadder – had the right, known as 'estover', to help themselves to wood. Each could take home as much as he or she could carry, although only the Wishfordians were entitled to cut greenwood. To maintain the entitlement, a delegation from each village had to dance their way into Salisbury Cathedral on Whit Tuesday where the Wishfordians cried out 'Grovely, Grovely and all Grovely!' and the Barfordians clamoured 'Grovely, Grovely, Grovely!'

In 1539, with the dissolution of Wilton Abbey, Grovely Wood and everything around it fell into the hands of Sir William Herbert, first Earl of Pembroke and builder of the great house of Wilton. At intervals thereafter various Earls of Pembroke tried to curtail the fuel-gathering forays into the wood, but the Wishfordians and Barfordians clung strenuously to their rights. In 1825 the elderly eleventh Earl, George Augustus Herbert, announced that he had had enough of the incursions, and banned them. A spirited Barfordian girl, Grace Reed, and three Wishfordian women resolved to resist the haughty Earl. Returning from Grovely with their armfuls of wood, they were summoned before the magistrates and locked up when they refused to pay fines. So furious was the outcry that the next day the Earl, or those who acted for him, backed down, and the quartet were released. Grace Reed lived another sixty-nine years in her cottage in Barford, warmed by proud Pembroke wood.

★ ★ ★

The Amesbury Turnpike Trust was formed in 1761 and was largely responsible for developing the first recognisable incarnation of the A303. At the time trusts were sprouting forth all over the place, charged with upgrading existing roads and building new ones. They were generally comprised of local business interests; and while investors undoubtedly hoped for a return through the tolls, there was also a strong element of public-spirited commitment to improving the infrastructure in pursuit of social as well as economic progress.

The driving force and chief investor in the Amesbury Trust was the third Duke of Queensbury, owner of Amesbury Abbey and the surrounding estates. Apart from loaning the Trust the considerable sum of £6000, the Duke paid for the rickety old wooden bridge over the Avon in Amesbury to be replaced by the elegant stone crossing that takes the traffic to this day. The financial returns on his loan were meagre in the extreme, and his heir, the absentee whist-mad fourth Duke, made repeated efforts over the next thirty years to shift the debt onto someone else; in vain, for by 1835 the Trust was more than £60,000 in the red. Nevertheless, from the point of view of everyone bar the investors, the Trust was a great success. A modest scale of charges – three pence per carriage, one penny per pack animal, ten pence per score of drove cattle; mail coaches, churchgoers, soldiers, electors and ploughmen free – offered the prospect of a safe journey across what had previously been one of the uncharted wastes of southern England.

The traveller who took the new road and came over the brow of the ridge rising from the west bank of the Wylye on any clear day between 1809 and 1825 would have been met by a bizarre spectacle on top of a wooded hill a couple of miles to the south-west. It was a monstrous octagonal tower 300 feet high – three quarters the height of the spire of Salisbury Cathedral – with eight Gothic spikes rising from the roof, the whole thing festooned with every species of stylistic extravagance and fancy. The tower formed the centrepiece of William Beckford's famous Fonthill Abbey, which was no abbey at all but a *folie de grandeur* dreamed up by one of the most reckless spendthrifts of that prodigal age.

Beckford, the fabulously spoiled only son of a fabulously rich owner of West Indian plantations, dazzled Europe with the publication in the 1780s of his Oriental fantasy *Vathek*, written – originally in French – when he was twenty-four. He commissioned the sham abbey and its tower after demolishing the vast mansion his father had built on the grounds that it was too conventional in design. The project consumed most of his fortune, and in 1825 the tower collapsed, an event widely interpreted as a judgement on Beckford's own ambitions.

Beckford's Abbey

To illustrate Beckford's notion of how to enjoy himself while impressing the locals, I cannot resist lingering for a moment with the report in the *Morning Chronicle* of the Fonthill Fete in January 1797. Ten thousand of the peasantry and assorted riffraff were admitted to the park for bread and strong ale. Polite aristocratic society would have nothing to do with Beckford after he was accused (falsely, in all probability) of seducing the teenage son of the Earl of Devon, so the best he could manage by way of the quality was the Mayor of Salisbury. His Worship and an assortment of lesser dignitaries were received by Beckford in a Turkish tent from which they watched a display of sports before retiring to the Grecian Hall to be served with roast beef ('the pride of Britons' according to the *Morning Chronicle*'s correspondent) and punch (the 'British nectar'). A succession of toasts culminated in Beckford's to 'Christmas Day, Twelfth Day, Old Times, and Old Names for ever, and may the ears of John Bull never be insulted by the gipsey jargon of France'.

Outside, the 'joy, gratitude and contentment' of the lower orders were expressed in repeated acclamations. This served to show, according to the *Morning Chronicle*, 'the vast influence which gentlemen of fortune and beneficent disposition . . . can still maintain in opposition to the effects of more modern habits and fashionable life . . .' In fact, needless to say, Beckford was loathed by his tenants and workers for his foul temper and habit of thrashing them as if they were indistinguishable from the slaves on the Jamaican plantations which provided his vast wealth.

★　★　★

Fonthill is a lovely spot, folded so discreetly into its vale that it reveals itself only when you are almost upon it. A narrow lake curves along it, full of fat carp that cruise the shallows leaving bow waves to spread lazily along the reeds. The water sometimes turns milky with pale sediment stirred by the springs on the bottom. The approach from the direction of the A303 is through Fonthill Bishop, a cluster of picture-book houses and cottages. The road passes beneath a monumental arch, one of the few of Beckford's absurdities to have survived, with gatehouses either side, urns, ballustraded piers and rough rustications. Further on is a sweet little cricket ground which slopes down quite steeply from the woods, with a wooden shack of a pavilion at one corner and big clumps of daffodils at mid-wicket/extra cover, and a pitch that looked to me as if it would play low and slow.

Lake at Fonthill

Beckford's Arch

Another view

On the far side of the lake is the site of Beckford senior's mansion, known mockingly as Fonthill Splendens. Its predecessor was destroyed by fire shortly after Alderman Beckford bought the estate. A still earlier house was the home of one of the wickedest earls in English history, and the setting of events so dark and sordid as to make Beckford's most lascivious Oriental masturbatory fantasies seem quite tame.

On 25 April 1631 Mervyn Touchet, second Earl of Castlehaven and master of Fonthill, was tried before twenty-seven of his peers in Westminster Hall, London, charged with rape and sodomy. On the first charge he was found guilty by twenty-six to one; on the second the majority against him was fifteen to twelve. Three weeks later he was beheaded on Tower Hill, Charles I having rejected all pleas for clemency. The case was the scandal of the age, the events leading to it regarded as so shameful that almost two centuries later, Sir Richard Colt Hoare could not bring himself to mention them – 'I shall not offend the delicacy of my readers by stating the cause of this trial,' he wrote with a shudder. Our age is less delicate, and the story has been told fully and with great fairness by Cynthia Herrup in the splendidly titled *A House in Gross Disorder*. I cannot resist dipping into it.

The house in question, Fonthill, seems to have run on hatred and unnatural lusts. The earl's accuser was none other than his own son and heir, James Touchet, one of six children by his first wife, the daughter of a rich London

Fonthill Splendens

The true por-
traiture of.

the Earle of
Castlehaven.

Wicked Earl

merchant. When she died, Castlehaven – having married money the first time – went for rank in the shape of Lady Anne Brydges, widow of Lord Chandos. She was twelve years older than he was, and after her arrival at Fonthill she soon discovered that her new husband much preferred the company of tobacco, heated wine, and his servants to that of his wife. One of the few matters on which they co-operated was in arranging a marriage between his son James, then fifteen or so, and her daughter by Lord Chandos, Elizabeth, then aged thirteen. The young couple could not stand each other.

By 1630 James had fled Fonthill. The state papers

record that he appealed 'for protection from the Earl, his natural father, to the Father of his country, the King's Majesty'. He laid complaint before the Privy Council, accusing his father of having unnatural relations with a succession of male servants, and of urging one of them, Henry Skipwith, to conduct an illicit liaison with James's stepsister and reluctant wife, Elizabeth. The Privy Council appointed a panel consisting of the Earls of Manchester, Arundel and Surrey, together with the Lord Chief Justice, Sir Nicholas Hyde, and the Bishop of London, William Laud, to investigate the goings-on in deepest Wiltshire. Further shocking allegations soon emerged. Lady Anne claimed that her husband had paid a page, Giles Broadway, £200 as an inducement to rape her. Her daughter Elizabeth said he had not merely encouraged Skipwith to have sex with her, he had watched them at it and had 'used himself like a beast' with another footman, Florence Fitzpatrick (male, despite his name). Yet another servant was accused of seducing Castlehaven's daughter Lucy. In his deposition, Henry Skipwith admitted offering to 'lie with the Earl', and said he had been ordered to have sex with Lady Anne as well as with her daughter.

Castlehaven's trial lasted one day. He seems to have made little or no attempt to defend himself. Cynthia Herrup is sceptical that he committed all the horrible acts of which he was accused, or even that he was legally guilty.

His punishment seems to have been determined as much by general horror at the licentious behaviour in the house under his charge as by the specifics. His conduct was seen as undermining the standards necessary to bind society together – in particular, he had abandoned his responsibilities as a father to his heir, as a husband to his wife, and as an English nobleman. Charles I, a paradoxical Puritan in matters of sexual propriety, was resolved that he should pay the ultimate price.

Five weeks after Castlehaven's execution, two of the large cast of misbehaving servants – Fitzpatrick and Broadway – were hanged at Tyburn for sodomy. Others were given terms of imprisonment. Son James became a doughty soldier in the Royalist cause, mainly in Ireland, where he died in 1684. The estate at Fonthill was awarded to one of Charles I's courtiers, Lord Cottington, of whom one contemporary, the historian Edward Hyde, first Earl of Clarendon, remarked that 'he left behind him a greater esteem for his parts than love for his person'. For ever afterwards the Castlehaven connection was referred to in hushed tones, or not at all.

★ ★ ★

One of my cycling circuits took me around Fonthill and over the A303 into Great Ridge Wood. A Roman road cuts through it and makes for pleasantly undemanding pedalling between the old oaks. After a while I cut down through Chilfinch Hanging towards the big road. Where the path emerged from the trees, the peace was fractured by a hell of a commotion ahead.

The mechanised and depersonalised character of farming today means that an encounter with humans in much of the countryside is a rare event. On a mixed farm like Rob Turner's at Winterbourne Stoke you will come across blokes attending to stock on a daily basis. But where arable rules, the chances of coming across anything more than the flight of birds, the popping of hare's ears above the corn and the occasional intrusion of a deer are remote. The arable fields are ploughed one day, fertilised another, sown another, sprayed another, and finally harvested on the fifth day of their active lives. For the remaining 360 days of the year they are left to themselves.

Tractor at work

When you do encounter men at work, their business is a far cry from the tillage of the fields in the traditional sense; more like slum clearance or a military sweep-and-burn exercise. The field of yellow rape below Chilfinch was shrouded in a dun cloud. On the flanks of the cloud were two 4x4s piloted by men steering with one hand and holding a phone or radio in the other. At the head of the cloud was a terrifying machine, a kind of agricultural Grendel, with a mouth as wide as a cargo ship furnished with revolving, slicing gnashers. One section of the mouth devoured the flowers, another the stalks. Everything apart from the dust was contained within the machine, where its digestive system separated and stored the different components of the crop.

High above the insatiable mouth, cocooned inside a bubble of air-conditioned glass, was the controller, the brains. He had headphones clamped to his ears to receive data from his outlying sentries. His hands gripped and pulled the levers, adjusting the height of the gnashing blades to the lie of the land. Ahead of him, the crop spread out in all its slightly fevered vitality. Behind stretched the trail of destruction – brown earth, stones, the stubble.

Close up the noise was deafening. No one waved to me, no one noticed me. The task of feeding the ravening machine demanded complete concentration and precision. It was relentless and pitiless: a very far cry indeed from the image of the farmer leaning on his plough to light up his clay pipe, ready to offer an opinion on whether the way the rooks were gathering might be a sign of rain before evening.

The A303 passes Great Ridge Wood and bisects a tiny hamlet called Chicklade. There is a handsome old house there once occupied by Neville Chamberlain's brother, and a rectory where T. E. Lawrence's brother lodged for a time – evidently a place for lesser-known brothers. From Chicklade the road rises over a ridge. Westward the land is, if not bright, different.

13

THE END OF THE PLAIN

From its start near Basingstoke, the road has been founded on chalk. Chalk has determined the character of the landscape. It shows beneath the pale grass and the growing barley and on the newly ploughed earth and the tracks of tractors and through the cattle-trampled mud beside the gates. It is the chalk that bestows on the streams their dazzling clarity, and with the chalk comes the flints that give the churches, old houses, barns and walls their look of strength and endurance. But now the road is finishing with the chalk.

Its western extremity is a bulge like a fist thrust out north of Fonthill. This is the end of Salisbury Plain, the rolling sea of grass on chalk that unfolds below Beacon Hill beyond Amesbury. Its last bastion, which drops with startling suddenness into the fields due north of Mere, is Whitesheet Hill.

End of the plain

It is a fine name for a place of very ancient occupation. The flint flakes of Mesolithic axes have been found there. A Neolithic camp was established on its north-western flank; inevitably William Cunnington thrust his inquiring nose into the accompanying group of barrows, in one of which he found a skeleton 'which grinned horribly . . . a singularity we have not encountered before'. An Iron Age hillfort came after the Neolithic camp, and a little way south of it. Among other innovations, the Normans brought rabbits to England, and on Whitesheet Hill are the remains of artificial warrens made to encourage the creatures to settle long enough to become rabbit stew. Across the top cuts an old road, possibly a very old road indeed, as it is identified by Mr and Mrs Timperley in *The Ancient Trackways of Wessex* as our old friend the Harrow Way.

I first cycled along it on a damp, dank morning that followed a night of rattling windows and beating rain. The ruts were filled with water and the chalky mud was as slippery as ice. Cloud hugged the slopes, blotting out the views, and apart from a couple of hardy dog-walkers I met no one. I came back on a breezy, sunny Good Friday, and the world and his dog were there. Squads of cyclists and droves of walkers passed me. Hang-gliders swooped over the hillfort. A game of rounders was in progress near the Neolithic camp. I sat for a time looking across to Stourhead and the wooded hill from which Alfred's Tower pokes its top. To the south-west the dark line of the Blackdown Hills formed the horizon. I could see a short stretch of the A303 over to the left, and its buzz was carried on the wind.

Where I sat, the ground dropped abruptly to the eastern edge of the valley that contains the infant Stour. The change in the texture of the landscape is almost as abrupt, and from my vantage point as clear as the day itself. To the south and west extends a greener, gentler land of clay and loam, the beginnings of the Vale of Wardour. Like Salisbury Plain, it is a mixture of pasture and arable. But the meadows are lusher, and the fields are noticeably smaller than on the Plain. Most of them are defined by hedges along the lines of the eighteenth-century enclosures, and the effect is a striking contrast to the wide, sweeping downs. The lie of the land is more intimate. There is no obvious pattern: hills bunch and drop into wooded vales seemingly at whim. The stone of the old buildings inclines to dun and coffee rather than grey. Flint becomes less common the further you go.

The A303 runs along the south flank of the chalk bulge that rises into Whitesheet Hill. It is right on the divide, and there passes at right angles over the A350 on a typically functional and aesthetically barren concrete bridge. There is no meeting of the ways, no inducement to east–west traffic to take notice of north–south traffic or the other way round, nothing to suggest that this could be one of the most ancient crossing-points in the civilised world.

You notice the 'could', I hope. Mr and Mrs Timperley asserted that this was the intersection between the two leading contenders for title of 'oldest road', the Great Ridgeway and the Harrow Way. The route they plotted for the Harrow Way has its intimate relationship with the A303 coming to an end about here. Between Weyhill and Thruxton the two are pretty much one and the same. At Amesbury the Harrow Way curves north across the Avon, south across the A303 at Longbarrow Crossroads, then follows the Grovely Wood ridge to Chicklade, where it is reunited with the road for a last few miles. At Willoughby Hedge – according to the account in *The Ancient Trackways of Wessex* – the Harrow Way leaves the A303 to deal with Mere while it sets off on a northern loop through Stourhead. It meets the A303 for the last time at Knoll Hill, between Wincanton and Sparkford. Thereafter its destiny is to the south.

Mr and Mrs Timperley believed as an article of faith that the Harrow Way and the Great Ridgeway and the other ridgeways were established long-distance routes that would have been known as such to prehistoric people. The proposition is that they formed a recognised transport system that would have enabled a man in Dover to contemplate doing business in Devon, or enabled a recent arrival from Europe to be directed to the ceremonials on Salisbury Plain. It arose from the natural desire to find something of ourselves in our ancestors when we ponder the deep past, and to locate systems and ways of thinking that we can recognise. The fact that archaeologists have found no convincing evidence to support it has done nothing to lessen its appeal.

The heritage and outdoor leisure industries, in particular, have embraced it with enthusiasm. The Great Ridgeway has been broken down into more manageable sections – the Wessex Ridgeway, the Ridgeway National Trail and the Icknield Way – which are promoted by the hiking associations and respective local authorities, and endowed with more or less fanciful historical associations. The underlying message is that your enjoyment will be enhanced by the thought that your boots are landing in the footsteps of the keen-eyed hunter-gatherers of old in the days when aurochs and wolves still roamed the land. There is no harm in it. As Hugh Davies points out in his *From Trackways to Motorways*: 'The flimsiness of the evidence for long-distance paths need not detract from the enjoyment of using them – after all their existence is part of our history even though evidence for their use as a means of reaching Stonehenge from far-flung parts of the island is no more secure than the idea that the monument was built by the Druids.'

In the case of the putative intersection of the Harrow Way and the Great Ridgeway where the A303 crosses the A350, it's a fair bet that there was an east-west track and a north-south track and that they met somewhere here and that several other tracks went off in various directions. That is how it was. Local people needed to get around and to do so they followed the ways their mothers and fathers and grandmothers and grandfathers had followed. These were along ridges that led to other ridges, routes that were well-drained and offered vantage points to see the lie of the land. In time they became tracks and the knowledge of where they started and where they went became common.

So it is wholly possible that I, Neolithic Tom Fort, might have been on my way one summer's day from my humble hutment on Two Mile Down to check on my animals on Charnage Down; and that I would have met an equally grubby, hairy-arsed fellow coming up the slope from the south, perhaps with a bag of pots or tools to trade; and that I would have asked him how life was in his equally humble settlement down the hill at East Knoyle. How the conversation might have developed from there it seems pointless to speculate.

East Knoyle is a very pretty village of stone and brick houses close enough to the A303 for convenience, far enough from it not to be troubled by its noise. Its stone church stands on a grassy knoll nestled among yews. An interesting display inside the door shows how it has been expanded and restored over the centuries since the Norman chancel was built. Dr Christopher Wren, father of Wren of St Paul's, was Rector of East Knoyle, and left his mark on the walls of the chancel in the unusual form of a series of plaster reliefs showing the Apostles attending the Ascension of Christ. On the north wall is a kneeling figure with hands upraised in prayer which is believed to be Dr Wren himself. An unswerving Royalist throughout those turbulent times, his artwork landed him in trouble when the Roundheads reached the village. They took a dim view of what they regarded as idolatrous image-making, and the soldiers turfed him out. He was accused of heretical practices by a Parliamentary commission and deprived of the living.

The other Wren

There is a modest tablet near the church door in memory of thirteen members of the Foliot family 'who for upwards of a century occupied Knoyle Down and other farms' – the last of them Anne Foliot, who died in 1867 at the age of eighty-six. The stained-glass east window recalls another family of the village. Paid for by members of both Houses of Parliament, it honours George Wyndham, 'Statesman, Orator, Man of Letters and Soldier'. It was dedicated by the Bishop of Salisbury on 9 May 1934, twenty-one years after its subject's death. The window makes no mention of the circumstances of his passing – understandably so, since Wyndham's cousin, the poet Wilfred Scawen Blunt, who knew a thing or two about such matters, alleged that it was caused by a heart attack brought on by energetic love-making in a Paris brothel.*

Much of the story of the Wyndhams of East Knoyle is the story of their famous house, Clouds. Widely regarded as one of the masterpieces of the late nineteenth-century

---

* A pompous marble memorial in the chancel records another East Knoyle association, this time with the Seymours, a junior branch of the Seymours of Wolf Hall. One of them, Henry Seymour, married as his second wife a French countess and took a house outside Paris, close to Louveciennes, where Louis XV had installed his favourite mistress, Madame du Barry, as châtelaine. She swiftly fell for Seymour's manly Wiltshire charms and they became lovers. He was moody and jealous, she was passionate and wholly indiscreet. In one of her letters she lamented: 'How cruel and unjust you are. Why must you torment a heart that cannot and shall not belong to any but you?' In August 1792, after the sacking of the Tuileries by the Paris mob and the detention of the French royal family, Seymour prudently hot-footed it back to England. His lover was less fortunate. Convicted of extravagant living and publicly mourning the King, Madame du Barry was guillotined.

Arts and Crafts movement, it stands a little way out of the village to the north, where today it serves as a treatment centre for alcohol and drug dependency. It was commissioned by George Wyndham's father, Percy, and designed by Philip Webb, a close friend and colleague of William Morris. Morris himself designed most of the fixtures and furnishings, including carpets, tablecloths, screens, curtains and upholstery. Edward Burne-Jones painted angels in the hall, the furniture was mostly Hepplewhite and Chippendale, the walls were panelled in unstained oak.

Clouds was a perfect period piece, universally admired. One night in the phenomenally cold January of 1891 a dozy maid given the job of cleaning an upstairs fireplace managed to tip live coals into a cupboard. The resulting fire reduced the house to a blackened shell, while the fire engines tried in vain to reach it on the ice-bound roads. Captain Carse of the Wiltshire Fire Brigade directed the futile attempts to contain the flames until he was prised from the ladder to which he had become frozen.

Nothing daunted, Percy Wyndham and his wife Madeline rebuilt Clouds as it had been (although without the Burne-Jones angels). It became the favourite weekend retreat of the artistically inclined and high-principled Tory toffs known as the Souls. Deep in the green Wiltshire countryside the Souls – who included Lord Curzon, Margot Asquith and Arthur Balfour as well as a gaggle of Wyndhams – cycled, played tennis, earnestly disagreed on

Irish Home Rule, and conducted discreet love affairs. These, according to Curzon's later mistress, Elinor Glyn, 'were never undertaken either for money or out of sheer lust . . . nothing was allowed to appear crude and blatant, and what were essentially ugly facts were made to seem beautiful and even admirable.'*

All the hopes of Percy and Madeline Wyndham and their friends were pinned on their eldest child, George. Seen by them and many others as a Prime Minister in the making, he had literary leanings but subordinated them to a political career that resulted in his appointment in 1900 as Chief Secretary for Ireland. Like many well-meaning Englishmen before and after him, George Wyndham was moved to a passion of pity for Irish misery and as a result became a victim of Irish tribal bitterness. He resigned after being accused by Unionists of betraying their principles. Disillusioned with public life, he retreated to East Knoyle where he adopted with gusto the life of a Tory squire: hunting, coursing hares, attending to his estate and the affairs of the Cheshire Yeomanry. He dabbled with writing, had his bust sculpted by Rodin ('a very great man . . . we run over the whole universe, lightly but deeply') and conducted a long love affair with the Countess of Plymouth, apparently with his own wife's approval.

George was forty-nine when he died. He drank too

* The exotic-looking Glyn was the subject of an oft-quoted ditty: 'Would you like to sin/With Elinor Glyn/On a tiger skin?/Or would you prefer/To err with her/On some other fur?'

much and suffered from depression and there was sadness on the part of the many who loved him that so much bright promise had not been fulfilled. His father had died two years before him, and his son – known as Perf – was killed in France a month after the outbreak of the 1914–18 war. Four other grandsons of Percy and Madeline Wyndham died in the conflict.

The last Wyndham to own Clouds was Dick, the oddest of the lot. Cyril Connolly knew him as Whips Wyndham, others as Dirty Dick or The Amateur Flagellant. He achieved a kind of immortality in Wyndham Lewis's notorious satirical novel *The Apes of God* in the character of Richard Whittington, a self-proclaimed painter of genius with a cupboard containing 'a perfect hedge of birches, drovers' whips, bamboos and martinets'. From the start Wyndham conceived a strong distaste for Clouds – possibly because he lived there during his brief and horribly miserable marriage. During the 1920s he sold as many of the contents as he could find a buyer for, and let the house (according to Wyndham Lewis, to 'rich Jews'). He painted adequately but not brilliantly, and spent his money on cars, aeroplanes, wine, modern pictures and girls prepared to put up with his keenness for handcuffs and instruments of correction.

Whips Wyndham's end combined wastefulness and absurdity in appropriate measure. After the war – in which he pottered about for a time as a captain in the Territorial Army before being overcome by alcoholism – he got a job as a foreign correspondent with a news service set up by

Ian Fleming. His first assignment was to cover the conflict in Palestine in 1948, where he was shot dead by a Jewish sniper after standing up to photograph a skirmish.*

★   ★   ★

Most rich men like to leave a mark. Sometimes – as with Clouds – it is quite discreet, a statement of taste and worth intended for family, friends and neighbours. Others are more public. William Beckford's vainglorious tower at Fonthill can be seen as a cry for attention, a plea to the society that preferred to ignore him to take him and his obsessions seriously. At Stourhead – across from Whitesheet Hill – is a monument that, on a clear day, is quite unmissable. It can be seen across a vast swathe of country, and was meant to be seen, not as a reflection of the glory of the man who put it there, but of its subject.

'I have one scheme more which will crown or top all,' the

---

* Wyndham's one success in life was a book called *The Gentle Savage*, which made something of a stir when it was published in 1936. He wrote it after a visit to southern Sudan, where an old Sandhurst chum, Jack Poole, was Assistant Commissioner. Liberally illustrated with photographs of the local Dinka tribespeople with no clothes on, the frontispiece was a painting by Wyndham of a Dinka herdsman holding a spear and displaying an impressive set of genitals. When Poole returned to England, Wyndham arranged a dinner for him in a room at the Savoy fitted for the occasion with palm trees, a camp-bed hung with a mosquito net, and two tall Africans with painted faces, spears, and loincloths in attendance. The guests were summoned by tom-toms to eat peanut soup, turtle fins, aubergines and pimenti, and pawpaw and mango fool. Afterwards they watched a film made by Poole of Dinka dances which was considered 'unsuitable for public release'.

banker Henry Hoare declared in 1762. The 'all' referred to Stourhead, the famous mansion and garden paradise he and his architects and designers had created along the vale where the Stour is born of six springs. By then the vision of house, lake, vistas of woodland and turf, obelisk, temples, grottoes, bridges and statues all blended into one glorious Classical unity was almost complete. A new king, George III, was on the throne. The messy and hugely costly Seven Years' War was over. A new age beckoned. How better to mark it, Hoare thought, than by remembering a previous age in which a great king – the greatest of them – had by his courage and wisdom and godly learning confounded England's enemies, brought peace to a war-sick people, fostered art and literature and the one true religion.

Alfred's Tower

He instructed his architect, Henry Flitcroft, to design a tower to stand, in Hoare's words, 'in that spot where Alfred settled his standard (in this day called Kingsettle Hill) after He came out from His concealment in the Isle of Athelney [near Taunton] and gave Battle and Defeat to the Danes.' Never mind that no one knows for sure where the standard was raised or where Alfred met the lords of Somerset, Dorset and Wiltshire and their men to begin the decisive march against the Danes; or, indeed, where exactly the battle took place (long referred to as Ethandune, its likeliest location is at Edington Hill on the northern edge of Salisbury Plain). Henry Hoare, a stout patriot, needed no convincing that the event that shaped the course of history took place on his land.

From a distance King Alfred's Tower is a dark finger raised from the woods that flow over the ridge above Stourhead. Close up it is a strange construction. Flitcroft apparently believed that its three-sided design, with rounded projections at each corner, would make it less likely to be blown over by the wind in its exposed position (another possible explanation of its shape is that the sides corresponded with the old boundaries of Dorset, Wiltshire and Somerset, which certainly come together hereabouts). It stands on a sandstone base and is built of red brick, rising 160 feet to a crenellated top with a bulbous projection at the southern apex. There is a statue of the King in a stone recess above the entrance, standing as if about to address his troops before battle with one arm across his breast and his sword at his side. According to Hoare's account, it was executed 'by a young lad of eighteen . . . sent from Bath, working from a model given to him, to the Admiration of all the Spectators'.

By the time the tower was finished in 1772, the bright promise of George III's first years was fading and the disastrous American War of Independence was looming. But even if Henry Hoare's hopes of a new Alfredian golden age were disappointed, his tower did not. It chimed in nicely with a new vogue for what connoisseurs weary of the symmetries of Palladianism were calling 'the sublime'. Height was an important element of sublimity because it excited awe, and few monuments had more of it than King Alfred's Tower. The association between it and its subject's lofty character and accomplishments was the cause of much satisfaction to its owner.

Whatever the architectural merits of Hoare's act of hero worship, the vista it offers is indeed sublime. The tower rises from a grassy terrace lapped by the ash and beech trees of Selwood Forest. To the east, beyond Stourhead, loom the whale-backed bare downs of Salisbury Plain. To the north and north-west spreads a patchwork of green fields, sharply defined by their hedges, dotted with farms and barns, dabbed with woods and copses, fingered by the darker, wandering lines of brooks and ditches. I could clearly make out Hinkley Point power station on the Bristol Channel thirty-five miles away, with the hump of Glastonbury Tor halfway between. Cadbury Castle stood out to the west, while to the south, reaching towards Dorchester, lay the Vale of Blackmore.

This is the heart of Wessex. Under Alfred, of course, it was the Kingdom of the West Saxons, a political entity formed sometime in the sixth century and gradually expanded until it covered much of what we know as Hampshire, Wiltshire, Dorset, Somerset and Berkshire. It had its capital at Winchester and was sufficiently powerful and cohesive to repel a succession of Viking invaders. The Saxons built churches as well as warships and defensive walls, and their language became the language of learning, developing into the Old English of *Beowulf* and the basis of the English we speak now. Under Alfred's successors Wessex annexed Mercia and East Anglia, so that by 927 AD there was a single kingdom of England extending from Northumbria to Cornwall. After the Norman invasion, Wessex ceased even to be an earldom, and vanished from the map.

But not the idea, apparently. If you believe today's Wessex enthusiasts – Wessexians? – this was merely dormant for a remarkably long time. A joint submission in 2002 from the Wessex Constitutional Convention, the Wessex Society, and the Wessex Regionalists stated: 'It is not possible to say whether during the centuries after the Norman Conquest Wessex remained in the region's folk memory or not. This is not the kind of information with which records of that time were concerned.' Quite so. On the other hand one might have thought that, had the

Wessex dimension been afloat, it might have got at least a mention from the one or other of the many poets, story-tellers, historians, antiquarians and fantasists active in the area over those centuries.

It took a novelist, Thomas Hardy, to put Wessex back on the map. Indeed, a map was included in the later editions of the sequence he called the Wessex Novels. It is pretty clear that Hardy regarded it as a marketing ploy rather than a deep-rooted response to a long-felt regional identity. In a preface to *Far from the Madding Crowd* he said that because a single county (which would have been his own, Dorset) did not 'afford a canvas large enough' to accommodate what he had in mind, he had 'disinterred' Wessex. 'The press and the public,' he wrote, 'were kind enough to welcome the fanciful plan, willingly joining me in the anachronism of imagining a Wessex population living under Queen Victoria.' Subsequently, rather to his irritation, his concept took on a life of its own: 'The appellation which I had thought to reserve to the horizons of a partly real, partly dream-country has, by degrees, solidified into a utilitarian region which people can go to, take a house in, and write to the papers from. But I ask all good and gentle readers to forget this . . .'

In vain. The dream-country evolved into a crusade. After Hardy's death a group of now largely forgotten poets, critics and assorted men and women of letters got together to produce a journal promoting his vision of a University of Wessex. Under the editorship of Vivian de Sola Pinto, it provided a mirror reflecting a sentimental, nostalgic yearning for a lost England. It was full of sonnets by the likes of Samuel Gurney Dixon: 'I watched a rain-cloud stoop with queenly grace/To greet the solitary sun-scorched hill' etc., and earnest ponderings on the nature of Wessex, usually referred to at some point as 'the heart of England'. Hardy himself was well aware that 'his' Wessex had been overtaken by the modern, urban industrial society. The rural world in which he grew up depended for its culture and community spirit on its isolation. Once that was broken down, the old ways became anachronistic curiosities clung to because of their sentimental associations.

The Annual Record of the Movement for a University of Wessex did not last long, but the sentiments behind it proved to have more stamina. In the 1970s the media's favourite eccentric aristocrat, the hirsute, polygamous Marquess of Bath, formed the Wessex Regionalists. Their cause was self-government for a Wessex enlarged to include Oxfordshire and Gloucestershire. Judged by the severe standard of electoral support, the impact of the Wessex Regionalists has been modest. The highpoint was the near-2000 vote achieved in Westbury in the 1979 election (Lord Bath himself contested Wells and got 155). The party fought seven seats in 1979 and ten in 1983. Since then its fortunes have waned to the extent that in each of the last six general elections it has fielded no more than one candidate, never doing better than the 223 votes gained at Devizes in 2017.

You might deduce from this that most people in Berkshire, Devon, Dorset, Hampshire, Somerset, Wiltshire, Oxfordshire and Gloucestershire do not regard themselves as having a great deal in common and are not interested in self-government. I am sure you are right, and the same goes for the rest of England. But the crusade does not die. The Wessex Society – patrons included the late clarinettist Acker Bilk, as well as Lord Bath – flies a bright red flag decorated with a wyvern, and proclaims the vigour of Wessex culture. This embraces the dialect – 'the purest form of English' – as well as cider and the melange of dub reggae, hip-hop, punk rock, acid jazz and techno disco music loosely known as the Bristol Sound. The Wessex Regionalists may struggle for votes but the Wessex brand is thriving. Wessex Water feeds the taps, Wessex Connect runs the buses, the Wessex Rivers Trust looks after the streams, Wessex Archaeology strives on behalf of buried heritage all over the country (Wessex Trains, regrettably, was swallowed up by First Great Western). Hardy's Wessex University never happened but there is a Wessex Institute of Technology in Southampton and several hundred businesses boast the Wessex marque. After a lapse of 900 years we even have an Earl and Countess of Wessex once again.

The idea of Wessex endures in a way that is different from that of Mercia, East Anglia and Northumbria. Its essence is a vague nostalgia for the disappeared past. One element might be Hardy's 'natural' rural society, a rough-handed peasantry bound together by ancient customs and shared dependence. Another might be personified by Alfred himself, embodiment of valour, chivalry, public spiritedness and Christian charity. There is an apprehension of a pure Englishness at work long ago, a feeling of something noble and selfless in ourselves that we have somehow contrived to mislay, and could perhaps – if we tried hard enough – rediscover one day.

★　★　★

After crossing the A350, the A303 runs down the side of Charnage Down towards Mere. There is a well-known watering hole in a lay-by there, the Willoughby Hedge Café, where you can get a splendidly filling breakfast at half the price you would pay at the Starbucks up the hill. There are loos and a picnic table and a grassy bank to lie upon; and if you ask her, the cheery lady doling out the bacon-egg-and-sausage baps will tell you how Chris Evans praised them on the radio and how Norman Tebbit used to stop by.

This stretch used to be enlivened by the appearance in an adjoining field of a life-sized bison made from plywood. For thirteen summers the creature surveyed the scene and advertised the presence of bison at a farm at West Knoyle. Then, in June 2007, the owners of the farm received a letter from some busybody at Salisbury District Council telling them to remove the beast or face a fine. 'It's bureaucracy gone mad,' the farmer's wife protested. Not so, droned the council spokesman. The bison was unauthorised, the location was an area of 'outstanding natural beauty', it might 'represent a distraction to drivers'. At that time, Little Chef's Fat Charlie still beamed moronically a couple of miles up the road, presumably no distraction at all. The mad pen-pushers won the day, of course, and the bison was carted off back to the farm, where I spotted it standing under an oak tree by the entrance, unloved and unheeded.

Does no one want a bison?

One late January afternoon, having tramped the A303 for many wearying miles past Fonthill and through Chicklade and as far as Fat Charlie's annoying face, I decided I had had enough of the noise. I took the lane that leads to West Knoyle. I turned off before the bison farm for Mere, whose lights were winking across the fields. The light was almost gone as I went through Charnage, which hardly even qualifies as a hamlet. But the footpath I was looking for showed up clear enough in the gloaming and I followed it through a herd of shadowy bullocks, reaching the outskirts of Mere as the church clock struck five.

I spent the night at the George, where the bed was comfortable, the bath big enough for me, and the water hot. Charles II is said to have dined there before he was Charles II, on his flight from defeat at the Battle of Worcester in 1651. We are not told what he ate, but I doubt if it could have been better than my breaded mushrooms followed by sirloin steak washed down by four pints of Badger Bitter.

14

ALL KNIGHTLY DEEDS

A little way out of Mere the A303 leaves Wiltshire and belongs for a few miles to the northern extremity of Dorset before entering Somerset. The brief Dorset phase is not recorded on the road signs and generally occasions little fuss. The one difference I noticed as I marched along the verge was that Dorset attends closely to its footpaths. At least three cross the A303 and each has a flight of brick steps leading up and down either side of the road, plus a marked cut through the central reservation, all of which must have cost someone a bob or two. The rambler still faces a somewhat anxious dash across the two carriageways, which here run straight and smooth, encouraging cars to scorch by. It requires a cool head, a spot of nerve, and a nice sense of timing to get it right.

A couple of paths lead to Dorset's northernmost village, Bourton. The Stour runs down to it from Stourhead, and although the stream is only a few feet wide it had enough latent energy to be exploited to Bourton's advantage. The mill listed in Domesday subsequently evolved into a complex comprising a flax mill and a foundry. More than 200 people worked there, and it was a proud moment in Bourton's history when a water wheel sixty feet high – then the largest in the country – was installed in the 1830s (some say it was the second-largest, but Bourtonians know better). The business was owned by a local family, the Maggs brothers, and towards the end of the nineteenth century it concentrated on the foundry where agricultural machinery, water pumps, steam engines and the like were manufactured.

The outbreak of war in 1914 meant a new role for the company, now Maggs and Hindley. A clever young engineer from Sunderland, William Mills, had developed a hand-held grenade known as the Mills bomb. Its serrated casing made it easy to grip and fragmented to lethal effect when it exploded. The troops were taught to adapt their cricketing skills to lob them at the enemy, and it is estimated that 70 million were used up to 1918. Factories all over the country went over to making the Mills bomb, among them the Bourton Foundry, although production there came to an abrupt halt on an infamous June day in 1917, when a tremendous thunderstorm set off a flood which destroyed much of the factory and washed hundreds of bombs far downstream.

By then the mighty water wheel was gone, and the company's fortunes subsequently went into decline. After various later incarnations – one as a dried milk plant – it closed in 2002 and was left to rot. It was a sad but evocative sight when I was there: abandoned rusting turbines and boilers and crankshafts, walls covered in witless graffiti, roofs collapsed, rubble and smashed beams heaped everywhere – all later cleared away to make room for a housing development. Just above the mill pool a surviving member of the Maggs family occupied a house with a pair of model Mills bombs on the gateposts. Outside the gate was an odd little tiled well-cover over a pair of blue china boots bearing the inscription, 'Faeces Tauros Sapientia Vincit'. My knowledge of Latin is not what it once was but even I could work out the sentiment, though why anyone should wish to commemorate the triumph of wisdom over bullshit in such a way was beyond me.

The Stour is hidden in a tunnel immediately below Bourton Foundry but emerges into the daylight a little way further on. I spent some time on the bridge inspecting it, for I can never resist a stream. Here it has covered two of the sixty miles that take it to the sea at Christchurch. It is very small and you wonder how – even in the days before abstraction when our rivers generally ran much fuller – it could ever have powered the mighty wheel. It flows quick and dark, although the water is clear: another clue to the transformation in the landscape between here and the chalkland to the east. The chalk has given way to a form of sandstone known as greensand which breaks down over the ages into fertile loam and clay. It makes for a greener, softer land.

From Bourton I followed the 'old' A303 out of Dorset and up a gentle but persistent hill to Wincanton. All roads south led to Stoke Trister, a village I imagined to be prey to congenital melancholy. I went into a café just off Wincanton's High Street for a bacon roll and a cup of tea. It was run by a young Portuguese man, and the TV was tuned to a Portuguese discussion programme. I sat next to a set of shelves stacked with dried beans and tinned fish and other foodstuffs from Portugal, listening to three Wincanton ladies discussing husbands and soap operas. I did wonder about the Portuguese dimension, but the provider of my bacon sandwich did not seem to understand my question.

Wincanton is, apparently, the only town in England to boast a twinning link with a fictional place – Ankh-Morpork, which features in the *Discworld* novels of Terry Pratchett. With the author's approval, some of the titles of the novels were adapted into street names in the housing development that now fills the space between the old market town and the A303 bypass to the south. Disappointingly, the twinning initiative seems to have been a marketing ploy dreamed up by PR people hired by the building company Wimpey, rather than a reflection of a particular burning enthusiasm among the people of Wincanton for Sir Terry's work. But the town has done its best to join in; for a time the local butchers rebranded its popular wild boar and cranberry sausages as Discworld sausages, and the Discworld Emporium in the high street advertises itself as 'the official Ankh-Morpork consulate'.

Never having read a *Discworld* novel and having no means to cook a banger, I did not linger. I had the sniff of older adventures and nobler chivalry in my nostrils.

★ ★ ★

There was a time, not so long ago, when it was still possible to believe that there had once been a King Arthur, a Camelot, a Round Table, a company of Knights.

The Reverend James Bennett was one such believer. For twenty-six years until his death in 1890 he served as Rector of South Cadbury, a village just south of the A303. As well as ministering to the souls of his little parish, Bennett had a passion for deciphering and dating ancient ecclesiastical rolls and legal documents, and was a dedicated member of the Somerset Archaeological and Natural History Society. In short, he was a model Victorian enthusiast for the past. In the words of the sweet and affectionate obituary in the Society's *Journal*, 'his vivacity and eager interest, readiness to receive and impart information, sunny good humour, with occasional vigorous thrusts and sharp retorts, but ever genial sympathy, will leave a long and pleasant remembrance of the friend who has been taken from us.'

For Bennett and others of his admirable breed, history was living tissue, and the past was a land peopled by flesh-and-blood heroes and villains. His imagination was stirred by the echoes of deeds of valour and chivalry. How could it be otherwise when the ramparts of Camelot rose from outside the very windows of his rectory?

Cadbury Castle – even more so than Yarnbury Castle, back up the A303 – is a natural stronghold, a place to fortify and look down on your enemies, not a place to relish attacking. It is shaped a bit like a conker, with sides whose testing steepness is concealed by a belt of sycamore and ash. It levels at the top into a smooth meadow like a monk's tonsure big enough in times past to have been worth ploughing, although it is now left to grass. Four lines of still formidable bank-and-ditch loop around the summit, with a break on the south-west side where the entrance was positioned.

Is it Cadbury? Or Camelot? Or both?

Henry VIII's itinerant recorder of the nation's wonders, John Leland, started the mischief about Camelot. He inspected Cadbury in 1542, and wrote his record thus:

> Sometime a famose town or castelle, apon a very torre or hille, wonderfully enstrengthened of nature . . . much gold, sylver and copper of the Romaine coynes hath byn found ther yn plouing . . . the people can telle nothing ther but that they hav hard say that Artur much resorted to Camalat.

'Hav hard say' hardly qualifies as reliable source material. Nor is Leland's citing of the nearby villages of Queen Camel and West Camel in support of his 'Camalat' any more convincing.

Leland's successor, William Camden, also reported that 'the local people call it Arthur's Palace', though he clearly did not believe them. The Druidical William Stukeley, a century and a half after Camden, asserted that the name Camelot 'generally obtained among the learned' and that 'the country people are ignorant of it.'

But Leland's seed germinated and took root. By the time James Bennett succeeded his father as rector, the country people believed entirely in Camelot and a great deal else. The hill, they said, was hollow – a gentle clap over the well on the eastern face could be clearly heard at a spring on the opposite side. The fairies, they said, lived there and left their gold behind them when the fitting of bells at the church forced them to abandon the hill. When the moon was full, they said, Arthur and his men rode around on horses shod in silver, and watered their animals at the well; and at Christmas came down to the village of Sutton Montis to use the spring by the church wall.

The rector listened to these tales and doubtless smiled. But his soul was roused. 'There is no smoke without fire,' he wrote about the legends. He went in search of evidence to support his conviction that 'the peaceful green mounds of Cadbury were once a living city, the very heart of the life of a gallant race of men.' He had a trench dug below the crown of the hill in which he found considerable quantities of pottery – and the deeper they dug, the coarser it became. From this Bennett deduced that 'the rude race that began it had to give way to another in a higher state of civilisation.'

But whose civilisation? Bennett also uncovered Roman coins. It was known that the Roman era had ended in the fifth century AD, and that the Saxon invasions had started soon after. But who came in between? Bennett posited a 'British' kingdom protected by the Mendips in the north, the great forest of Selwood in the west, and 'the trackless valley of the Stour' to the south. After the taking of Sarum (Salisbury) by the Saxons in the middle of the sixth century, the Britons had withdrawn west making Cadbury their new capital. Their leaders were 'such men as the race has loved to sing of in the story of Arthur, Geraint and all the noble knights.' But the Saxons would not be denied. Arthur beat them at Mount Badon, which Bennett placed at Badbury Rings in south Dorset. They came again, and were beaten again, at Cathbregion (Cadbury). Back they came, and at last they triumphed and bested the great British king, who was slain and whose body was carried to Avalon (Glastonbury).

Bennett located the last stand of the ancient Britons and their leader in a little valley to the south-east of Camelot/Cadbury. The place is called Sigwells, from 'siege-quelle' which he translates as 'Victory Springs'. He imagined 'the Saxon host panting and weary from the long, hot fight here stopping a while to drink' before chasing the enemy up the ramparts of Cadbury and slaughtering them where they stood. In a field called Westwoods at the foot of the western side of Cadbury were trenches filled with the bodies of men and boys. 'Here, it seems,' wrote Bennett, 'we have the graves of the last of the Britons of Camelot.'

The rector's castle of imagining was built on a shifting sand of dubious chronologies and dodgy etymologies. But he had unwittingly stumbled upon one important clue. Later analysis of the pottery he found showed that Cadbury had indeed been occupied in pre-Roman times as well as by the Romans themselves. Ploughing of the crown of the hill in the 1950s turned up more remains, some Neolithic and some Iron Age, but most intriguingly some fragments of pottery contemporaneous with pottery found at Tintagel in Cornwall and dated to the fifth or sixth century AD. This was the age of the Round Table. Back onto the public stage galloped Arthur, Launcelot, Geraint, Merlin and the rest.

Between 1966 and 1970 the secrets of Camelot were laid bare by a team of archaeologists led by Professor Leslie Alcock of Cardiff University. They were able to show that the hill had been occupied for several hundred years before the Romans arrived. For some unknown reason it had been unused for much of the Roman period. Then – thrillingly – it was reoccupied around 500 AD and remained in use for the best part of a century. During that period the fortifications were mightily strengthened with a stone top or even an added wall. A gatehouse was built at the south-west corner over a cobbled access road. At the highest point of the hill, the archaeologists revealed the foundations of a great timber hall, inevitably named Arthur's Palace.

The coincidences were almost too good to be true. At the very least, Cadbury/Camelot had been the military headquarters of a powerful and wealthy warlord, and it took no time for the Arthurian connection to be made. Thousands of tourists gathered to watch the digging. Some colourful and excitable press coverage was exploited in a calculated fashion – principally to attract funds – by the organisers of the dig, who called themselves the Camelot Research Committee. Professor Alcock himself, in a book which he wrote at high speed as soon as the excavation was over and called *By South Cadbury Is That Camelot*, referred to Camelot as 'a place that never was.' But what about Arthur? The spirit of the Reverend James Bennett must have been in the air, because Professor Alcock declared himself a believer.

In later years he came to regret his boldness, as a succession of medievalists and archaeologists exposed each and every one of the written sources attesting to the historical Arthur as being riddled with absurdities. Arthur the great king who fought the Saxons and defended the ancient British virtues has steadily receded into the mist. But Arthur the legend, Arthur the fabulous, Arthur the idea – that Arthur is immortal.

What was President John F. Kennedy's favourite song? It came from Lerner and Loewe's Arthurian musical extravaganza:

> Don't let it be forgot
> That there once was a spot
> For one brief shining moment
> That was known as Camelot.

Soon after Kennedy's funeral his widow gave an interview to Theodore White during which she played the song over and over again. White wrote later that Kennedy's association with Camelot 'represented a magic moment in American history when gallant men danced with beautiful women, when great deeds were done, when artists, writers and poets met at the White House, and the barbarians beyond the walls held back.'

I feel that the erstwhile rector of South Cadbury and the assassinated American president would have recognised each other as kindred spirits.

North Cadbury stands across the A303 from South Cadbury. It is not as imposing, but still represented a taxing ascent at the end of a trudge that had begun the day before beyond Wylye, and when the one bus of the afternoon to the railway station at Castle Cary was imminent. It has a fine church and an even finer manor house, Elizabethan in origin, whose high windows look to Camelot across the ceaseless movement of the road. Apart from the traffic noise, North Cadbury is a quiet place and there was not a soul to be seen when I came into the village with a good ten minutes before the bus was due. It has two main streets, one heading north, one breaking off to the east. But which had the bus stop?

Eventually I spotted a postman doing his deliveries and I urged my blistered feet after him as he negotiated his van from house to house down the street past the church. When I finally caught up with him and gasped out my question he was nonplussed. Bus? He'd never seen one of them, certainly not down this road, mate. Maybe back on the main road. I lolloped back to the other road and heard the bus before I saw it breast the hill. I waved my arms like a shipwrecked mariner hoping for rescue, and the driver

– surprised, I think, to encounter a fare in North Cadbury – took pity on me.

Between the Cadburys the A303 curves north to circumvent Sparkford. The roundabout signifies the end (or beginning) of what is – at fourteen miles – the second-longest stretch of dual carriageway after Popham–Amesbury. It thus tends to be the target of much resentment on the part of westbound drivers and their passengers and, conversely, a place of liberation for those heading east. Between Sparkford and the start of the Ilchester bypass three miles or so further west, the road reverts to humble single-carriageway status. The Mere–Sparkford dual section was completed by the opening of the Bourton bypass in July 1992. Although no one realised it at the time, this was to be the last major upgrading of the A303. Thereafter the great vision of the London–Penzance highway was sucked into the morass of the Stonehenge issue and swallowed as if it had never been.

A similar fate overtook the road-building ambitions of the Blair government. For a while the snappy talk of 'smart choices' and 'better use options' was matched by the allocation of very considerable funds for construction. As Joe Moran has pointed out, the term 'road-building' had become dirty and was replaced by less provocative expressions – 'widening', or 'enhancement' or 'extension' or just 'improvement'. Enormous projects for widening the M25, the M6 and the M1 went through without fuss or fanfare. Labour's spending on roads was twice that proposed in the Tories' *Roads For Prosperity* blueprint. But they were canny enough to make a tenth as much noise about it.

Nevertheless the intractable realities continued to squeeze the network. The number of cars on the roads continued to increase in line with disposable incomes. Congestion worsened, but no more than any other government, Blair's would not look this situation in the face. In 2006 Alistair Darling was elevated from Transport to the Treasury, to be replaced by Douglas Alexander, another Scotsman, although not in the same league for lawyerish dullness. Alexander was keen to make a splash with exciting initiatives, among which was a £10 million project to introduce road-charging. 'If we do nothing we simply face eternal gridlock,' Alexander said grimly. They did nothing.

We knew then, as we know now, as a child could have told them, that there is one way to alleviate congestion, and that is to deter people from driving; in effect to ration it. But to do so requires a resolve – a courage, if you like – that no government has been able to summon. Blair and his ministers walked in fear of the loud and bolshy voice of Mondeo Man Middle England. This was regularly heard in the columns of the *Daily Mail* and the *Daily Express*, and pretty much non-stop on websites set up by the likes of the ABD, the Alliance of British Drivers. The ABD is for 'drivers who THINK for themselves', and its mission is to speak out fearlessly and at high volume on behalf of the bullied and exploited and previously mute British motorist. The ABD fulminated against fuel tax, speed bumps, the traffic police and their mobile speed checks, the hated cameras, environmental campaigners (particularly those of the global warming tendency), and the reluctance of the powers-that-be to spend enough on building new roads. The mention of road tolls is sufficient to send the ABD's committee of Mondeo Men wild.

Mr Alexander and his colleagues immediately lost their nerve. He did what ministers do when trying to disguise inaction as a dynamic, carefully considered and meticulously costed new policy, and ordered a review. By the time it was completed and published, Mr Alexander had been shunted off by Gordon Brown (at last Prime Minister) to take charge of International Development. His replacement was Ruth Kelly, previously regarded as one of the party's rising stars but at that time – July 2007 – levelling off in preparation for disappearing from the political landscape altogether. The review found that the Department of Transport's procedure for considering and adopting new road schemes was a joke. Any relationship between projected and actual costs was accidental. The programme set out by Tony Blair in 2004 was unaffordable. The words in his foreword – 'where it makes economic sense . . .the long-term solution lies in the sustained programme of investment and innovation started under this government and the courage to take difficult decisions' – chimed with more than usual hollowness. The appendix to the 2007 review listed a modest number of projects that would proceed, mainly for widening motorways. The A303 did not feature.

★ ★ ★

Beneath Sparkford Hill the road heads south-west for Ilchester. To the north unfolds a flat, tranquil tract of green, hedged fields broken by patches of woodland and traversed by narrow, wandering lanes. The exception is the rulered line of the Fosse Way, which cuts north-east towards Shepton Mallet.* A dark little stream, the Cary, winds an unhurried course through the meadows north-west of the junction between the Roman road and the A303 at Podimore. It lends its name to a place of extraordinary, almost unreal beauty.

It is called Lytes Cary, the first part of the name belonging to the family that occupied it for 500 years until financial pressures proved too much for them in the middle of the eighteenth century. Different Lytes left their mark at different times: the little three-windowed chapel built in 1343; the manor house and Great Hall with its beefy chimney-stacks, dating from the fifteenth century; the oriel, entrance porch and parlour added in the reign of Henry VIII. They are built of the local blue lias stone, and of hamstone from the Ham Hill quarry, a few miles down the A303. Over the centuries they have grown together as

* Perhaps the best-known Roman road in Britain, the Fosse Way extends more than 180 miles between Exeter and Lincoln.

if they had risen from the dark Somerset soil. Together with the severely formal gardens and the orchard added in the early twentieth century, they – in Pevsner's words – 'blend to perfection with one another and the gentle sunny landscape that surrounds them'.

Lytes Cary

The Lytes were an English family of a particular kind. They were not aristocrats, they did not aspire to assist in empire-building or slaughtering the monarch's enemies, they did not seek to ally themselves with powerful dynasties. They were gentry, intensely proud of their lineage and their land, and were generally content to stay quietly at home, glorying in their bloodline, attending to their tenants, their acres and their fine old house. They were clever, educated, and somewhat prone to innocuous battiness.

The only one to cause any ripples beyond Somerset

was Henry Lyte, who was born in 1529. According to the famously venomous diarist Anthony à Wood, Henry travelled extensively abroad after leaving Oxford and became a 'most excellent scholar in several sorts of learning'. In 1578 he published his *Herbal, or History of Plantes*, which was based on his own translation, extensively annotated, of a Dutch text. It was a mighty volume of more than 700 pages and was popular enough to go into several later editions.

Henry Lyte's other published literary work was a much more modest and eccentric affair. It consisted of twenty-six small pages, one of which bore a portrait of Queen Elizabeth and another a woodcut of the Lyte family crest, a chevron with three swans beneath another swan with the motto *Laetitia et Spe Immortalitatis*.* It was called *The Light of Britayne, a Recorde of the Honourable Originall and Antiquitie of Britaine*, and it attempted to prove, through the author's ingenious etymological deductions, that the British were descended from the Trojans. Two subsequent treatises – both unpublished – developed the theme. Henry Lyte also compiled a table which showed how 'Lyte of Lytescarie sprang from the race and stock of Leitus (one of the five capitaynes of Beotia that went to Troye) and that his ancestors came to England first with Brute' – 'Brute' being Brutus, a descendant of the Trojan hero Æneas, whom Henry

---

* 'Through joy and in hope of immortality'.

Lyte credited with the founding of Bruton, a town north-west of Castle Cary.

In a history of the family published in 1910, Sir Henry Maxwell Lyte commented of his Trojan forbear: 'How a man capable of such scholarlike work as the translation of Dodoen's *Herbal* could occupy himself with fancies of this sort is a psychological problem.' I could not have put it better myself.

Limington Church

A few miles south of Lytes Cary, on the other side of the A303, is a village called Limington. There is a nice old church there, with a sturdy, square tower. Two effigies lie side by side in the north chapel: those of Sir Richard de Gyverney, Lord of the Manor in 1329, and his wife Gunnora. Sir Richard is in full armour, with bascinet, vambrace, couters, hauberk and gambeson (the knightly idioms are irresistible), and there are flecks of the original turquoise paint still visible.

But Limington's chief claim to notice does not reside in the recumbent knight and the fair Gunnora, but in the rector instituted – so the parish register records – on 10 October 1500. He was the son of a butcher, born in faraway Ipswich, and his destiny was to become the most powerful figure in the country after the king himself (and there were those who disputed that order of precedence). Thomas Wolsey secured the living at Limington because it was in the gift of the Marquess of Dorset, whose sons he tutored at Oxford and on whom he lavished his considerable talent for flattery. Subsequently Wolsey accumulated clerical offices as other men collect butterflies or pewter mugs, and he was not inclined to boast of the rectorship of an obscure parish in Somerset. But he could not shake off the place altogether: a story connected with it stuck to him like a birthmark.

It was said that one day he attended the fair at Lopen, a village down the Fosse Way to the south-west; that he was drunk and excessively merry; even that he pinched a female bottom or two. His conduct came to the attention of the Sheriff of Dorset and Somerset, Sir Amyas Paulet, a distinguished soldier who had fought for Henry VII against the Yorkist rebels at Stoke Field in 1487. Sir Amyas ordered the boisterous rector to be placed in the stocks by his feet, an indignity made all the worse because, under the law, he had no right of jurisdiction over a priest. Wolsey did not forget.

The historian Clarendon takes up the tale: 'When Wolsey mounted the dignity of Chancellor of England he was not oblivious of the old displeasure ministered unto him by Master Paulet but sent for him and after many sharp and heinous words enjoined him to attend upon the council until he were by them dismissed . . . so that he continued within the Middle Temple the space of five or six years or more.' Other reports suggest that Sir Amyas was accused of fomenting heresy through his position as Treasurer of the Middle Temple. Eventually he was able to appease Wolsey by paying for a splendid new gateway for the Temple which prominently displayed the Chancellor's badge.

'Who would have thought,' commented Clarendon sententiously, 'that when Sir Amyas Paulet punished this poor scholar that he would have attained to be Chancellor of England considering his baseness in every condition . . . these be wonderful works of God and fortune.'

Indeed they be.

★ ★ ★

So to Ilchester on the old road, the A303 far enough away to the north to be inaudible. It was a long plod in the fading light of a February afternoon, much of it past the high fence surmounted with razor wire that defends the Royal Navy Air Station, Yeovilton. These days the likelihood of a ground attack against our military installations seems remote, but they all have these fences, so there must be a reason.

These places are very distinct; they could not be confused with a university, say, or a boarding school or prison or some other institution where people live and work. It's partly to do with the glimpses of blokes and occasionally women in uniform, partly with the fondness for displaying military memorabilia to remind passers-by what their business is – in the case of RNAS Yeovilton, a superannuated helicopter here and there. They are also distinguished by their disorderly appearance, which is curiously at odds with the model of the serviceman or woman on parade. There is no planning, in the conventional sense of trying to make a large complex appear tidy and vaguely pleasant to the eye. Everything at Yeovilton – offices, accommodation blocks, runways, football pitches, fuel tanks, hangars – looks as if it had been thrown down wherever the need for it has arisen, by people with their minds on other matters. The resulting mess is a statement: we have the space, we help ourselves, we haven't the time for looking nice.

As the darkness gathered, the orange lights lining the perimeter of the base and the roadways and verges and standing at every corner grew brighter. Overhead, the granite sky was pricked by the clear front lights and winking red tail-lights of Lynx helicopters returning from training flights. I passed the main gates, guarded on either side by mighty anchors that once held HMS *Ark Royal* and HMS *Eagle* steady against storms and tides as they defended the nation's interests across the Seven Seas. My hips and knees ached and my blisters – one on the ball of each foot – smarted as my steps slowly closed the distance between me and the beer, the sustaining food and the welcoming bed for which my soul was yearning.

Outside RNAS Yeovilton

15

ROMAN WAYS, BLOODY ASSIZES

It may be that Edward Hutton had a bilious attack or suffered some kind of outrage when he visited Ilchester in preparation for writing his *Highways and Byways in Somerset*. Normally a warm-hearted as well as a splendidly inquisitive guide, he does not have a good word to say about the place. 'An ancient decayed town with very little to interest the traveller' is his grumpy verdict. He concedes that Ilchester had 'some importance' in medieval times, due to its position on the Fosse Way. But now (in 1912), Hutton says, it is once more what it was when the Romans built the road, namely 'a poor and unimportant village'.

He quotes John Leland, who found it 'in wonderful decay as a thing in a manner raised by men of war'. Of the old buildings and monuments described by Leland, three of the four parish churches, the Roman walls, the town gate, the Dominican Priory, the Augustinian nunnery, the Hospital of St Margaret, the almshouses, the Guildhall and

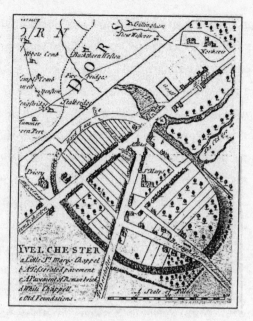

Ilchester, 1736

even the gaol – all had been destroyed. Hutton makes it sound like a charge sheet. Only the Church of St Mary Major ('small . . . contains little to attract us') and the Market Cross ('merely a fine and lofty pillar crowned by a sundial') had survived Ilchester's neglect of itself. Its sole glory, Hutton declares, is the memory of its one great son, the medieval scholar and mage Roger Bacon.

Hutton's deepest scorn is reserved for Ilchester's Roman pretensions – 'a fictitious greatness . . . that never belonged to it,' he snorts. He was plain wrong, although he was not to know it, since the excavations that revealed Ilchester's very considerable importance as a Roman trading centre did not begin until the late 1940s and were not fully described until the 1980s. In fact *Lindinis* or *Lendiniae* was a substantial walled settlement built around a junction between the Fosse Way and two other roads – one leading to Dorchester, the other going north-west – with a grid of residential streets and ribbon development leading to suburbs on the higher ground to the south-east and north-west. By the fourth century AD Ilchester covered an area of fifty acres. Its centre was densely filled with stone dwellings, some of which boasted that defining measure of Roman affluence, mosaic floors. Evidence has been uncovered pointing to the existence of a glassworks, metal works, builder's yard and at least one farm. River trade almost certainly played a major role in the town's commercial life. Several cemeteries have been identified, one containing at least 1500 dead Romans.

Unlike Edward Hutton, I warmed at once to Ilchester. This may have had something to do with finding a friendly bed-and-breakfast which provided me with a limb-caressing hot bath, a mattress sprung ideally between resilience and give, and a sustaining fried breakfast (home-made fig jam with my toast) that set me up perfectly for the next day's labours. It may also have had something to do with the steak-and-ale pie and several pints of Great Bustard Bitter that I put away for supper in the Bull Inn. My opinion was most certainly influenced by Ilchester's river, which flows in from the east, chatters cheerfully beneath its handsome seven-arched stone bridge, and winds away past one of the Roman cemeteries.

Edward Hutton was not much of a water man, though very strong on churches. He notes bridges but does not linger on them, which shows he cannot have been an angler. To me a bridge with water underneath it is simply irresistible, and I enjoyed Ilchester's both on the evening of my arrival and on the morning of my departure – my one complaint being the amount of traffic using it, presumably generated by the Yeovilton base.

Ilchester persists in calling its river the Ivel, while everyone else prefers to call it the Yeo. Ilchester has antiquity on its side – Ivel is of Celtic origin – but not much else; and one wonders why it does not call itself Gifelecestre (as it was in the fourteenth century) if it is so keen on the old names.

Call it Ivel or Yeo

Whatever you call it, the stream alternates pleasingly between still, reedy pools and speedy shallows, the water clear over a dark, marly bed and highly suggestive of good artisan fish like chub and perch. It is eventually subsumed into the Parrett at Langport away to the north-west. The Parrett is one of the few rivers in this country on which commercial fishing for elvers, infant eels, still takes place. Since eels migrate far up rivers, as well as to the Sargasso Sea, an eel connection for Ilchester (?Eelchester), may be presumed. As a keen eel fancier myself, you may imagine that my interest quickened when I came across a reference to the Ilchester Eel Fair. I pictured a quaint celebration of country ways with its origins lost in the mists of time – perhaps a procession with eel spears to a favoured spot on the river, or an eel dance or eel song. To my disappointment, I found out that the Eel Fair was a recent and short-lived promotional exercise dreamed up with the ostensible objective of raising money to restore a dilapidated eel trap somewhere upstream, although in the end the funds went to provide flowerbeds on one of Ilchester's roundabouts.

For a long time Ilchester was Somerset's official county town. As such it had the county gaol, which stood on a damp piece of ground on the east side of the Ivel/Yeo just downstream from the bridge. Hutton complained that it was entirely gone by 1912. In fact some fragments of wall do survive, but nothing to suggest the imposing scale of this grim institution where up to 270 inmates – men, women and children – were confined until its eventual closure in the 1840s.

The town was also the appointed scene of executions. Traditionally these took place on common ground beside the road and were the occasions of riotous merrymaking on the part of the locals, who called them 'hang-fairs'. In time, the scenes of drunken disorder became such that the authorities ordered the gallows to be moved to the gaol, where they were installed on top of the entrance block. The decision prompted one Ilchester innkeeper to declare: ' Damn me if Ilchester is worth living in without there are hang-fairs and good elections' – the latter reference was to its reputation as one of the rottenest boroughs in the land. A good view could still be had, however, either from the wharves across the river or from the bridge, which was invariably packed with spectators on execution days.

Between 1808 and 1822, Ilchester Gaol was run by William Bridle, previously chief mate on the *Retribution*, one of the convict ships moored in the Thames off Woolwich. The seventeenth of May 1820 was an evil day in the life of Mr Bridle. At ten o'clock that night he took delivery of one of the most notorious troublemakers in the kingdom. He had no inkling of it at the time, but it was the prelude to his eventual ruin and disgrace.

The prisoner was Henry Hunt, widely known as 'Orator' Hunt. Described by Captain Gronow in his celebrated *Memoirs* as 'a large, powerfully-made fellow who might have been mistaken for a butcher', Hunt was the son of a well-to-do Wiltshire farmer. As a young man he quarrelled with his father, married the daughter of an innkeeper in Devizes, had two children by her before eloping with his best friend's wife, and served a prison sentence for challenging the colonel in charge of the Marlborough Troop to a duel. He later joined William Cobbett, John Horne Tooke, Sir Francis Burdett and other reforming spirits in challenging the political establishment, and embarked upon a career as a tub-thumping firebrand whose creed embraced universal suffrage, the repeal of the Corn Laws, annual parliaments and voting by ballot.

William Bridle, Gaoler

On 16 August 1819, Hunt was due to deliver some rabble-rousing to an enormous crowd that had gathered at St Peter's Field in Manchester. The local magistrates, fearful of a riot, banned the meeting. When that order was ignored they ordered a mounted force drawn from the Manchester and Salford Yeomanry to arrest Hunt. The horsemen charged the crowd with swords drawn. At least eleven people were killed and between 400 and 700 were injured in what the radical newspaper, the *Manchester Observer*, dubbed the Peterloo Massacre. Hunt himself had his trademark white topper bashed in, but escaped the mêlée unhurt. He was charged with sedition, and the following spring was sentenced to spend two years at Ilchester Gaol.

Initially the Orator seemed content with a quiet life of confinement, and devoted himself to writing his incredibly prolix and tedious memoirs (the three volumes he managed to complete got him no further than 1812). But his nature was to make mischief wherever he could, and a year after his arrival at Ilchester, a London printer produced a one-shilling 24-page pamphlet entitled *A Peep into a Prison – or the Inside of Ilchester Bastile*. It was anonymous, but everyone knew that the author was the prison's most celebrated inmate.

Society in Hunt's day expected their prisons to be severe, horrible places. But the picture he painted shocked – and was carefully designed to shock – their hardened hearts. Indecencies between male and female prisoners in church on the Sabbath; debtors 'having connexion' with their wives in the privy or on a table in the tap-room; carousals, dancing and gambling on election nights; boys as young as seven sharing a bed with male inmates, one of them a convicted bestialist; cruel and unusual punishments, including shaving a manacled prisoner's head and applying an 'irritable pungent' to blister it and chaining a man's hands to his feet so that he 'resembled a parachute'.

Hunt also laid formal charges against Gaoler Bridle. Among the twenty-one accusations were: gross neglect of duty, drunkenness, gambling, 'swearing horrid oaths', absence from Divine service, dancing with 'women of the town' on election night, encouraging 'drunkenness, debauchery and riot', cruelty, stealing prisoners' provisions, embezzling candles, compelling boys to sleep with men, fathering at least one bastard, and altering the Occurrence Book to 'hoodwink the magistrates'.

Bridle did his best to defend himself. He produced his own account, under the snappy title *A Narrative of the Rise and Improvements Effected in His Majesty's Gaol at Ilchester in the County of Somerset Between July 1808 and Nov 1821 under the Governance and Superintendence of Wm. Bridle, Keeper.* The substance of his defence was that Hunt had turned against him after the withdrawal – by order of the magistrates, not Bridle – of exceptional privileges, which had included daily visits in his room from his mistress, Mrs Vince, and the provision of 'dinners, wine and other liquors' from the town. The result was 'a crocodile egg of mingled falsehood and villainy . . . all malice and perjury'.

It was no good. The Orator may have been hated and reviled by the Establishment, but he was listened to. He was a Somebody. Poor Bridle was a Nobody and in December 1821 he was dismissed.

The following year Hunt was released and resumed his mission of agitation, forming the Radical Reform Association with William Cobbett, although the two of them later fell out in fine agitating fashion. In 1830 he contrived to get himself elected as MP for Preston, but he soon managed to infuriate his constituents by declining to support Lord John Russell's Reform Bill on the grounds that it did not go far enough. Following his defeat in the 1833 election, the Orator concentrated his energies on the manufacture and marketing of annatto, a colouring for cheeses, as well as a new kind of boot polish. In 1835 this exceptionally quarrelsome man died of a stroke and was buried at the insistence of his mistress, Mrs Vince, in her family vault, much to the fury of her relatives.

As for the wretched William Bridle, information is scant, as you might expect with a Nobody. But there is a pathetic footnote to his life in the form of a newspaper cutting dated 12 September 1843. It records that Bridle – 'an elderly man of good address but evidently reduced to great distress' – appeared before Bow Street magistrates in London charged with using his crutch to break a window at the Home Office. The accused told the court that he had taken the action because of his state of destitution. He embarked upon an account of his undoing at the hands of Henry Hunt, which, he said, had led to his ruin. He was ordered to pay a fine of six shillings or spend six days in prison.

In that same year Ilchester Gaol was closed, and its inmates were moved to Taunton and Shepton Mallet.

★ ★ ★

The Fosse Way approaches Ilchester from the north-east as the A37, bisects it partly as an unclassified road and partly as the High Street, and departs south-west as the A303. On the OS map its name is inscribed in antique script, as if it had somehow retained its classical roots. In fact it is no more than a modern functional highway – a fast modern functional highway in the case of the A303, which has dual-carriageway status restored to it for several miles between Ilchester and South Petherton. The map also shows it pretty much dead straight, which – being Roman – it should be, since the one thing every child knows about the Romans is that they built straight roads. (There is an underlying assumption, which is that straightness equalled efficiency which equalled superiority in battle, which equalled conquest over nations reliant on winding paths and tracks.)

Actually the Fosse Way section of the A303 is not straight. If you stand on the bridge over it near Tintinhull you can see that it curves perceptibly this way and that. Furthermore, when Fosse Way and A303 part company at South Petherton, the Roman road becomes a very minor country lane heading south-west; and between the villages of Lopen and Dillington you get a excellent view of its alleged straightness. It quite clearly wiggles, in the way a ribbon or piece of string wiggles when pulled taut and then let drop. It is direct, undeniably so, but straight it is not. It follows the way of the track that preceded it, and why would it not? They were efficient, those Romans, but they were not fanatics for straightness.

Straight? I think not

I walked west from Ilchester not on the road but along the Monarch's Way,* across flat meadows where the early frost sparkled around and in between knots of sheep. I could hear the tearing, rending noise of the A303 over to

* So designated in the 1990s because the man who would be Charles II took it to flee the country after being beaten by Cromwell's forces at Worcester.

my right. A couple of times a rise in the ground interposed itself between it and me to silence the racket, and I could then hear the birdsong from the hedgerows. From Tintinhull I took a lane that led towards a place of ancient usefulness, Ham (once known as Hamdon) Hill. It rises quite steeply above the A303 in the shape of a pasty or bloomer loaf lying at right angles to the road, and forms the northern extremity of a ridge of limestone that extends towards Yeovil. It thus looks north across the flatlands between the Parrett and Ivel/Yeo rivers. Ham Hill has been occupied and exploited since Neolithic times, and probably longer. Three miles of ramparts encircle the top, doubtless breached and repaired many times until the Romans finally dislodged the local tribe, the Durotriges, and pacified the whole region by force.

The hill had much more than just military value. The evidence is all around you if you wander the heights, which are pitted and gouged and excavated into a moonscape of ridges and hollows. A sheer stone face shows the scars left by tools: picks, wedges, hammers, adzes. The hill is built on a type of sandstone known as hamstone, which has been dug here for more than two thousand years, and is still being dug. The Romans used it to make the Fosse Way, and when the road-builders returned to widen the A303 they sent trucks up Ham Hill to remove 25,000 tons of spoil to make the foundations. But it is as a building material that hamstone has made its distinctive imprint on this part of England.

The architectural writer Sir Simon Jenkins has called it 'the loveliest stone in England', and one of its charms is that it suits the humblest cottage as well as the mightiest mansion. In this second category belongs Montacute – 'that glorious great house', as Edward Hutton called it – which rises in a vale immediately to the east of Ham Hill. It was built to reflect the wealth and self-esteem of Sir Edward Phelips, Speaker of the House of Commons and one of the prosecutors of Guy Fawkes under James I. Montacute's wonders are well enough known, but its incomparable general effect owes much to the stone from the quarries above it. In sunlight the building glows as if the blocks had somehow been made from clear honey. In shadow the glow fades, but the warmth is magically retained. It is soft stone, soft enough to be cut easily into ornamental features, and its texture is slightly roughened, like home-made fudge – vanilla, rather than coffee or chocolate. It is ardent, generous stuff.

The problem with Montacute, as with so many great piles, is that it was built to be lived in and no one lives there any more. It is a National Trust museum, beautiful beyond description and lovingly looked after, but lifeless – more of a monument or a document than a house. The Phelips family clung on there for 300 years, then left because one of them went off his head and gambled away the family fortune. Besides, who would want to live in a place so vast, so echoing, so impossible to heat?

The glory of Montacute

Montacute from below

The answer, for a while, was the ineffably vain and proud Lord Curzon, who considered it a suitable symbol of his enormous grandness. In 1916 he asked his mistress, the romantic novelist Elinor Glyn, to supervise the refurbishment and furnishing of Montacute. Curzon himself was required in London, attending to matters of state and reserving what little spare time he had to conduct an affair with a wealthy American widow, Grace Duggan. It was a pinchingly cold winter. Elinor Glyn shivered in Somerset, feeling neglected. Newspaper deliveries were somewhat patchy out in the sticks and Montacute had no telephone, so it was not until 17 December that Glyn read in *The Times* of six days beforehand the announcement that Curzon was to marry his American lady.

'Oh, that he whom I adored,' she wrote, 'whose nobility I treasured, whose probity I worshipped, could prove so faithless and so vile.' Who would have guessed that romantic fiction was her calling?

Hollow Lane

A sunken lane leads down from the back of Ham Hill to Montacute. I cycled down it one evening to view the great house. Late sunshine lit the beeches soaring above the high banks but where I was it was gloomy enough for dusk. Walls of dark earth held up by slabs of hamstone and pale writhing knots of tree roots rose twenty feet on either side. They had been munched and nibbled by the action of water over the ages, and were splashed with thick mantles of ivy and ferns. High above me the branches clasped each other. I felt squeezed, slightly threatened.

It may have been down Hollow Lane that Betty Hayne rolled one snowy night when she missed her footing during a blizzard and turned into a snowball by the time she reached the bottom. There she was found the next morning by her husband with her pipe still going, giving rise to a ditty called *The Snow Dumpling*:

> He was mazed such a smoke from a snowball to see
> He gave it a kick – Lor! How stared he
> When out bundled Betty as brisk as a bee.

Although stone is still quarried from Ham Hill, its main function these days is as a place of recreation. It is managed as a country park by the county council, and offers mountain biking and horse riding, and swarms with dogs and their owners. There is a stone pub where the dog people meet for coffee and beer, the inside of which smelled more strongly of dog than anywhere I have ever been.

A circle of stones stands in a flattened grassy bowl near the northern edge which is frequently mistaken by visitors for a lesser-known, miniature cousin of Stonehenge. In fact it was put up in 2000 to mark the two millennia of stone-cutting on Ham Hill. An innocent enough idea, you might think, but not in the eyes of the vicar of the village of Stoke-sub-Hamdon, the Reverend Peter Kerton-Johnson. At his behest the parochial church council requested the removal of the circle on the grounds that it would inevitably attract pagans wishing to engage in outlandish and revolting rituals. Drawing on his experience as a priest in Africa, Mr Kerton-Johnson hinted at the possibility of children being used as sacrifices, described the flat stone at the centre of the circle as a mockery of the Lord's Table, and quoted a passage in the book of the Prophet Jeremiah referring to Israel's pagan neighbours engaging in sexual acts on hilltops in order to put them in touch with their primitive gods.

Looking down on Ham Hill and its stones

Mercifully this terrifying vision of orgiastic Druidism seems to have remained where it originated, in Mr Kerton-Johnson's imagination; either that, or the pagans have been unusually discreet in their observances. I tend to agree with a long-departed stalwart of the Somerset Archaeological and Natural History Society, Richard Walter, who was moved to deep reflection by contemplating the history of Ham Hill. 'This classic spot,' he wrote, 'which resounded with the clang of arms and the clamour of consanguinary strife is now the retreat of rural quiet and silence . . . It is a matter for grateful felicitation that we are now living in an era when the progress of civilisation, the march of intellect, above all the benign influence of Christianity have rendered such fortresses unnecessary.' You don't often come across the word 'consanguinary'.

The views from the hill are glorious: to the line of the Mendips in the north, to Alfred's Tower in the east, to the Dorset downs in the south, to the Blackdown Hills in the west. More mundanely, it looks down on a long stretch of the A303. I sat for a time by the war memorial watching the traffic pass. The road seemed possessed by some mysterious and irrepressible vitality. All around, the green Somerset countryside was still and tranquil, and through it cut this channel of ceaseless noise and motion. So many cars and trucks, so many drivers, so many people in a hurry to get somewhere to do something. That's all you could tell of them, that they were in a hurry.

★ ★ ★

The old part of Stoke-sub-Hamdon is an attractive advertisement for the qualities of the hamstone, but the charms diminish as you reach the modern developments down the hill towards the A303. To the west of the village are fields densely packed with blackcurrant bushes, from which – so I was told by a Ham Hill dog-walker – Ribena obtain the fruit for their famous cordial. As a toddler my younger son was so addicted to it that he began to turn purple from the inside out. 'I want Bena,' he would yell, and then sob and shake with grief when we told him he couldn't have any. Ribena was credited with having kept the nation's children healthy during the 1939–45 war, when it was distributed free, although more recently it has been accused of promoting tooth decay and even obesity.

Beyond the blackcurrant bushes the lane peters out close to where the A303 crosses the River Parrett on an ugly concrete bridge. On the north side of the bridge, a little flight of steps leads down to a curious memorial set into the side of the structure. It comprises two very small statues or reliefs with facial features entirely worn away. The figures are said to be those of a boy and girl who were drowned in the river some time in the seventeenth century, and were originally incorporated into the stone bridge which was replaced when the A303 was dualled in the 1970s. Who they were and the circumstances of their deaths remain unknown. But ignorance did not inhibit one of the lesser lights of late eighteenth-century poetry, one Mr Gerrard, from composing an affecting elegy on the subject entitled 'Petherton Bridge'. This stanza conveys something of the flavour:

Boy and girl

See'st thou the limpid current glide
Beyond yon bridge, my hapless theme,
Where branches fringe its verdant side
And willows tremble o'er the stream

The poet imagines the pair – 'two smiling infants . . . sweet victims' – coming to play at 'the flow'ry margin'; one rolling 'headlong in the deep . . . beneath the doling tide'; the other stretching forth 'his little hand' but in vain; 'they both descended swift as thought . . . their lives dissolved in one embrace, their mingled souls flew up in air'.

It is powerful stuff.

* * *

The Ilminster bypass is one of the minor oddities of the A303. All the other major upgradings, starting with the Andover and Amesbury bypasses, were dual carriageway as a matter of course. But the Ilminster section, completed in 1988, was restricted to two lanes supposedly wide enough to permit overtaking (subsequently re-marked into three, with the central one reserved for passing). The decision not to dual it was justified at the time by projections of traffic use which, as usual, proved to be hopelessly wide of the mark, but was in fact a matter of cheese-paring economy. The result was the worst of several worlds. The stretch is fast but not fast enough, and the overtaking lane has incited folly, leading to numerous nasty accidents. Furthermore, the use of concrete to form the top layer instead of asphalt causes the passing wheels to make a horrible, high-pitched noise.

At the time of construction, space was left for widening if and when the comprehensive upgrading of the A303 ever happened. Years later the Highways Agency came up with a route for the new highway from Ilminster to Honiton and beyond. It was to be in part brand new, in part adapted existing road: all of it dual carriageway and all of it through the Blackdown Hills. An alliance of groups – including the National Trust, the Friends of the Earth and the Council for the Protection of Rural England – joined forces to oppose it. They pointed out that the Blackdown Hills was a designated AONB – an Area of Outstanding Natural Beauty, which would be a lot less outstanding if the road went ahead. An alternative was suggested, to forget about the A303 and instead widen the A358, which went north-west from Ilminster to meet the M5 at Taunton. It was less direct, comprising two sides of a triangle rather than one. But it would be much less destructive of cherished views and ancient woodland and hedges, and less disruptive to colonies of bats, communities of newts and dormice, and the wanderings of otters. It would also be a lot cheaper.

Traffic models were commissioned. Engineers were sent forth to measure and calculate. Exhibitions were staged and consultation exercises organised. Public money was dispersed in every direction save that of building a yard of new road. The Transport Secretary, Alistair Darling, scratched his silver thatch, arched his dark eyebrows, furrowed his brow; and in November 2004 plumped for the A358 scheme.

That was the day the A303 dream finally expired. As it turned out, the A358 widening also bit the dust, because no funding for it could be found. By the time Gordon Brown finally got his nail-bitten fingers on the fag-end of the Labour administration, building roads had receded out of sight in the 'vision for Britain' that he strove with such painful lack of success to articulate. It was a sign of the times that the Conservative manifesto for the 2010 election did not mention the subject. How far we had travelled in the twenty years since *Roads for Prosperity*! The coalition's Transport Secretary, Philip Hammond, said that the primary objective was to manage the existing road network more efficiently. To that end £6 billion would be spent over four years. A mere £2.3 billion was earmarked for new schemes and for completing those in progress.

An era had ended.

* * *

The old and the new A303 diverge again a couple of miles east of Ilminster. The bypass loops around the town to the north, while the old road – now without a number at all – meanders through the Seavingtons, St Michael and St Mary. Before it finally gets to Ilminster, it passes through Whitclackington, an insignificant place with a fine manor house and a handsome hamstone church.

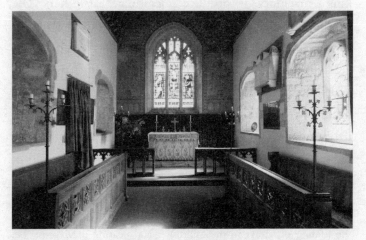

Whitelackington Church

From the fifteenth century onwards the foremost family in these parts were the Spekes. The one familiar and famous Speke was John Hanning, discoverer of the source of the Nile, who is buried a mile or two away at Dowlish Wake.* Earlier Spekes were generally content to attend to their lands and offices and keep the peace. Generally, but not always.

The 1680s was a troubled time in England. Conspiracies erupted like pustules on the body politic. Spies slipped back and forth between London and the Continent. Catholics and Protestants were once again at each other's throats, and the most absurd falsehoods about either were readily believed. Charles II was still on the throne, no more the swaggering star of his youth but a querulous, touchy, unpredictable shadow of his former confident self. For all his bedroom swordsmanship he had failed in a king's first duty, to produce a legitimate male heir. The nearest he had come was his eldest bastard, the Duke of Monmouth. Monmouth was a darling; brave, charming, graceful and athletic. Charles loved the lad but saw his faults – lack of brains and even more acute lack of resolute character – and refused to approve him as his heir. Others, determined to prevent Charles's obstinately and fanatically

---

* There is a marble sarcophagus in the church there carved with his gun, sword and sextant and the inscription A NILO PRAECLARUS. The Union Flag that once fluttered at Jinja on the shore of Lake Victoria hangs next to it, near a weird stained-glass window depicting the finding of Moses in the bullrushes and bearing the words: 'Let These Bones Live'.

Papist brother James from succeeding, continued to promote Monmouth's claims.

In 1680, five years before Charles II's death, the dashing young Monmouth embarked upon a quasi-royal tour of the West Country. According to his nineteenth-century biographer, George Roberts, he was 'caressed with the joyful acclamations of the country people, who came from all parts twenty miles about, the lanes and hedges being everywhere lined with men, women and children who with incessant shouts cried "God Bless King Charles and the Protestant Duke".' At Whitelackington the crowds were so enormous that several sections of the fencing around the estate had to be removed to let them in. Monmouth's party were welcomed by the squire, George Speke, and took refreshment beneath the spreading branches of a famously big sweet chestnut.*

Monmouth's reception in the West Country was viewed with alarm in London. He was spoken to severely by his father, and following the discovery of the so-called Rye House Plot to assassinate Charles and James, was expelled into exile in France. Five years later he was back, just as handsome and dashing as before, but this time on a mission of deadly seriousness. Charles was dead, finished by a stroke while shaving, and vindictive, bigoted James was in his place. Now was the time, Monmouth convinced

---

* The tree survived the Great Storm of 1703 but was finally upended by a hurricane on Ash Wednesday 1897, although its gnarled and withered stump still lies in a field near the church.

himself, to sweep the servant of Rome off the throne and sit on it himself. In June 1685 he sailed into the harbour at Lyme Regis, having sent word ahead to his supporters in Taunton to prepare themselves for rebellion.

The news reached George Speke at Whitelackington. Although he had fought on the Royalist side in the Civil War (and had been imprisoned and heavily fined by the Parliamentarians), in common with most other Englishmen from both sides of that great divide he viewed the prospect of a Catholic on the throne with righteous horror. Speke and his elder son John were both members of the notorious Green Ribbon Club which met at the King's Head in Chancery Lane, London. The members drank a great deal, carried a life-preserver known as a Protestant Flail, and for several years organised a procession each November which climaxed in the burning of an effigy of the Pope at the Inner Temple gate – a spectacle said to have been greeted with a shout so prodigious that it could be heard in Catholic Paris, or even Rome itself.

George Speke declared himself too old to fight again, but sent John with forty men to join the rebellion. From Lyme the Duke, his signature black plume waving above his broad hat, rode to Axminster, then Chard, then Ilminster. The streets of Ilminster were thronged with his men – hardly an army, more a raggle-taggle mob of untrained farm labourers, weavers, shop-keepers and idlers intent on plunder and easy rewards. Each wore a sprig of green in his cap. 'A Monmouth, a Monmouth and the Protestant religion,' they cried. The Duke smiled and waved. But one who observed him closely detected a 'settled melancholy' on those graceful features. Among those who greeted him in Ilminster that day was George Speke's younger son, Charles. Unlike his father and elder brother, Charles Speke had no aptitude or inclination for plotting, but he offered his hand to the Duke when the Duke offered his.

From Ilminster the rebels advanced to Taunton, where Monmouth denounced James as a Popish usurper and declared himself King. A fortnight later the enterprise came to its predictable, ghastly end on the peat-bog of Sedgemoor. Most of Monmouth's forces were slaughtered. He himself fled, but was found three days later cowering in a ditch near Ringwood in Hampshire with some peas in his pocket, the only food he had been able to find. He was conveyed to the Tower where, on 15 July, he laid his handsome head on the block. The executioner, the infamous Jack Ketch, struck five times at his neck with the axe while the crowd bayed for blood; then resorted to a butcher's knife to finish the job.

A dreadful revenge was taken on the rebels who survived Sedgemoor. Twenty were strung up in the market place in Taunton and, while the drums beat, their hearts were cut out and burned and their other remains were boiled in pitch and hung about the gates and walls of the town. Similar scenes were enacted in Exeter, Bridgewater and elsewhere. At the end of August the Lord Chief Justice, Judge George Jeffreys, was appointed to head what became known as the Bloody Assizes. Between the beginning and end of September he conducted a series of show trials at which 300 people were condemned to death and almost a thousand were sentenced to be sold as slaves for transportation to the West Indian plantations.

The penultimate of these spectacles was held at Wells in Somerset. Among the several hundred prisoners paraded in carts through the streets was Charles Speke. For the crime of having shaken the Duke's hand he was condemned by Jeffreys to hang in Ilminster market square, together with eleven other sons of the town. When the major of dragoons who had arrested him ventured to suggest that the real culprit was his brother John, and that Charles's life might be spared, Jeffreys came up with an answer worthy of this legend of judicial infamy:

'No, his family owe a life. He shall die for his namesake.'

16

COACHING DAYS

They were cramped, claustrophobic and filthy. Sleep was possible, comfort not. A seat inside was extremely expensive, and to our way of thinking the journeys would have seemed intolerably slow.

Yet Georgian England was proud of its stagecoaches. William Cobbett, generally more inclined to carp than to praise, said that next to a foxhunt 'the finest sight in England is a stagecoach ready to start'. And its arrival was almost as good – 'the horses all sweat and foam, the reek from their bodies ascending like a cloud, the whole equipage covered in dust and dirt'.

There was a splendour about them: the burnished maroon body of the coach, the royal cypher picked out in gold, the Cross of St George or Scotch Thistle or Shamrock and Star, the high, thin wheels painted scarlet or Post Office red; the coachman in tall hat and dark cloak, whip in gloved hand; and the horses, usually four but sometimes six of them snorting in their harnesses, their hooves clattering on the stony road. They had romance and dash and colour. But that was not the point of them. The point was that they enabled a social and economic transformation to take place.

The development of the coaching trade breathed a new life into England's slumbering market towns. William Chaplin, who saw the potential early, built a business that covered every major route out of London, employed 2000 people, and turned over £500,000 a year. His and other enterprises required support from what we would call service stations, stops where very large numbers of horses could be watered, fed and stabled, and passengers could be dined or breakfasted at speed and at highly unsocial hours. Coaching inns sprang up along all the trunk roads of the time. They were spacious establishments with cobbled yards and rows of stables, where a traveller could get a pint of sherry and a mutton chop at one in the morning and clear his plate and be off within a quarter of an hour. They became features of the landscape, and their landlords and landladies familiar and well-loved figures.

There was another dimension to the stagecoach revolution. They diminished distance, eroded isolation, and mentally and physically expanded the horizons of those who could afford the fares. Within a generation the well-to-do family that had previously been quite content to rusticate inconspicuously on their country property was taking the waters in Bath, a seaside holiday in Weymouth, and the season in London. The stagecoaches changed the way people thought about life and the world around them. They were crucial to the economic upheaval that was to turn Britain into a nineteenth-century superpower. We talk about the railways, but the coaches came first and led the way.

First of all, however, came the roads. In the 1720s it took four days for a coach to reach Exeter from London. Long-distance travel was an arduous affair, to be undertaken only if the business was very pressing indeed. In dry weather the roads were rutted and pitted and thick with dust. When it rained they became sluices of mud and water. Even with the appointment in the 1750s of the first turnpike trusts – associations of local businessmen and landowners which undertook to build, improve and maintain roads in return for being able to charge tolls – matters improved only slowly. In 1752 the *Gentleman's Magazine* observed of the London–Exeter road (the current A30 via Salisbury) that 'they do not know how to lay a foundation, nor make the proper slopes and drains; they throw a heavy mass of huge loose stones into a hole . . . which then make the best of their way to the centre of the world.'

But the Scottish engineer John Loudon McAdam knew. Through years of patient experimentation, he learned that if a road was slightly raised and cambered, if it was provided with adequate drains and culverts, and if it was constructed in layers of hard stone broken into small, angular fragments, it would over time become compacted and consolidated into a solid structure that would take any amount of rain and wear. Parliament appointed him General Surveyor of

Roads, and the turnpike trusts seized upon the principles he had set out in his two definitive books, *A Practical Essay on the Scientific Repair and Preservation of Roads* and *The Present State of Road Making*. All over the country old roads were transformed and new ones were cut. While the surveyors measured and the navvies dug, families sat by the roadside beating and bashing the blocks of stone into bite-sized pieces. And the stagecoaches picked up speed.

Historically the London–Exeter road was one of the small number of indispensable highways radiating out from the capital. It gave access to the important wool centres of the south-west, as well as to the ports of Falmouth and Devonport. The way was via Brentford, Hounslow, Staines, Egham, Bagshot, Basingstoke, Andover, Salisbury, Yeovil and Honiton – the route of the A30. During the 1750s it was parcelled out between various turnpike trusts which did their best, given the pre-McAdam technology, to improve and maintain it. But there was an alternative – shorter and potentially quicker – waiting to be exploited. It lay across Salisbury Plain.

The Andover Trust started the ball rolling by turnpiking what was to become the A303 as far as Thruxton. The Amesbury Trust took it over there, and between 1761 and the late 1770s extended it all the way to Willoughby Hedge, where the Wincanton Trust stepped in. Thereafter the Ilchester Trust, the Ilminster Trust, and Honiton and Ilminster Trust all played their parts, so that by 1809 the new way to Exeter was complete.

It took some time for its advantages to be recognised. The mail coaches continued to go via Salisbury, and the proto-A303 was used mainly by local traffic. But an Ilminster man, William Hanning, became fired with a vision: to turn the road that ran through his town into the main highway to the west, and thus to knock the A30 Salisbury route off its perch.

The Hannings were farmers, originally tenants of the Spekes of Whitelackington. They made good, very good indeed, so much so that they took over the bulk of the Dillington estate from the Spekes. It included a fine house previously occupied for a time by one of our less exalted Prime Ministers, Lord North, who married a Speke and is chiefly remembered for having inadvertently provoked the American War of Independence by refusing to lift the hated duty on tea.

The Dillington estate cost John Hanning £83,000 in 1795 (at least £8 million at today's prices), and by the turn of the century his son William was in residence at Dillington House. The Hanning fortunes evidently continued to prosper, because in the 1820s William had the place rebuilt and expanded into a very considerable mansion. It is hamstone, with slender mullioned windows and a slate roof bristling with clusters of high, octagonal chimneys. The sombre east front looks out over a formal garden, with the landscaped park beyond. Because of the slope on which the house stands, the west front is much less grand and more welcoming, and very lovely when the lowering sun warms the honeyed stone. The entrance is on the west front, and Hanning had the drive curve away up the slope and off in a southerly direction to meet the road between a matching pair of hexagonal gatehouses.

Dillington House

He was the driving force within the Ilminster Turnpike Trust. Out of his own pocket he subsidised the use of what became known as the New Direct Road by the main West Country carrier of goods, Russells of Exeter. A colleague of Hanning said of him that 'he talked largely of not regarding a few thousands loss if he can make his road (as he calls it) the Great Western Road.' The Russell Flying Waggons, as they were known despite an average speed of 3 m.p.h., reverted after a while to the alternative route via Yeovil and Salisbury, but soon some of the stagecoaches were trying out the New Direct Road.

But Hanning had ambitions beyond mere horse-power. He was one of a group of wealthy landowners and entrepreneurs seduced by the visionary enthusiasm of one of the unsung heroes of nineteenth-century technological advance, Goldsworthy Gurney. A Cornishman by birth, a doctor by training, and an inventor by inclination, Gurney had developed a steam-powered version of the stagecoach. In its final version it actually consisted of two vehicles connected by a rod, the front one containing the engine and manned by the crew, and the second carrying the passengers and the coke and water.

On 28 July 1829, at 4 a.m. Gurney, accompanied by two assistants, steered the steam-carriage out of the yard of the Cranford Bridge Inn on the western fringe of London and onto the road that led to Bath. His brother Thomas, two more engineers, and two of the backers sat in the passenger vehicle. Two horse-drawn conveyances were in the little convoy: one a phaeton carrying Hanning and the other chief investor, Sir Charles Dance, the other loaded with extra fuel. Initially the horses forged ahead while the engine puffed and clanked, but well before Maidenhead was reached, steam had amply demonstrated its superiority over horse muscle. At a steady 14 m.p.h. Gurney's creation powered its way triumphantly to Bath, its progress interrupted only by an encounter with a pile of bricks near Longford and by a rowdy demonstration from a drink-inflamed mob in Melksham, during which a stoker was knocked unconscious and the inventor himself was wounded in the head by a flying flint.

The word spread, and on the return journey enthusiastic crowds turned out to get a glimpse of the thundering iron beast. The townsfolk of Reading were so impressed that the mayor put on a civic reception. Back in London, Gurney and his backers glowed in anticipation of the triumphs to come. Hanning ordered eight of the steam-carriages for a new Exeter–London service, upping his overall investment to £10,000. Sir Charles Dance bought three at £800 each and began a four-times-a-day service between Cheltenham and Gloucester. The stagecoach proprietors began to be alarmed and – assisted by turnpike operators and corrupt magistrates – decided that Gurney's great venture represented a serious threat to their comfortable monopolies.

They paid for a layer of loose gravel a foot thick to be deposited on the Cheltenham–Gloucester road, into which the steam-carriage's wheels sank, bringing it to a halt. At about the same time new tolls were introduced: two pounds for a steam-carriage, four shillings for a stage-coach. Gurney and his sponsors raged and ranted against this blatant act of protectionist trickery. After a leisurely investigation a parliamentary committee agreed with them, but took no action to rectify the injustice. Gurney was financially cleaned out, and turned his fertile mind to other projects.* As for William Hanning, he died in 1834, his

---

* Gurney subsequently adapted the concept of the steam jet that had powered his carriage to a fire-fighting device, and eventually took charge of ventilation and lighting at the House of Commons for which work he was knighted.

dream of watching his own steam-powered carriages passing his gates on his road still unfulfilled.

But the road proved its worth. The coaching companies on the Exeter run began to switch to it because it was shorter and quicker. The *Subscription* – known affectionately as the *Scrippy* – began using the New Direct Road in 1819. In 1831 a race was arranged between it and its rival, the *Defiance*, which ended in a virtual dead heat after covering the 170 miles in thirteen hours. The deaths of several of the horses from exhaustion was considered a price well worth paying.

In 1835 Mrs Nelson, the formidable landlady of the Bull in Whitechapel, established a daily service featuring the *Exeter Telegraph*. It left Piccadilly at 5.30 each morning 'to the cries of Jewboys selling oranges and cedar pencils at six pence a dozen', as Anthony Trollope's elder brother Thomas recalled. There was twenty minutes for breakfast at Bagshot, thirty minutes for dinner at the Deptford Inn at Wylye. It reached Exeter at 10.30 p.m., a journey time of seventeen hours. In response to the success of the *Telegraph*, William Chaplin put his *Quicksilver* on the New Direct Road. It left St Martin–le–Grand at 8 p.m., reached Andover at 2.30 a.m., Amesbury at 3.39 a.m., Ilchester at 7.50 a.m., Honiton at 11 a.m., and Exeter at 12.34 p.m. From there it proceeded to Devonport, reached in an overall time of 21 hours 15 minutes, with 23 changes of horse.

'The *Telegraph*', proclaimed an advertisement placed in

the *Plymouth and Devenport Herald* on 12 January 1839, 'is admitted to be the most punctual coach with regard to time in all England'. Nothing would stop it, not even the memorable snowstorm of 27 December 1836, when the coachman – having reached Amesbury through the blizzard – resisted all entreaties to give up, had fresh horses harnessed, and battled on through the drifts up Thruxton Hill to Andover. Thomas Trollope described in his autobiography (rather prosaically called *What I Remember*) a furious pace between Ilminster and Ilchester: 'four miles in twenty minutes and a trace broken and mended without any interruption – the performance was the *ne plus ultra* of coach-travelling.'

But the heyday was short-lived. The railway reached Exeter in 1845, cutting the journey time from London to eight hours. Some coaching towns became railway towns; others – like Amesbury – returned to their slumbers. Many of the coaching inns closed. Coachmen, ostlers, grooms and stableboys were laid off. The turnpikes fell into disrepair and their trusts were wound up. Funds for maintaining the roads dried up. Half a century after the *Telegraph* and the *Quicksilver* had made their final runs, William Hanning's New Direct Road was described in a gazeteer as 'a rough green track strewn with flints . . . cyclists are advised to ride in the grass margins.'

★ ★ ★

Ilminster is a rather pleasant town which would be even more pleasant had not the elected representatives of the people seen fit to allow Tesco to deposit a spectacularly ugly supermarket in its centre. It stands not far from the market square where poor Charles Speke swung at the end of a rope: a hulking square block faced in pale, liverish brick with a layer of red brick at ground level. A white awning supported on tubular steel hangs over the entrance, which is reached through what the design brochure calls 'a landscaped courtyard' – in reality a paved thoroughfare to the car park with the public lavatories, in matching sickly yellow brick, on the other side. Over the doors is the Tesco banner in red and blue showing a pound being snipped with a pair of scissors, with the legend 'Every Little Helps'. There is another banner on the wall: 'From schools to charities we work with our community to support local causes – EVERY LITTLE HELPS'. A few yards away a flight of steps leads to the spanking-new premises of the Ilminster Bowling and Tennis Club, over-looking emerald rectangles of turf as smooth and flat as billiard cloths.

The saga of how Tesco got the store that Tesco wanted convulsed the town and filled the pages of the local paper, the *Chard and Ilminster News*. It was also chronicled by a well-known journalist and part-time Ilminster resident, Rosie Boycott. Ms Boycott[*] had a weekend home on the Dillington estate and for a time ran a smallholding there. She produced two books about her endeavours, which – as

---

[*] Now Lady Boycott, a cross-bench peer.

can happen when they arise from virtuous intentions and complete absence of experience – went sour over time. She eventually abandoned her efforts to make a going concern of her vegetables, chickens and Gloucester Old Spot pigs, took a £200,000 hit (painful details shared with readers of the *Daily Mail*) and got a new job as advisor on sustainable food to the Mayor of London, Boris Johnson.

She had some harsh words for Ilminster's councillors, and harsher ones still for the supermarket leviathan itself. The councillors may have smarted, but Tesco hardly blinked. It deployed its proven strategy of combining blandishments with veiled threats, and routed its opponents. When Somerset District Council dared to object to a proposal to shift the position of the store and to alter aspects of its hideous design, its members received a letter warning them that continued refusal would place them 'in a vulnerable position', and that they would lose any resulting planning appeal. At the same time the bowling and tennis club were offered facilities beyond their wildest imaginings. A colony of slow-worms was tenderly removed from the site and found a quieter home elsewhere. In November 2007 the store opened. 'We are determined to be good neighbours,' a Tesco spokesman said.

More than four years on it has become just another part of the town, and the story is over. Rather like a new road, it has lost its ability to shock and outrage. The people of Ilminster have learned to use it, and no longer recoil from its remarkable unloveliness. It may well be that the dire predictions of local shopkeepers about the impact on their trade were unfounded. Ilminster still has a butcher's, a greengrocer's, a wine merchant and two delicatessens, which is not bad in these desperate times. The weekly market survives somehow and the town also boasts a theatre (the Warehouse, showing *A Day in the Death of Joe Egg* when I passed through) and a church which our friend Edward Hutton considered 'as noble and glorious a building as is to be found in Somerset'. 'A man born within sight of such a thing,' Hutton mused, 'may consider himself fortunate if, in his last hours, he may see it again.' As a fleeting visitor, I can testify that the beauty of the Church of Our Lady, Ilminster, certainly counterbalances the barbarism of Tesco – without, unfortunately, being able to cancel it altogether.

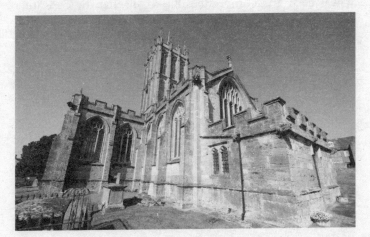

Ilminster Church

★ ★ ★

Those turnpikers of old knew a thing or two. Their business model was simplicity itself. They put up the money to make the road usable, and auctioned the right to collect the tolls to a third party. The third party hired the pikemen to collect the money, and fitted them out in their high glazed hats, corduroy breeches, white aprons and white stockings. The road users paid according to distance and mode of travel. It was not cheap – an inside seat on the *Telegraph* between Exeter and London in 1832 cost three pounds ten shillings, rather more than the equivalent first-class rail fare today. The system was far from perfect. It offered plentiful opportunity for dodgy dealing, and – unlike the railways when they came – it rarely produced a decent return for investors. But at least the principle behind it was clear and comprehensible to all: that the consumer pays for what is consumed.

Then the state took over, and that link was broken. During the first age of the automobile, the state funded a halting expansion of the road network from general tax revenues. Motorists paid taxes for their motoring, but there was no direct correlation between those proceeds and expenditure. As the car habit took ever deeper hold, governments came to rely upon progressive increases in the duty on fuel to pay for things that had nothing to do with transport. The motorist became a revenue milch cow, to be appeased by regular additions to the nexus of motorways and upgradings of other major roads.

The first age of motoring ended around 2000. By then it had become apparent that no government could afford to maintain its unspoken contract with the motorist. Car use had risen to a level far beyond the capacity of the road system to deal with it. At the same time the potential for increasing that capacity had almost been used up. There was no uncontentious space left for roads; and anyway the hostility to the principle of building them had become too great for a democratically elected administration to overcome or circumvent. Furthermore the financial cost was beyond bearing.

But the motorist was still being bled, and was becoming restive. In 2000 the simmering sense of grievance among road users boiled over into a series of protests by lorry drivers and farmers. They blockaded fuel depots and blocked roads, causing the more excitable commentators to forecast economic paralysis around the corner. The duty on petrol had risen to 80 per cent of its total cost, making it the most expensive in Europe. At the same time the programme for providing new roads was grinding to a halt. Alarmed as much by the bellows of outrage from the *Daily Mail* and the *Daily Telegraph* as by the bolshiness of the hauliers, Tony Blair froze the tax element of the cost of petrol and ordered a review of the long-term future of road transport.

This was carried out by a committee chaired by the economist and government advisor, Sir Christopher Foster, under the aegis of the research arm of the Royal

Automobile Club. The results were published two years later under the title *Motoring Towards 2050*. Blair himself contributed a preface in which he called the document a 'valuable contribution to the debate' – a debate which, he said, he was looking forward to hearing (meaning, 'no action then, not in my time').

Much of *Motoring Towards 2050* consists of sober forecasts: road traffic to rise by a half if capacity is increased so that congestion remains at present levels, by a third if not; journey times to rise by a fifth; and so on. No government, the report says, ever keeps promises to expand the road network. To keep congestion at current levels would require spending at four or five times the level proposed in Labour's (subsequently abandoned) Ten Year Plan. Improved management – measures like variable speed limits, narrower lanes, reserving lanes for cars with two or more occupants – might give a 10 to 15 per cent increase in capacity.

Sir Christopher Foster and his colleagues were clearly confident that they saw into the heart and mind of the British motorist. The value we place on the freedom given us by the car is very deeply rooted, they noted. What matters to us is where we live, and we do not care how far we have to travel to get to work, nor – by extension – how long we have to spend in our cars to get there. Fortunately the waiting will be made more bearable by the car of the future, a steel or aluminium cage covered in a lightweight skin of aluminium or plastic, powered by hydrogen fuel cell, which will largely drive itself in the infrequent intervals between queuing. This will leave those inside free to take advantage of multi-media facilities – or perhaps to read *Autocar* or to go to sleep. Even so, the gradual annexation of more and more of our hours of consciousness by our enslavement to our cars will cause resentment and unrest.

There is only one answer: more road. New roads, wider roads, parallel roads, roads in tunnels, roads on stilts above other roads. The starting point for the wise men of the RAC – doing nothing, they said, 'has nothing to recommend it' – was Labour's Ten Year Plan, which proposed thirty new bypasses, eighty £5 million-plus schemes, two hundred smaller projects, and the spending of £30 billion on the backlog of maintenance. This, they judged, would be insufficient to contain congestion at current levels. The alternative – defined as 'high provision' – would see all 'strategic' roads widened, new roads in tunnels provided where necessary, and motorway capacity more than doubled. The cost: £30 billion a year.

At this point I think we can bid farewell to the RAC panel of experts, just as they take their leave of the firm ground of reality to float skywards in pursuit of their asphalt Utopia. To be fair to them, their brief was not to account for taxpayers' money and balance the demands of the health budget against the defence budget, but to dream the dream. Nevertheless the melancholy truth is that their efforts were wasted. The report was redundant even as it was published. Labour's Ten Year Plan – which the experts regarded as inadequate – was jettisoned because everything in it was turning out to cost twice as much as forecast. Given the present condition of the public finances, it does not require a supercharged intelligence to work out that investment on the scale envisaged in *Motoring Towards 2050* is not going to happen.

So what will? If the RAC panel are right, and car use and ownership simply continue on their upward path, paralysis beckons. If our enslavement is unbreakable, the time is not far off when commuters will hardly have time to get home from work before they have to leave again. They may be right – certainly thus far there is not much sign of the general sense of grievance at traffic jams translating into behavioural change, nor of the cost of motoring deterring people from doing it.

In a book called *After The Car*, published in 2009, two sociologists, Kingsley Dennis and John Urry, argued that the car system had reached a point of 'self-organised criticality' and was 'ripe for tipping'. They looked ahead to a world in which mobility was organised for us, where 'software will become as crucial as physical capacity'. They presented three models for the future direction of human society. In one we retreat into local self-sustaining cells where homes, workplaces, schools and sources of food are close together, and from which we would rarely need to depart. Another is what they called 'regional warlordism', where global connections are broken down, nation states crumble, tribes compete for energy sources, and long-distance travel ceases because it is too dangerous. The third envisages 'digital networks of control' in which software systems determine how and when people move around. Travel is in small, light, self-driven pods, people are allocated carbon allowances, and physical travel is increasingly replaced by 'virtual travel'.

Is it possible that we can think more carefully about when and where we drive? Such a giant shift would almost certainly require coercive as well as persuasive measures. But coercion is already woven into the fabric of our driving. We are coerced into wearing seatbelts, stopping at traffic lights, observing speed limits, parking in prescribed places. The 'freedom' of the car is a self-evident fraud. The RAC, the AA, the roads lobby, the car lobby, Mondeo Man, Jeremy Clarkson, the opinion-grinders at the *Daily Mail* – they would have us believe that to restrict our use of our car is to assault a fundamental human right – tantamount to restricting the amount of fresh air we breathe or the amount of nonsense we may talk. Why? Why is using the road any different from helping yourself to any other commodity. You help yourself, and when the supply is exhausted the commodity is no longer available.

Or perhaps I am missing some profound philosophical absolute. It's happened before.

★ ★ ★

Apart from a half-mile section bypassing the village of Marsh, the A303 beyond Ilminster follows the same line that it did in the turnpike era, and is generally not much wider. Its eighteenth-century character acts as a mildly sardonic commentary on the ambitions of a past generation of road-builders, as well as on the wilder fantasies of *Motoring Towards 2050*. In the grand plan, this should have been exalted into a big, wide, fast superhighway to Honiton and beyond. Instead it is no different from any other unimproved, meandering country A-road – except that it is expected to deal with a volume of traffic that at busy times is way beyond its modest capacity.

The Ilminster bypass peters out at Horton. The road narrows and becomes more winding as it climbs into the Blackdown Hills. The countryside is lovely. It rises and falls in a green sea of rounded ridges and wooded vales. Little streams twist and turn along the creases. The soil is loam and clay, overlaid with rich pasture broken into irregular fields by tidy hedgerows. In most of the grazing fields at least one mature oak has been left, presumably to give the animals shade on hot days. The effect is very pleasing.

I stopped to look at the minute Church of St Barnabas at Ham, a hundred yards or so up a little lane off the A303. Built of sturdy light grey stone which I presumed to be chert, it was once a barn but was converted to serve the spiritual needs of the residents of Ham who were apparently reluctant to walk the two miles there and back to the nearest church at Combe St Nicholas. There were not many of them, which was just as well because the building is no more than twelve yards long and half that wide. They still hold services twice a month there, but not in winter because there is no electricity.

A little way on I passed a faint echo of an old battle cry, in the form of a broken sign hanging from a gate on which the words DUAL THE A30/303 could be made out. There is a junction ahead with a minor road leading south to Chard and north to Taunton – the devil for accidents, according to the *Chard and Ilminster News*, but very quiet when I walked past. A spacious roadside inn called the Eagle stands close by, where I had a welcome pint and a ham ciabatta before plodding on down the hill towards Marsh.

It was a day in mid-March, balanced between winter and spring. The hedgerows were largely bare of leaves but the daffodils were out and it was warm enough to walk in shirtsleeves. The traffic was very light, and on occasions ceased altogether for up to a minute. On one occasion I stood still right by the A303 and clearly heard a blackbird sing, and then a cow bellow from the field below.

Devon welcomes you as you reach the Marsh bypass, although car drivers don't notice because they are too intent on slamming their feet down on their accelerators to wrest the maximum possible overtaking advantage from the short stretch of dual carriageway. Somerset also offers a welcome to those coming the opposite way, which is good of it (Hampshire, pay attention!). The border between the two counties is formed here by the Yarty, a river I had never heard of before but which looked distinctly trouty.

Slow down

Beyond Marsh the A303's designation as a strategic highway to the west becomes absurd. There is a testing little hill which leads up to a 90-degree left-hand bend signalled in advance by a 20 m.p.h. speed limit sign. Twenty miles per hour! How is the mighty London–Penzance Trunk Road fallen! The sweet Devon air is filled with the dissonant hubbub of hissing brakes, grinding gear changes and straining engines as the trucks pant their way around the obstacle, hardly able to summon ten miles per hour, let alone twenty. The road's spirit does not recover. It limps up and along Sandpit Hill and crawls into Newcott.

Newcott struck me as a bit of a non-place, but there was a garage and next to it a large roadside diner, the Newcott

Chef. As such it sported a white-on-red logo strikingly reminiscent of Fat Charlie – so strikingly that Little Chef were moved to bring a fatuous and unsuccessful legal action to get it changed. 'Simply better, definitely quicker', the Newcott Chef boasted challengingly from beneath his bulging white hat, until he was sent packing and it was rebranded as an American Bar & Grill under the name Route 303.

No, I'm not Fat Charlie

The end is close.

17

THE END OF THE ROAD

And it comes without even a whimper.

But first there is Annie's Tea Bar. Annie is Annie Harris, a silver-haired, motherly type with a West County accent moulded in Ilminster. The tea bar is a seasoned caravan whose very fabric is impregnated with the fumes from the bacon sarnies and full breakfasts – fried bread or toast, black pudding 50p extra – that she has been dispensing for the past dozen or so years. On my travels I have disposed of a good few of Annie's breakfasts, and I can testify that they infallibly cheer up the dreariest morning and induce a sense of lasting well-being.

She is a friendly soul, Annie, and so is her friend Carol, who shares the duties. When I stopped by in the early spring of 2011 they were getting excited about going to London for the wedding of Prince William and Catherine Middleton, which was Carol's treat for her friend. Their pleasure at the prospect of getting a glimpse of William and Kate was as warm and nourishing as the bacon sizzling on the griddle.

It's hard work for the pair of them, on their feet all day, and Annie is not in the first flush. But she likes the chat with her regulars, giggles at the suggestion that she should put croissants on the menu ('they can have toast instead of fried bread if they're worried about their health') and clings to the belief that she should really have been on the stage instead of flipping eggs.

Her smile fades if you mention the Highways Agency. For some reason they took away the loos that used to stand further along the lay-by from the tea bar. It was a blow to Annie's trade and she does not forget or forgive. The Agency's sign ahead of the lay-by does not hint at the existence of her enterprise. There is a WC on it, crossed out, a P for parking, a picture of a bench, and an I for information. This refers to a panel which may once have displayed titbits of interest to passers-by, but whose graphics and words are now as faded as a medieval fresco.

Annie on the left, Carol on the right, breakfast behind

The setting is splendid. The lay-by and Annie's Tea Bar* stand on the edge of a ridge that drops steeply into the valley of the River Otter – Coleridge's 'dear native brook . . . wild streamlet of the West'. Somewhere down there, out of sight, is the village of Upottery. This was once the seat of William Pitt's friend and loyal colleague, the famously long-winded Henry Addington, who served in six governments, prompting his fellow politician George Canning to remark: 'He is like the smallpox – everyone is obliged to have him once in their lives.'

---

* Annie subsequently departed into a well-earned retirement, leaving Carol in charge. Carol has now left as well and Annie's Tea Bar is now Emma's Café – its character unchanged, its welcome as warm as ever.

Beyond the river a white lane wanders up the slope past Baxter's Farm towards yet another Beacon Hill. To the left is curiously named Braddicksnap Hill, with Hartridge beyond. Whitewashed stone cottages and white bungalows are dotted around the edges of the fields, some pasture, others ploughed for barley and rape. Neat, flat-topped hawthorn hedges lead to much less neat copses. It is a good place for a road to die.

There is no sense in the A303's sudden demise. It is done in, swiftly and without fuss, by its old rival, the A30. Back at Popham this historic highway was usurped by the upstart newcomer and relegated to a thankless penitential plod past Stockbridge, Salisbury, Shaftesbury, Sherborne, Yeovil, Crewkerne and Chard. It waits a long time for its revenge. A short stroll beyond Annie's Tea Bar it strikes back.

In the end is my beginning

The means of dispatch is what road enthusiasts refer to as a TOTSO, an acronym for Turn Off To Stay On. It is a junction at which two roads become one, and the number of the lesser of them – the one that gives way – becomes that of the unified route. A simple diagram makes it obvious:

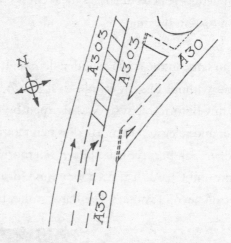

Clearly the Turning Off To Stay On applies only to east-bound traffic wanting to take the A30 for Chard rather than the A303. But whichever way you look at it, the designation of the single road born of the junction as the A30 is whimsical.

I asked the Highways Agency for an explanation, but it preferred to remain silent. The subject has been debated at length by contributors to the SABRE (Society for All British and Irish Road Enthusiasts) website, several of whom are as foxed as I am by this numerical anomaly;

although – as is often the case with enthusiasts – there is little agreement on how it should be corrected. Comparable oddities abound across the land as a consequence of the adoption in the 1920s of a numbering system which at the time promised order and logic, but which, as the road network evolved, grew instead into a thicket bristling with absurdities and inconsistencies.

Computer power could, of course, now give us a truly coherent and rational system, if we wanted one. We don't. We are used to the muddle we have, and the upheaval and expense that would accompany a root-and-branch reform are too frightful to contemplate. As Joe Moran points out, it matters not that the system makes no sense, because motorists do not navigate by road numbers anyway.* The survival of numerical quirks does no one any harm and provides a ready source of interest and amusement to the members of SABRE and like-minded groups.

The upshot of the TOTSO near Annie's Tea Bar is that the A303 expires without a murmur of protest, and the A30 marches on in triumph past Honiton. It experiences a temporary reversal in its fortunes when it is subsumed into the M5 to the south of Exeter, but it soon springs back into life. Thereafter it sweeps around the north edge of Dartmoor, past Okehampton, Launceston, Bodmin and Redruth towards Penzance and its own last rites at the tip of mainland Britain. For most of the way it is a fine, wide

---

* For more on this absorbing subject the reader is referred to Moran's *On Roads* pages 57–72.

dual carriageway – close to what the A303 would have been had the original masterplan been realised.

As it is, the A303 is left as a rump, an unmourned victim of changing attitudes and bureaucratic inertia of the small-minded, tight-fisted, mean-spirited variety. It does a job, not brilliantly but adequately. Considering the high ambitions that attended its conception, it is a disappointment. For roughly a third of its way it is on the grand scale. For a further third it aspires to grandeur and fails to reach it. And for its final stretch it abandons any pretence of aiming high and settles for meandering mediocrity. The A303 is the transport equivalent of a great public building project – a cathedral, an opera house, a bridge – begun with ample funds, tremendous intentions and the sound of trumpets; subsequently left unfinished because the first visionaries were succeeded by smaller, spiritually poorer men.

It is unfinished business, the A303, and likely to remain so. The odd thing is that we rather like it for that. The A30 that takes over the way to the west is big and fast and goes through some epic scenery. But it is bland. It lacks character. It does not inspire affection as the A303 does. We British have a soft spot for the gallant failure. We admire the gallantry and we feel for the failure. Maybe that is why this highway to the sun – when it shines – retains a special place in the hearts of those of us who know what it is to pass the walls of the Great Shed and the ramparts of Camelot, and to creep past the bluestones of Stonehenge.

BIBLIOGRAPHY

Alcock, Professor Leslie, *By South Cadbury Is That Camelot*, Thames & Hudson, 1972.

Allison, William, and Fairley, John, *The Monocled Mutineer*, Quartet, 1979.

Augé, Marc, *Non-places: Introduction to an Anthropology of Supermodernity*, Verso 2008.

Belloc, Hilaire, *The Old Road*, Constable and Co., 1911 (available as free download).

Buchanan, Colin, *Mixed Blessing: The Motor in Britain*, Leonard Hill, 1958.

— *Traffic in Towns*, Penguin, 1964.

Chandler, John, *The Amesbury Turnpike Trust*, Wiltshire Industrial Archaeology Society, 1979.

— *The Amesbury Millennium Lectures* (ed.), The Amesbury Society, 1979.

Chippindale, Peter, *Stonehenge Complete* (new edition), Thames & Hudson, 2012.

— *Who Owns Stonehenge?* (ed.), Batsford, 1990.

Cunliffe, Barry, *Wessex to 1000 AD*, Longman, 1993.

Dakers, Caroline, *Clouds: The Biography of a Country House*, Yale University Press, 1993.

Davies, Hugh, *From Trackways to Motorways: 5000 Years of Transport History*, Tempus, 2006.

Defoe, Daniel, *Tour Through the Whole Island of Great Britain*, Dent, 1962.

Dennis, Kingsley, and Urry, John, *After the Car*, Polity, 2009.

Dudley, Geoffrey, and Richardson, Jeremy, *Why Does Policy Change?*, Routledge, 2000.

Featherstone, Mike, Thrift, Nigel and Urry, John (eds.), *Automobilities*, Sage 2005.

Greene, Harry Plunket, *Where the Bright Waters Meet*, Excellent Press, 2007.

Harper, Charles G., *The Exeter Road*, Chapman and Hall, 1899 (available as free download).

Herrup, Cynthia, *A House in Gross Disorder*, Oxford University Press, 1999.

Hill, Rosemary, *Stonehenge*, Profile, 2008.

Hoare, Sir Richard Colt, *Ancient History of Wiltshire*, W. Miller, 1812.

Hudson, W. H., *A Shepherd's Life*, Nonsuch, 2005.

Hutton, Edward, *Highways and Byways in Somerset*, Macmillan, 1919.

— *Highways and Byways in Wiltshire*, Macmillan, 1917.

Huxley, Aldous, *Along the Road*, Chatto & Windus, 1925.

Johnson, Boris, *Life in the Fast Lane*, Harper Perennial, 2007.

McKenzie, W. A., *Motormania*, Cassell, 1972.

Masters, Gerry, *Ilchester*, available from Ilchester Museum.

Moran, Joe, *On Roads*, Profile, 2009.

O'Connell, Sean, *The Car in British Society*, Manchester University Press, 1998.

Raper, Anthony, *The Weyhill Fair*, Barracuda, 1988.

Rolt, L. T. C., *Landscape with Machines*, Longman, 1971.

Rowntree, Paul, *From Trackway to Trunk Road: A History of the A303*, 2004 (unpublished).

Sawyer, Frank, *Keeper of the Stream*, Unwin Hyman, 1987.

Setright, L. J. K., *Drive On: A Social History of the Motor Car*, Granta, 2004.

Smith, the Reverend Alfred, *Birds of Wiltshire*, R. H. Porter, 1887.

Thorold, Peter, *The Motoring Age*, Profile, 2003.

Timperley, H. W., and Brill, Edith, *Ancient Trackways of Wessex*, P. Drinkwater, 1983.

Woodbridge, Kenneth, *Landscape and Antiquity*, Oxford Clarendon Press, 1970.

Worthington, Andy (ed.), *The Battle of the Beanfield*, Enabler Publications, 2005.

Wyndham, Richard, *The Gentle Savage*, Cassell, 1936.

ACKNOWLEDGEMENTS

My thanks must go first to Colin Midson, who had the idea for this book, and coaxed it from me with great enthusiasm, tact and good humour, as well as providing ingenious maps of the road; and second to my friend, Jason Hawkes, who is Britain's leading aerial photographer, but consented to stay earthbound to take the pictures of the A303. I also owe a considerable debt to Paul Rowntree, for making available to me his invaluable history of the A303, thereby saving me a great deal of hard graft.

I would also like to thank my agent, Caroline Dawnay, at United Agents, for her unfailing support, and Sally Partington, who showed that the discipline of rigorous copy-editing was far from moribund, and thus helped make this a much better book than it would otherwise have been. I am most grateful to Jim Fuller for letting me reproduce two of the classic photographs of Stonehenge taken by his grandfather, Thomas Lionel Fuller. David Rymill, archivist with Hampshire Archives and Local Studies, helped with the illustrations of the construction of the A303; and Gill Arnott, of the

Hampshire Museums and Arts Service, enabled me to reproduce the map of the Weyhill Fair. Gerry Masters, historian of Ilchester, gave me a copy of his collection of miscellanea which is full of good things. Rob Turner, of Winterbourne Stoke, gave generously of his time to enlighten me about farming past and present.

I am grateful to the staff of the Hampshire Record Office in Winchester, the Wiltshire and Swindon History Centre in Chippenham, and the Somerset Heritage Centre in Taunton. Without them and their like the kind of book that I enjoy writing would not be possible. I would also like to thank my former wife, Linda, and my friend, Simon Walters, for their A303 memories.

Finally, I thank my wife, Helen, for her support and endless tolerance.

INDEX